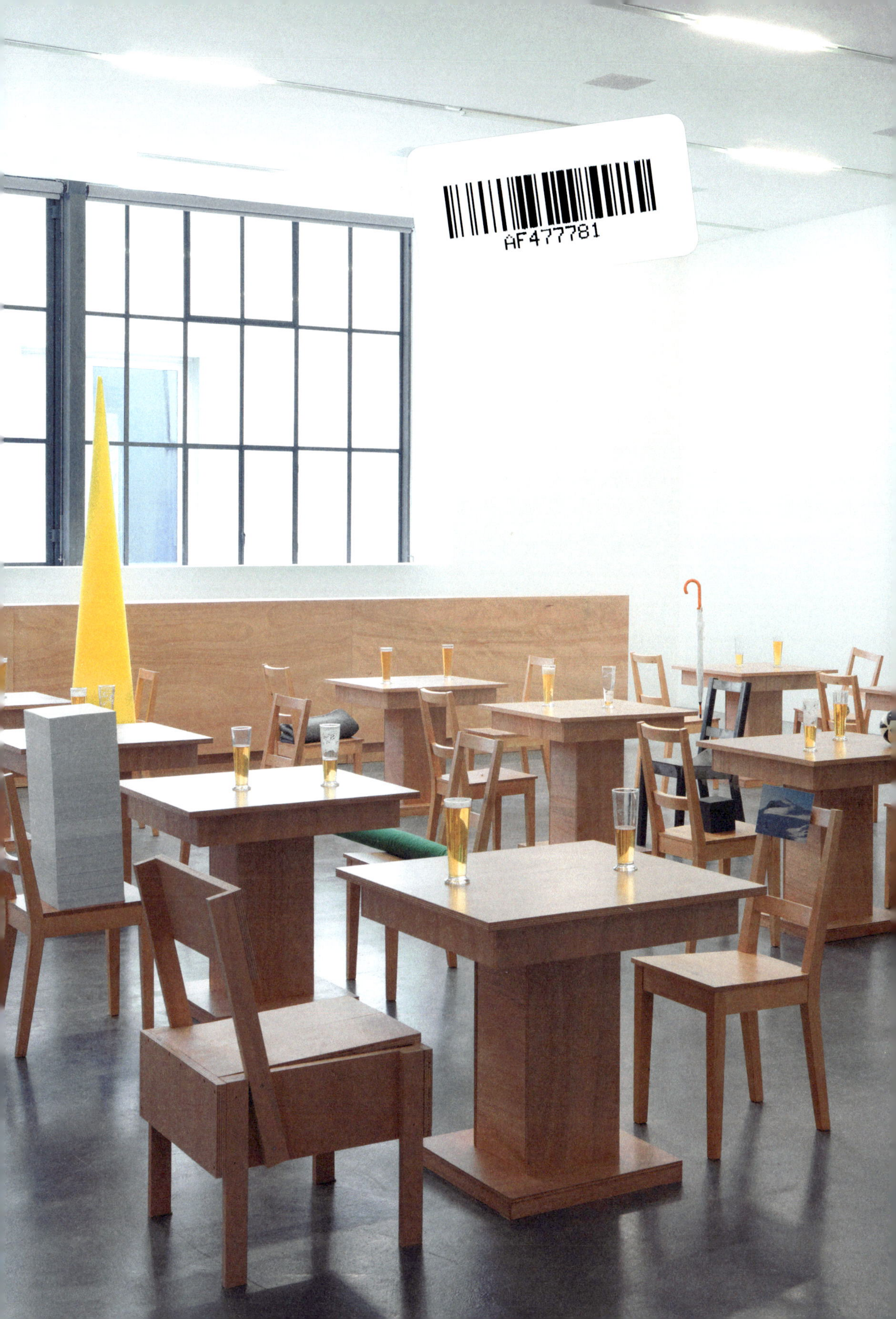
AF477781

Bar Restaurant

Bar Restaurante

Twenty-four different sculptures (geometric shapes, flour, clay, iron, stacks of journals, etc.) are "sitting" on chairs drinking beer. The liquid disappears from the glasses through an invisible system created by the artist. A waiter moves through the installation and continuously refills the glasses with a very good, cold beer.

Bar Restaurant / Bar Restaurante, 2010 / 2013
Waiter, ice, beer, glasses, fabric, pearl, clay, iron, wood, flour, bronze, salt, ink, paper, water, hidden mechanism
Dimensions variable

Courtesy of the artist / Sammlung Migros Museum für Gegenwartskunst
Photography: Stefan Altenburger Photography
Views: Migros Museum für Gegenwartskunst

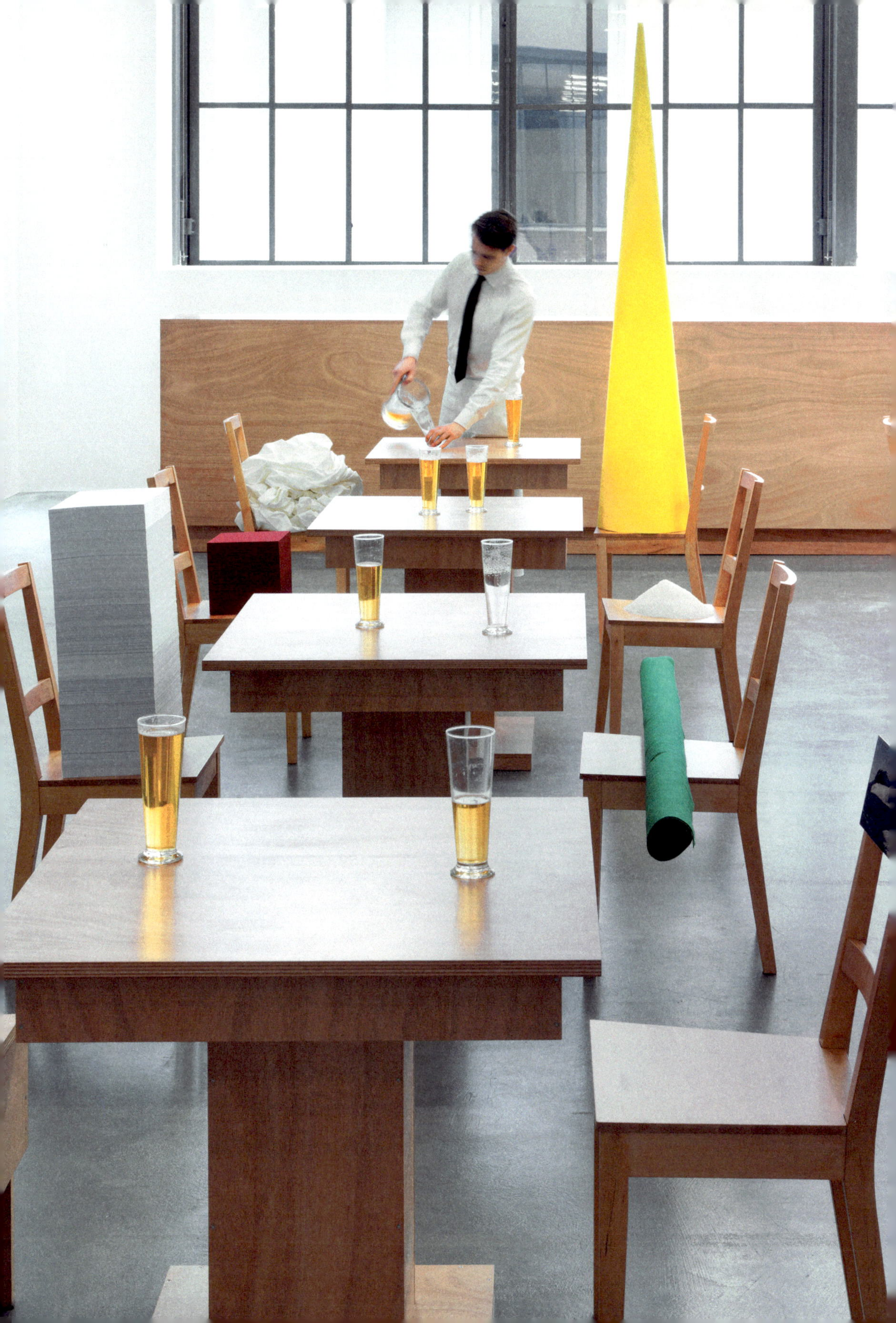

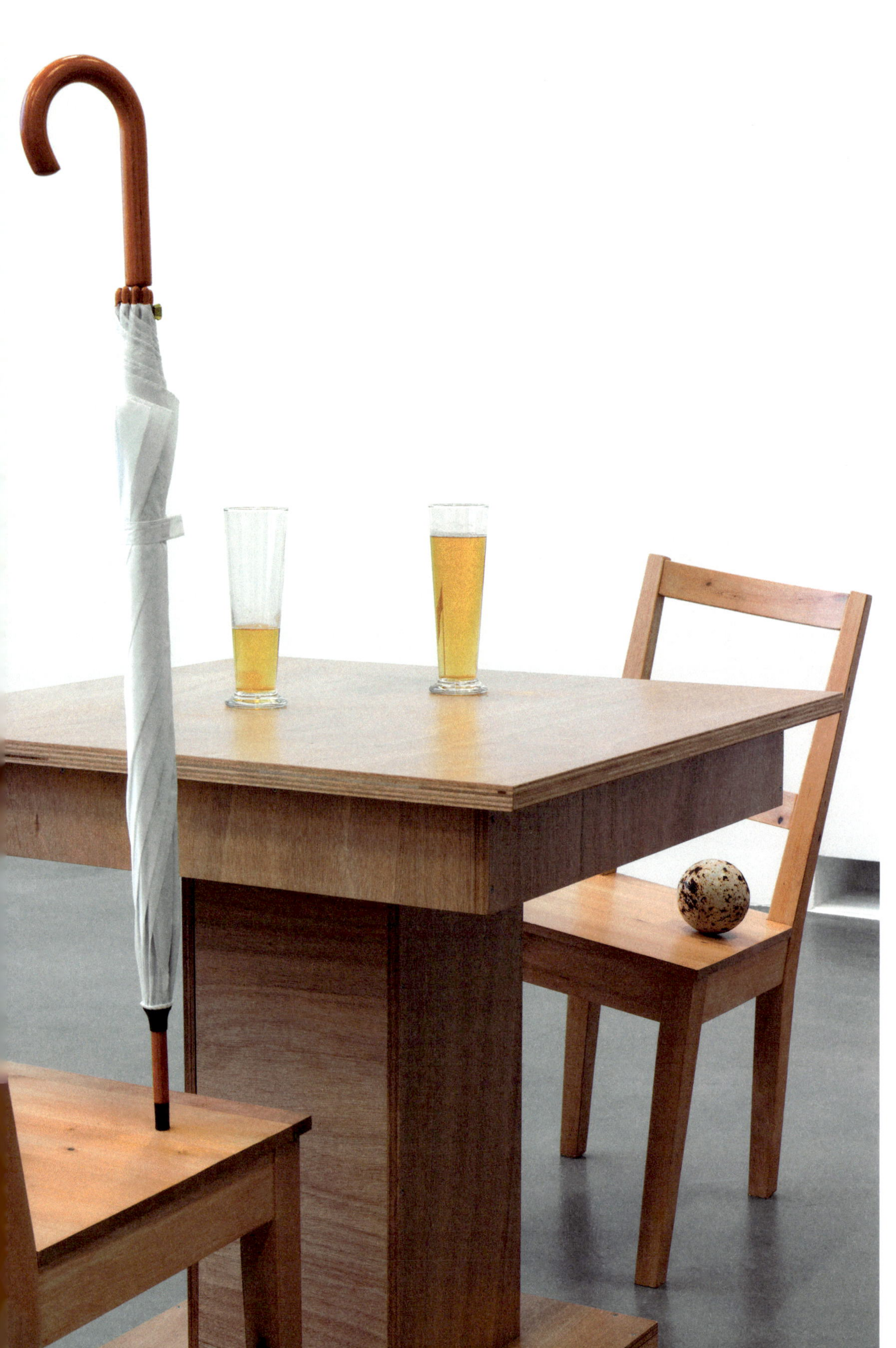

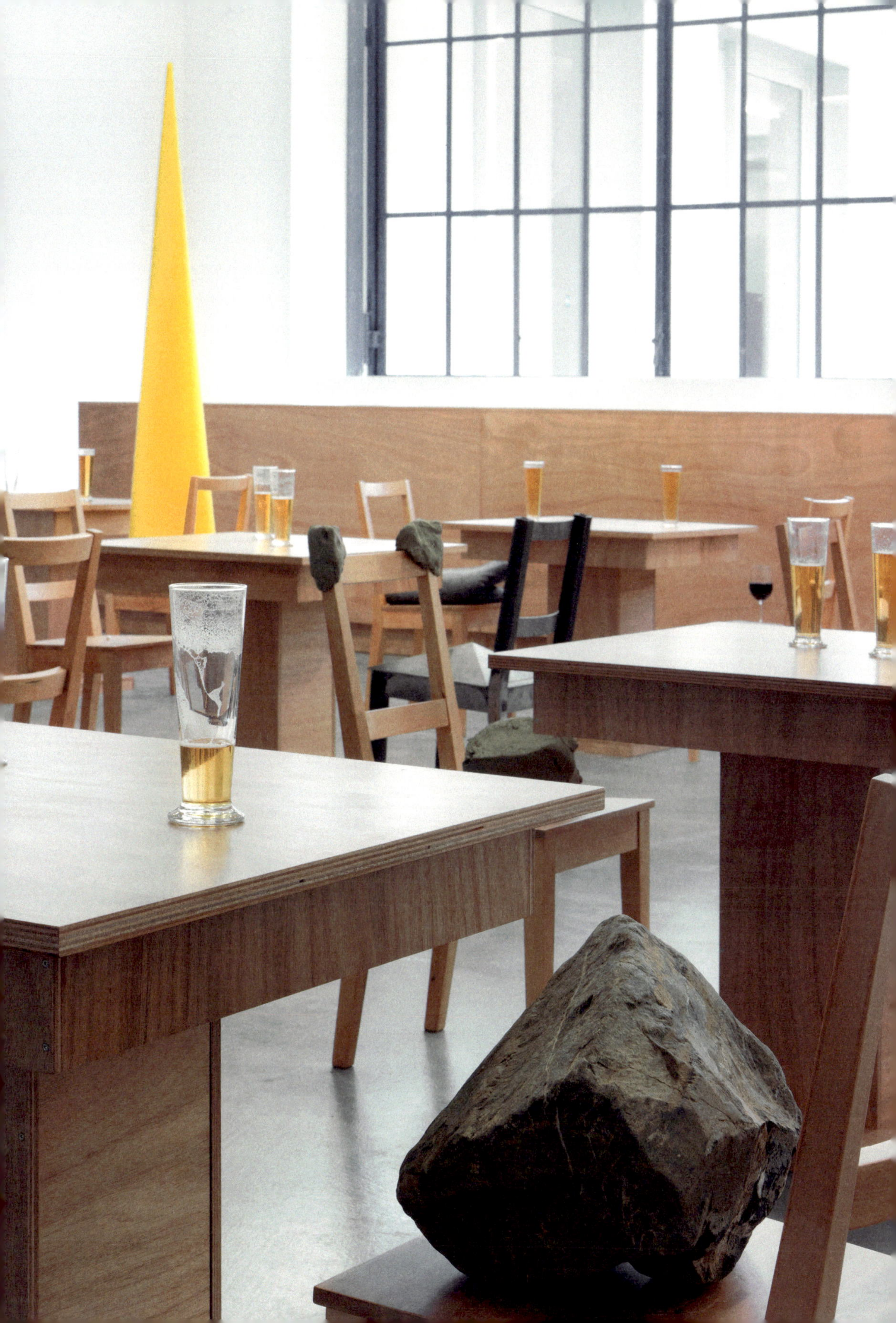

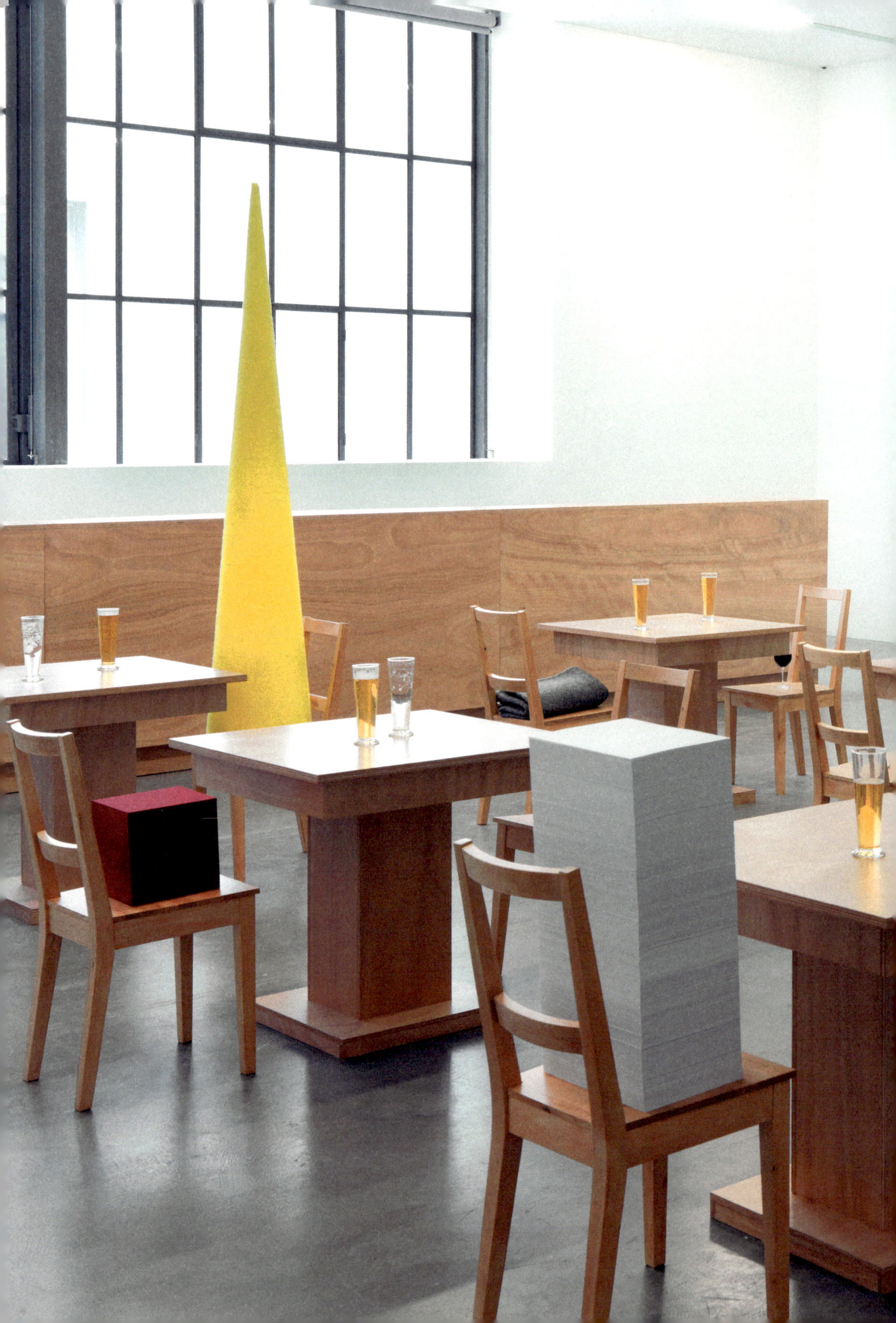

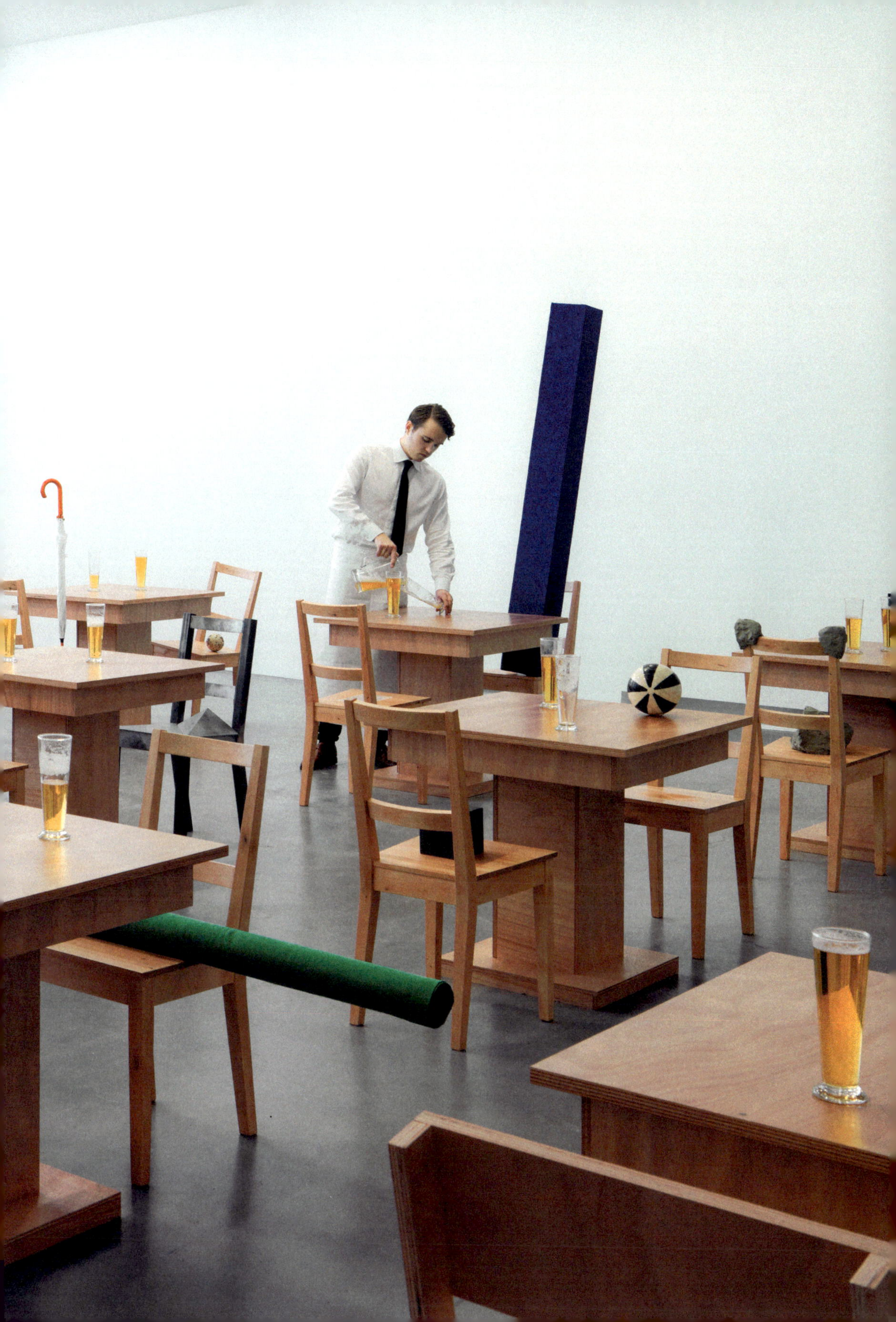

The Naked Magician

O Mágico Nu

A man is wearing an elegant magician's outfit, except that the sleeves are peculiarly short, suggesting that his tricks are not hidden. He is engrossed in his studio making all sorts of sculptures, drawings, and experimental images with the materials he finds there. An accumulation of objects fill the shelves and hang from the walls and ceiling. As viewers enter, they find themselves immersed in an intense space of concentration and information. Half the shelves stand straight, while the other half are in complete chaos, almost collapsing on the floor. In the strange atmosphere, the movement of things seems frozen. The magician never stops laboring.

The Naked Magician / O Mágico Nu, 2008 / 2010 / 2013
Magician, fabric, iron, wood, clay, tools, glasses, water, paper, fabrics, inks, flour, minerals, Chinese porcelain, mint, fireworks, plants, umbrellas, notebooks, books, comic books, instruction manuals, oil, alcohol, scotch, unidentified material, geometric shapes, cuckoo clock, bay leaves, sugar, wine, prosthesis, a stuffed rat, a small elephant, water from three different rivers, rubber, pollen, sodium bicarbonate, chocolate, petrol, iron ore, vitamins, hair, fragrances, postage stamps, a barometer, rulers, bamboo sticks, roses, silverware, coffee, empty eggs, brass bell, globe, deck of cards, hot glue, glue
Dimensions variable

Courtesy of the artist, Photography: Stefan Altenburger Photography, Gregor Staiger
Views: Migros Museum für Gegenwartskunst

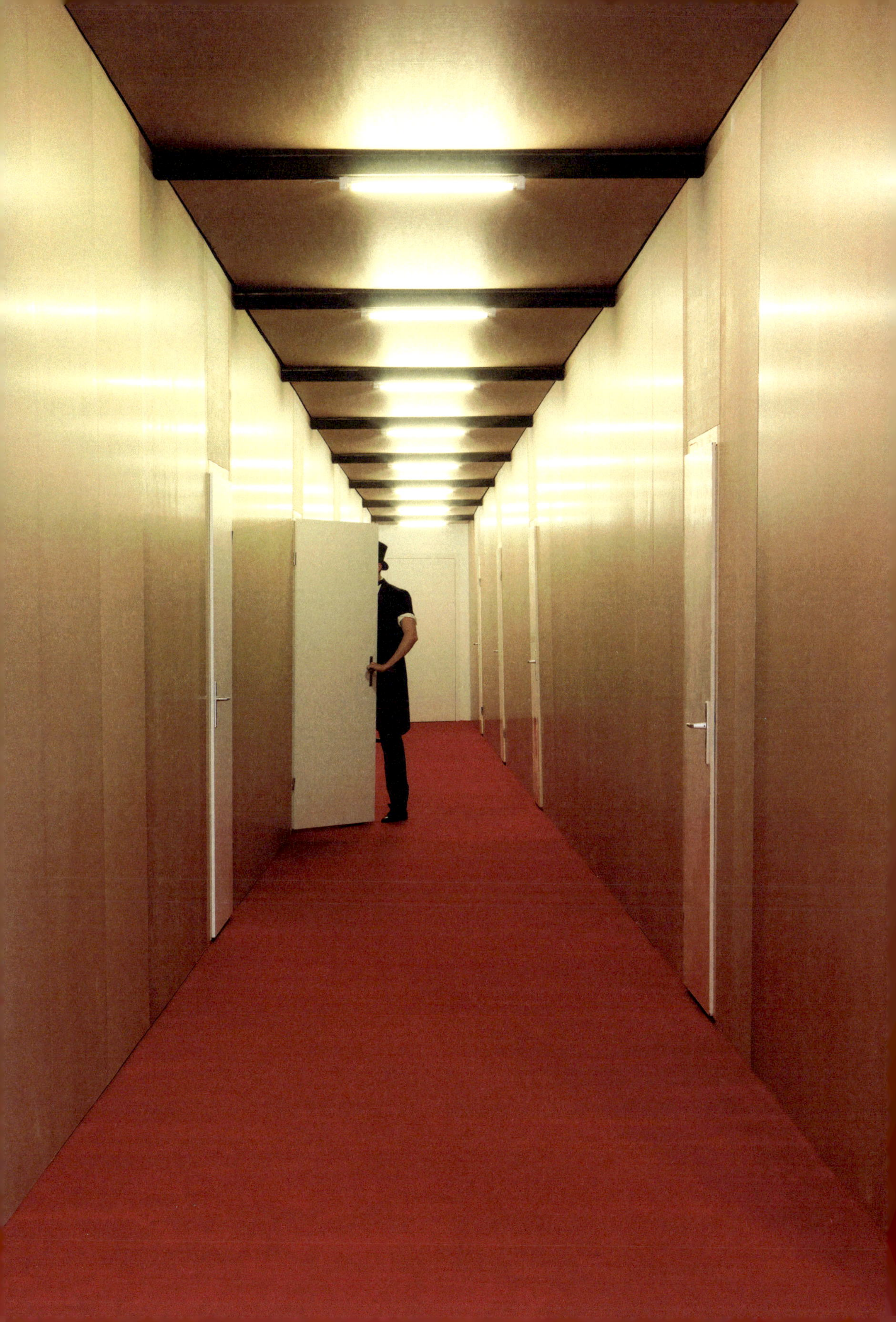

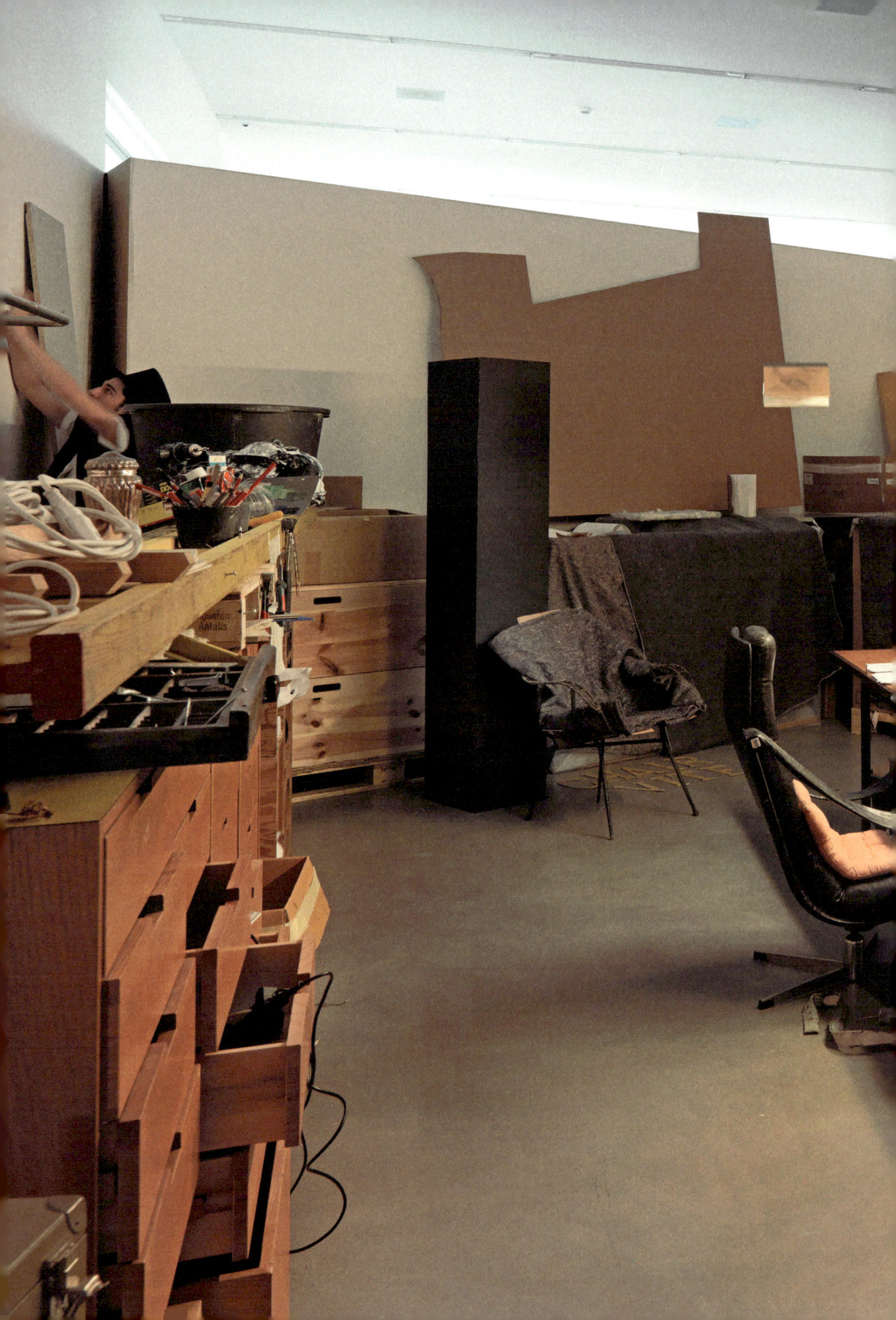

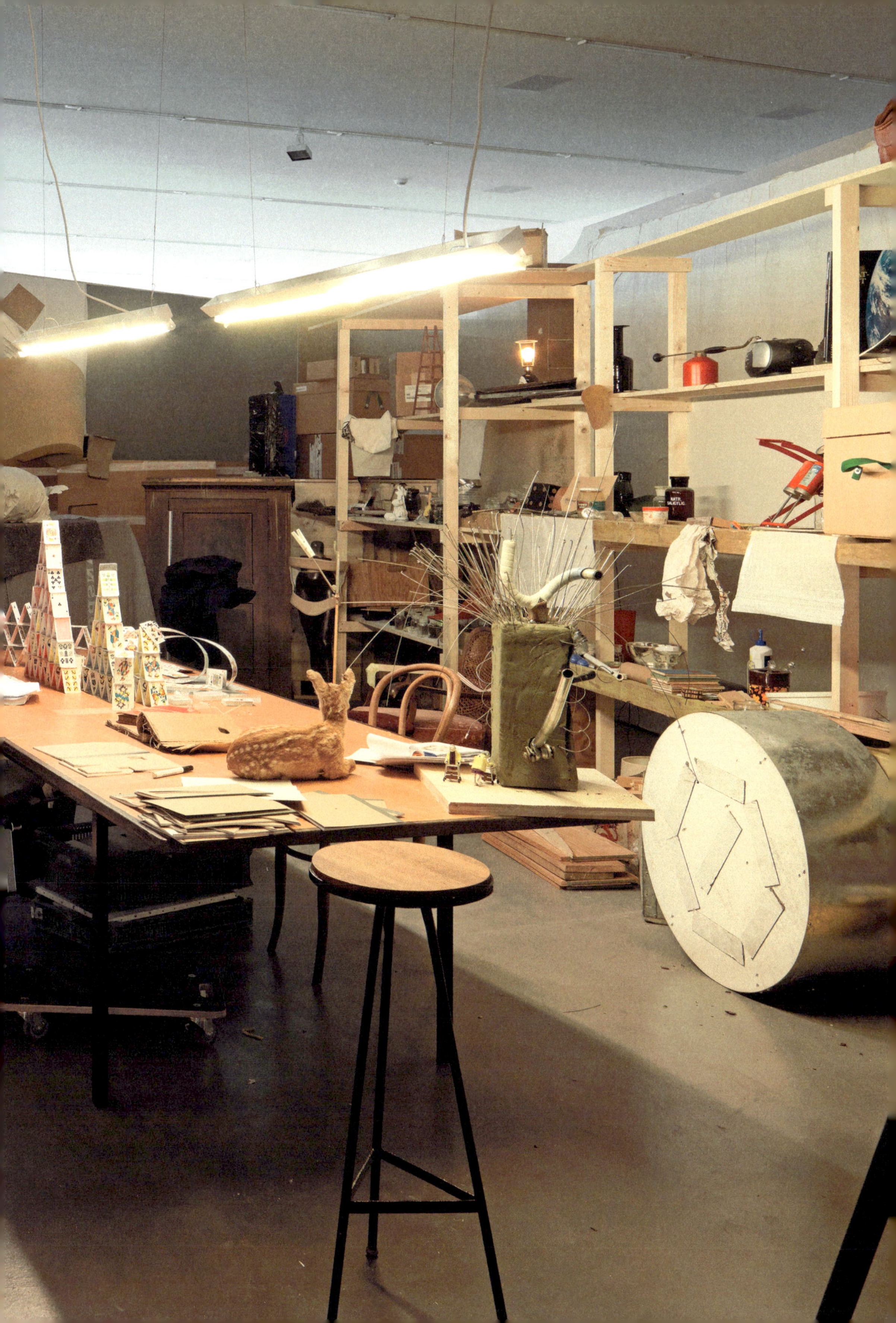

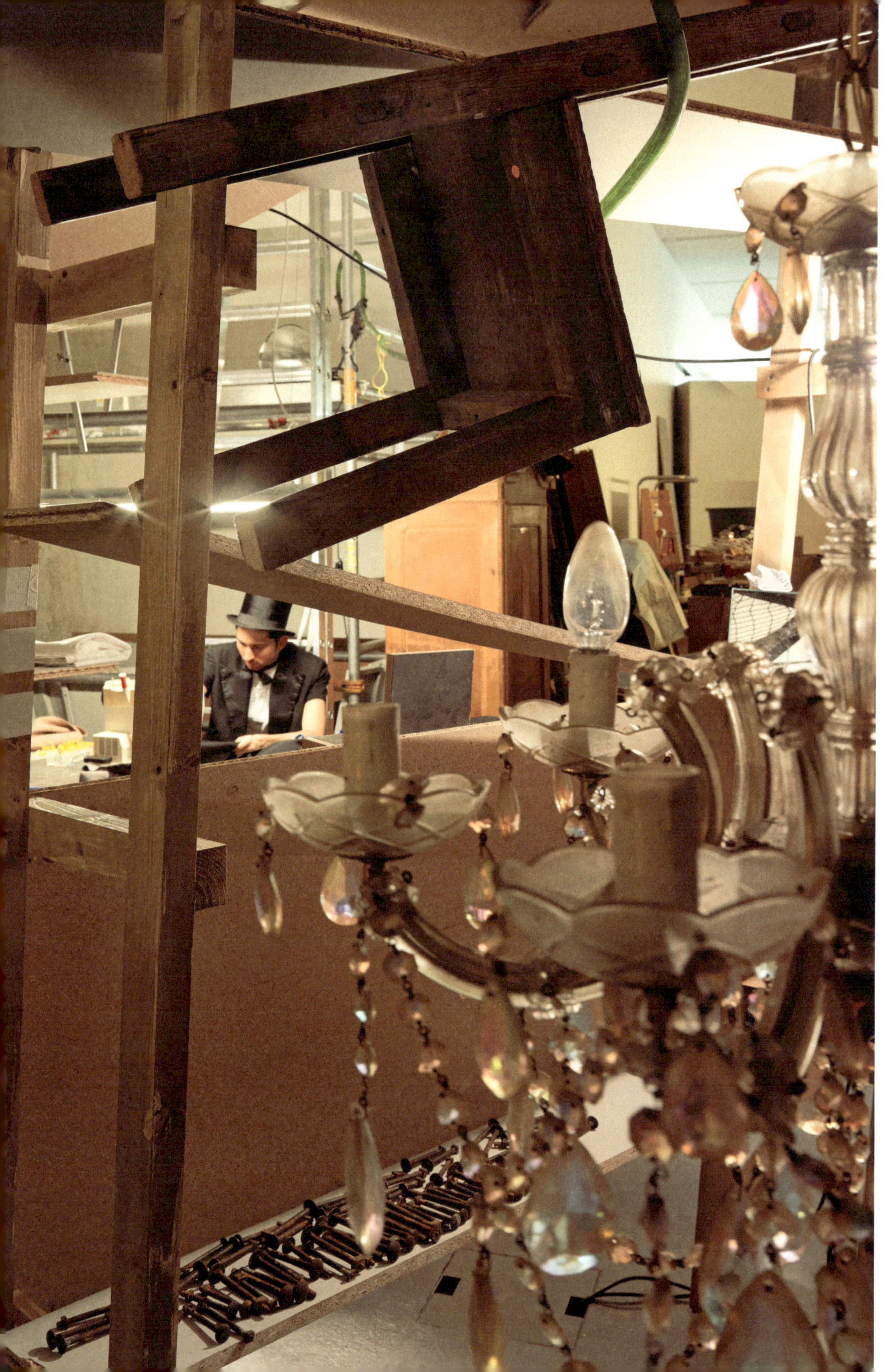

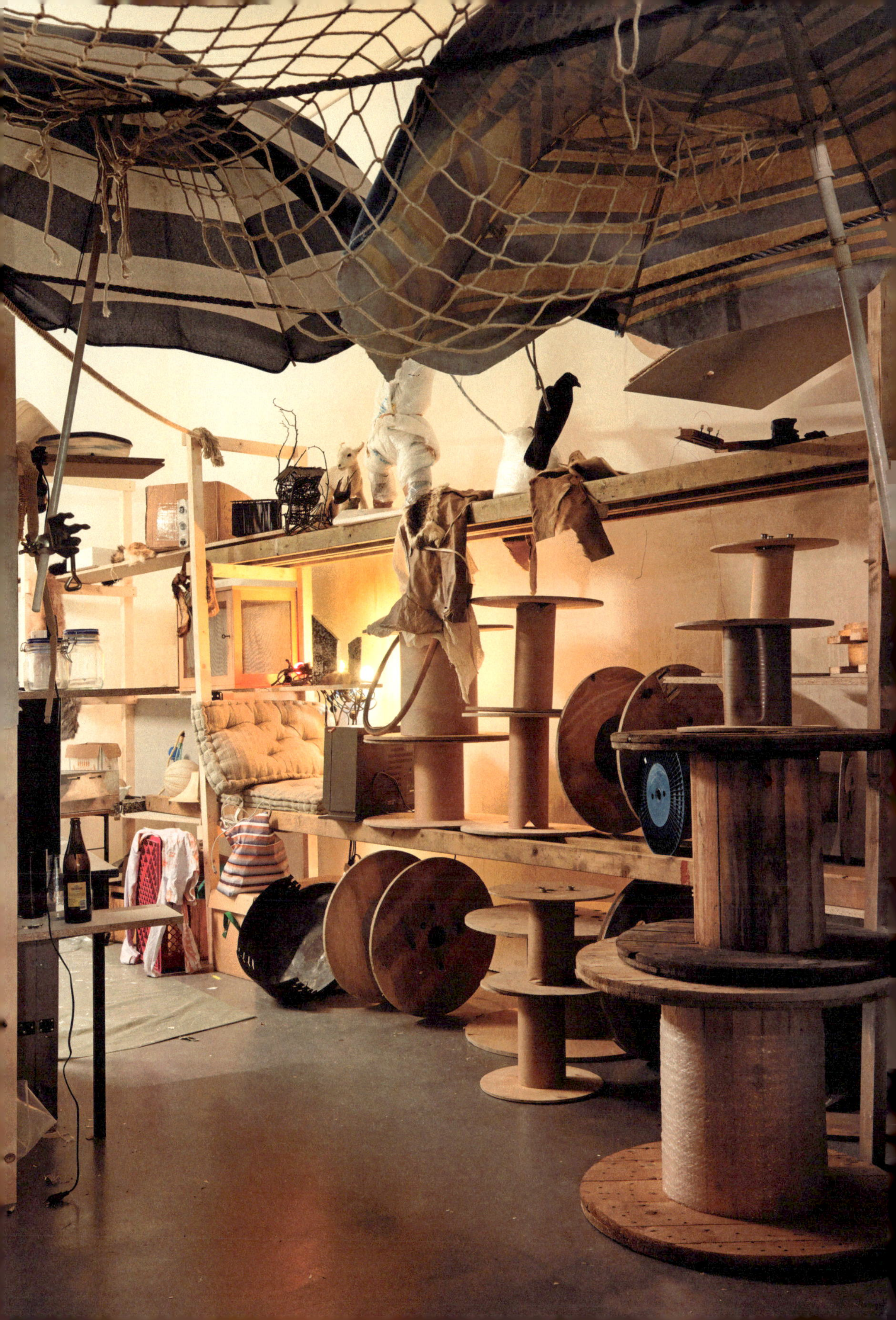

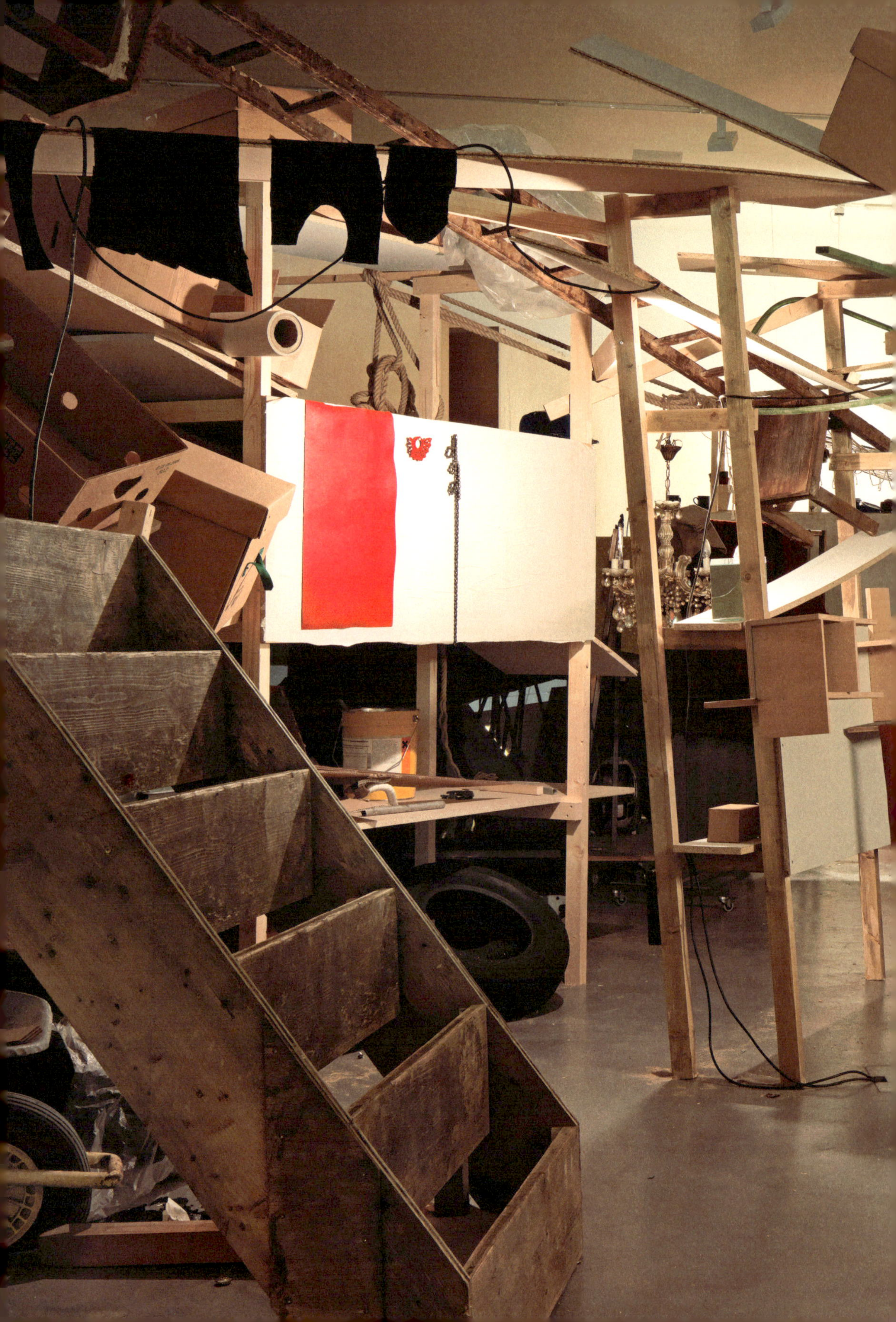

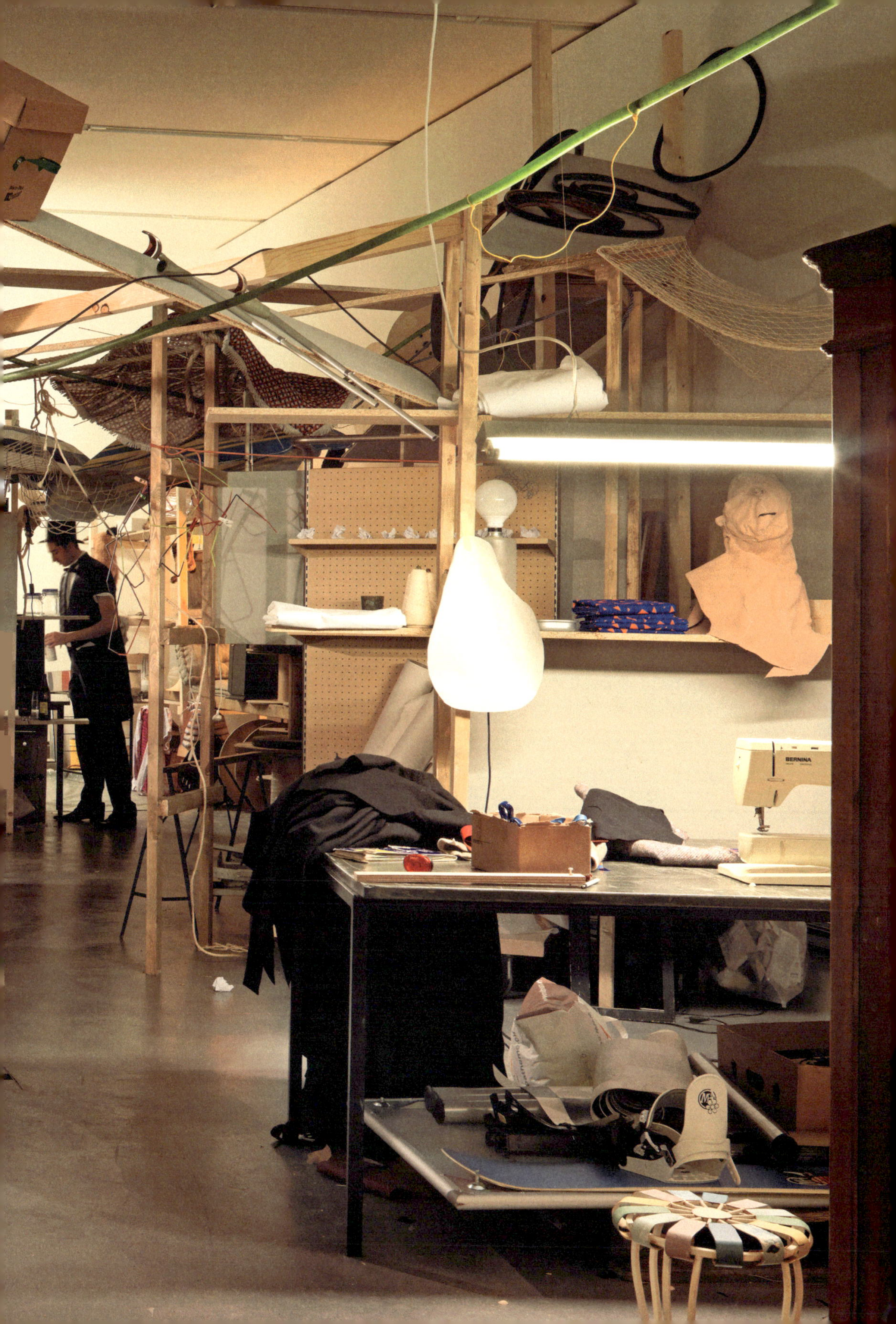

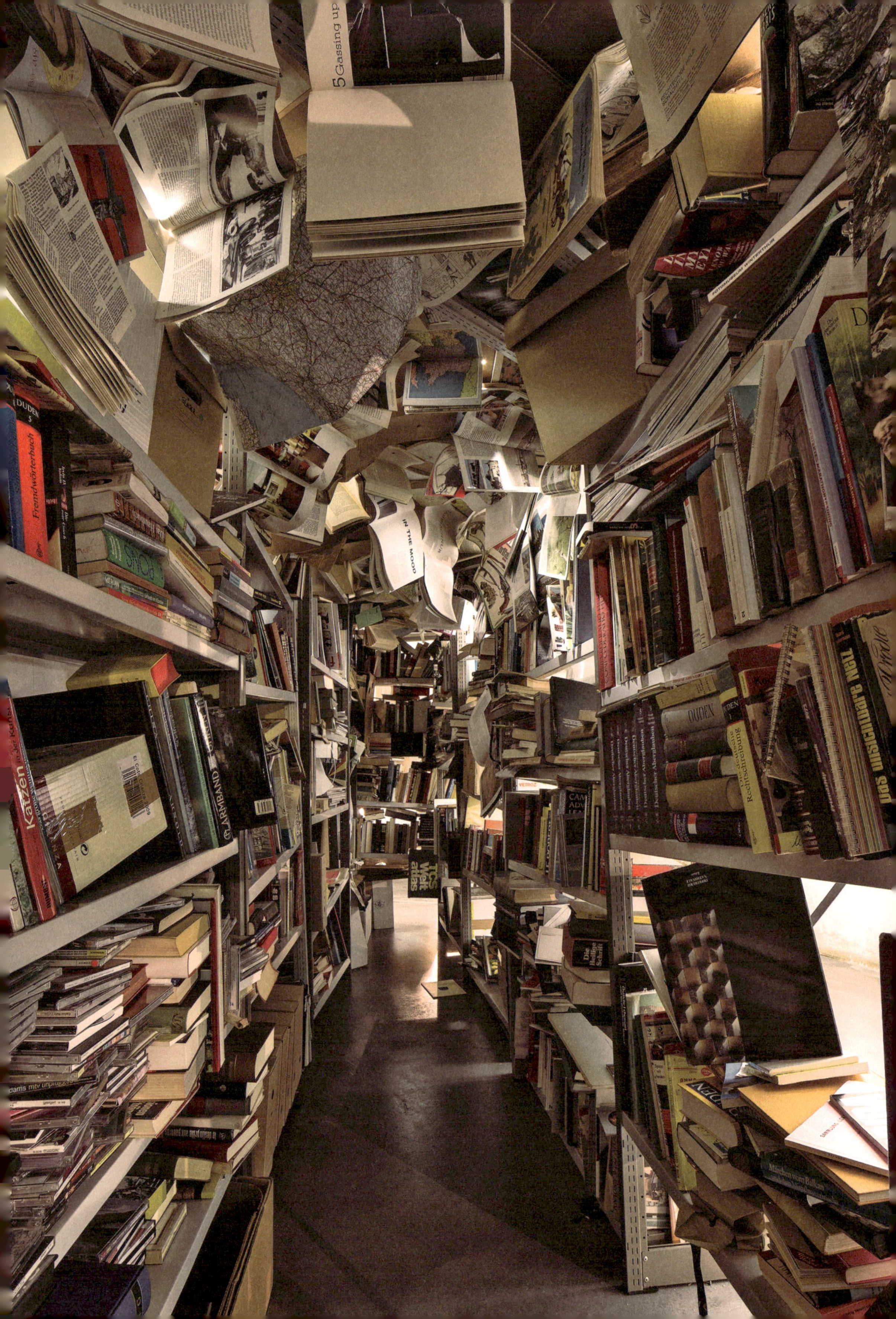

Laura
Lima

Published by

Migros Museum für
Gegenwartskunst
&
Bonniers Konsthall
&
JRP|Ringier

Contents

Heike Munder

*Impulses
of Resistance*

21

Nature creates similarities. One need only think of mimicry. The highest capacity for producing similarities, however, is man's. His gift of seeing resemblances is nothing other than a rudiment of the powerful compulsion in former times to become and behave like something else. Perhaps there is none of his higher functions in which his mimetic faculty does not play a decisive role.

Walter Benjamin, "On the Mimetic Faculty" (1933)

An atmosphere of mystery and opacity fills the room. A cluster of shelves forms the framework in which the action is set and turns the exhibition space into a universe apart. An overabundance of different materials such as books, tools, stacks of paper, and sculptures crowd the racks, floor, and tables. The shelves look as though in free-fall, as though they were collapsing upon themselves, and yet are frozen in mid-motion. At the center of this apparent disorder stands a man wearing a tailcoat with the sleeves cut off: a magician in his studio. Deeply absorbed in thought, he ceaselessly rearranges his utensils or creates new objects.

Laura Lima's *O Mágico Nu* (*The Naked Magician,* 2008) invites the visitor to the exhibition to become a silent observer of, and participant in, this scene. We intrude upon a situation that seems secret and arouses our curiosity. We can wander around the room and closely examine the things we find—the magician, meanwhile, goes about his business, undisturbed. There is something impenetrable about the situation: on the one hand the visitor observes a scene of ordinary and mundane work—sorting and arranging—while on the other hand the chaos and the objects look as though they came from a different sphere, an "otherworld" that, as the anthropologist Susan Greenwood puts it, is part of the "magical field" to whose experience and description she has dedicated her scholarly work.[1] In and of themselves, the rational world of work and the sphere of magic are incompatible universes: magic is generally regarded as a supernatural phenomenon that exerts influence over things, events, and living beings by communicating with supernatural forces and nature spirits.

---

1   See Susan Greenwood, "The Experience of Magic," in idem, *The Anthropology of Magic* (Oxford: Berg, 2009).

In recent years, magic has been big in the popular media. One need only think of Harry Potter, a student at a school of wizardry, or of British and American television shows like *Bedlam, Being Human,* or *Angel.* What all these narratives have in common is that they examine the classical question of "good versus evil" through the looking glass of white and black magic. In the Western world, magic and the magical are interpreted as an alternative world that is sharply in conflict with religious belief and accordingly subject to denigration. Yet the secularized Western societies show a growing interest in powers and explanations that exceed the rational level. How might we explain this trend? Most countries of the global Northwest—in Europe as well as North America—are informed by a cast of rationality and morality whose roots Max Weber uncovered in his major studies on the sociology of religion: *The Protestant Ethic and the Spirit of Capitalism* (1904–1905) and *Die Wirtschaftsethik der Weltreligionen* (The Economic Ethic of the World Religions, 1915–1917). According to Weber, the non-rational and extrasensory was pushed to the margins, especially in the era of modernization and industrialization, the period in which modern capitalism took shape: rationalization also implied a disenchantment of the world. Weber and his followers observed an overarching historical shift away from magic and toward a "philosophical breakthrough" (Talcott Parsons), toward ideas of salvation that, in the Western perspective, transcend the bounds of magical thinking in their relation to time as well as in their conceptions of morality and rationality. Another aspect of this historical process is the shift Weber conceptualized as "intellectualization and rationalization," which constitutes a space of possibility: "The increasing intellectualization and rationalization do *not,* therefore, indicate an increased and general knowledge of the conditions under which one lives. It means something else, namely, the knowledge or belief that if one but wished one *could* learn it at any time. Hence, it means that principally there are no mysterious incalculable forces that come into play, but rather that one can, in principle, master all things by calculation. This means that the world is disenchanted. One need no longer have recourse to magical means in order to master or implore the spirits, as did the savage, for whom such mysterious powers existed. Technical means and calculations perform the service. This above all is what intellectualization means."[2]

---

2 Max Weber, "Science as Vocation," in *From Max Weber: Essays in Sociology,* trans. and ed. by H. H. Gerth and C. Wright Mills, new ed. (Abingdon, U.K.: Routledge, 1991), p. 139.

According to Weber, the rise of those Christian religious tendencies for which he coined the term "inner-worldly asceticism" was a particularly decisive turning point. Rejecting contemplation and idleness, this active asceticism called for the application of possessions to necessary and practically useful purposes and regarded the world and society as imperfect realities that were thus in need of further development. On the moral plane, which it strongly emphasized, it sought to "tame what is creatural and wicked" in the individual, primarily through discipline and work in a worldly vocation. It fostered a view of life in which the Cartesian idea of the separation of body and mind associated with the Enlightenment became widely accepted and the mind achieved supremacy over the body. A methodically rational conduct of life widened the gulf between mind and body. A concomitant separation from the natural world reinforced the idea of authority and control over nature, which originally rested on religious foundations but was eventually set on an openly economic and political basis. These forms of the conduct of life demonstrate characteristic features of Western modernity. Conversely, the residents of an increasingly rationalized and administrated world developed a strong yearning for the restoration of the connection between mind and body as well as a renewed appreciation of intuition and sensory experience. In the Western world of the twentieth century, this tendency articulated itself in the spiritual quest for meaning that spawned youth, sub-, and counter-cultures, ecological movements, and phenomena such as the New Age movement and diverse variants of neo-paganism.

Other cultures have more smoothly integrated the spiritual register, and hence mysticism and magic—for instance, in the archaic form of natural religion, in conjunction with the desire to establish connections to the "otherworld"—into everyday life and religious practices. In Brazil, for example, a Catholic tradition to which magical elements are not alien to begin with shows such syncretism with Candomblé, an Afro-Brazilian religion imported by West African slaves. Candomblé knows the worship of multiple deities, and one form of contact with them is through rites involving possession in which the body is the scene of the surrender to the gods. This physical engagement with religion helps believers merge the rational and the mythical-magical sides of life in ways that feel natural. This aspect of an integrative religion provides an obvious and fascinating point of departure for a discussion of *The Naked Magician*'s work and other pieces by Lima with a view to "magical-religious" phenomena (Greenwood). One feature of such practices is their tendency to include aspects of imitation and mimesis. The magician hopes to obtain effects by channeling forces through an imitation of things.

The human or animal body plays a special role in the enactment of these moments of mimesis in Lima's works. It becomes the stage of her actions, as in the body of work *Homem/carne=Mulher/ carne (Man=flesh/Woman=flesh,* 1994–). In her theory of ritual, Mary Douglas had already regarded the physical body as a microcosm of society.[3] There is, at first glance, something strange about these actions, something arcane. The humans or animals appear as extras who are present for the entire duration of the exhibition (and replaced by substitutes when necessary).

In the first piece in this body of work, Lima took a cow from the hill country outside Rio de Janeiro to the city and pastured it on a beach for a day. The unusual sight in a public place led local residents and visitors to ask themselves a number of questions. Was it chance that had brought the cow here, or perhaps the decree of spirits or gods? For *Dopada (Doped,* 1997), Lima had a woman dress in a white robe, take a strong sleep-inducing drug, and lie down in the exhibition space. A crocheted, tubelike object constituted what seemed like an organic connection between her head and the wall of the building. In *Gelatina (Jelly,* 1997), a little girl in a white dress played in a basin filled with red jelly until her dress was stained red from top to bottom. The sullied girl triggers dark and sinister associations in the spectator that contrast with the childlike play with red jelly. And what is going on inside the woman resting on the floor in an immaculate white dress as the visitors circle around her? Or what does it mean that, in *Marra (Fighting,* 1996) two naked men are wrestling each other in the exhibition space, connected by a cloth hood sewn together to cover both of their heads? The blindfolded combatants charge at each other as though evil powers had found a suitable scene for their strife.

All of these works of art use the body as the central means of expression. The focus of interest is on what a body seemingly controlled by archaic powers may accomplish. But what are these powers the works bring to bear? Do they originate in an "otherworld," or are they mere fictions and imitations? If the latter, to which effects? Should we ascribe a distinct consciousness to the human beings, or are they utterly under the sway of remote powers? This question

---

3   Mary Douglas, *Purity and Danger: An Analysis of Concepts of Danger and Taboo* (London: Routledge & Kegan Paul, 1966).

is posed most vividly by the work *O Puxador Paisagem (The Landscape Puller,* 1999): a naked human body is tied to the architecture by rubber bands. Its powerful movements look like attempts to preserve the structure in an invisible equilibrium, braving imperceptible forces. Lima herself emphasizes that she treats things and humans as peers; such refusal to distinguish is reminiscent of animism, a variant of magical conceptions that regards things as possessing a soul as well. Lima's objects become organic and are thus bodies no less than her human actors.

The discourses on magic that emerged in the nineteenth century provide several explanatory models that can help us understand what is opaque about Lima's art. The debate over magic was shaped not only by sociological theorists of religion like Weber and Durkheim, who "demystified magic," but also by early anthropologists such as Edward Tylor and James George Frazer. Frazer's theory of sympathetic cultures knows two principles: the "law of similarity" and the "law of contact." The former describes the power of imitation; the second, the magic of contagion effected by touching an object. Both taken together constitute sympathetic magic. A little later, Émile Durkheim framed his hypothesis of the all-pervasive opposition between the sacred and the profane, which was also directed against the concept of sympathetic magic. "A religion," he argued, "is a unified system of beliefs and practices relative to sacred things, that is to say, things set apart and forbidden."[4] Durkheim advocated a functionalist understanding of religion as a source of meaning and identity that a society creates and controls.

Despite some similarities, magic and religion differ considerably. Magic, too, knows sacred objects with which humans engage in specific practices and rituals but that are otherwise untouchable. Yet Durkheim and, even more forcefully, his student Marcel Mauss drew a clear distinction between religion and magic in one respect: according to Mauss's theory, magic does not tie a community to rules and memberships. On the contrary, he argues, magic is individualistic in nature, foregrounding the performance of rituals for individual and worldly purposes.[5]

---

4   Émile Durkheim, *The Elementary Forms of the Religious Life*, trans. by Joseph Ward Swain (London: Allen and Unwin, 1976), p. 47.

5   See the reconstruction of the ideas underlying the classical sociological theories of magic in Randall Collins, "The Four M's of Religion: Magic, Membership, Morality, and Mysticism," *Review of Religious Research* 50, no. 1 (2008), pp. 5–15.

Susan Greenwood and Michael Taussig are exponents of a more recent anthropological approach to the question of magic. Their theories devote greater attention to the body as a scene on which magic is enacted and identify positive aspects of magic as well. In his essay "The Golden Bough: The Magic of Mimesis," Taussig discusses Frazer's sympathetic engagement with sacred objects as well as the power of substitutes and their direct touch: the mimetic faculty is "the nature that culture uses to create second nature, the faculty to copy, imitate, make models, explore difference, yield into and become Other. The wonder of mimesis lies in the copy drawing on the character and power of the original, to the point whereby the representation may even assume that character and that power."[6] In exploring the idea of mimesis, he also draws on Walter Benjamin's and Theodor W. Adorno's theory of adaptive behavior, which focuses on the ability of humans to assimilate to their environments. Yet Taussig goes beyond the observation of a purely reactive impulse, emphasizing the active aspect of human praxis and the pleasure we take in transforming and shaping something that then magically behaves like the original. The man in *The Landscape Puller* really seems capable of maintaining the architecture in balance.

Greenwood studies magic in a broader sense than Durkheim or Mauss. In her book *Magic, Witchcraft and the Otherworld,* she connects the findings of an ethnographic field study on occult practices she undertook in 1990s England, based on participant observation and her own involvement in magical experiences, with academic discourses on magic in the field of anthropology;[7] in this context, she complements the discourse on her exploration of the "otherworld" and the spiritual-magical components she experienced with a perspective that departs from the rationalism of science. The latter regards magic primarily as a pseudoscience full of fallacies, or else as a special variant of the egocentric quest for healing or salvation in this world. Greenwood, by contrast, believes that the rituals of magic are of interest first and foremost as a site of resistance to the rationalism of secularized society. Durkheim, she argues, was on to something: rituals serve as sources of the collective mobilization of energies, but they also allow for dissociation from the ordinary world of everyday life and help establish contact with the "otherworld." In this context,

---

6   Michael Taussig, *Mimesis and Alterity: A Particular History of the Senses* (New York: Routledge, 1993), p. xiii.

7   Susan Greenwood, *Magic, Witchcraft and the Otherworld: An Anthropology* (Oxford: Berg, 2000).

the figure of the magician also acts as a mediator. He occupies a place between the two spheres, abiding in so-called "intermediary worlds." Though magicians who appear in the popular media not infrequently develop elaborate "personae," Greenwood regards their practices as a serious attempt to balance positive and negative cosmic forces, which are understood to underpin white[8] and black[9] magic.[10]

This balance of the power of magic as a resistance to the hegemony of purposive rationality and mimesis, which, as Taussig writes, teaches us that we are to a certain degree capable of transforming the world itself, is where Lima's works are situated. *The Naked Magician,* to return to the work with which I began my remarks, accepts—without passing judgment—this dialectic between positive and negative energies as well as between the world ordered by reason and the magical universe informed by intuition and the experience of spiritual forces. For life, according to this logic, is profoundly dualistic. The magician immersed in his work in Lima's performative installation focuses forces and energies that originate in a time and space outside the mundane sphere of ordinary life. And yet he is in touch with this sphere through all five senses of his body.[11] His working environment appears to be in perpetual commotion, a chaos in space defined by the union of creation and destruction. This atmosphere of intense concentration enables his mind to attain an alternative state of consciousness that lets him connect to the "otherworld," which, in the perspective of magical experience, must be read as a domain of spirits, deities, and demons. That is also what cutting off the sleeves demonstrates. He has nothing to hide—this is not about "cheap" illusionist legerdemain.

In an early action entitled *RhR* (1999–2001), an acronym for *Representative-hyphen-Representative,* Lima founded an exclusive society, not unlike a secret cult. The members wore special robes when they convened for ritualized actions specifically designed for each occasion;[12] the meetings were held at irregular intervals over the course of the society's three-year existence, often in

8   Greenwood mentions the American writer Starhawk (b. 1951) and the Welsh occultist and theosophist Dion Fortune (1890–1946) as exemplary protagonists of white magic.

9   The British occultist Aleister Crowley (1875–1947) is probably the best-known representative of black magic.

10   Greenwood, *Magic, Witchcraft and the Otherworld,* p. 2.

11   See Charles T. Tart, ed., *Transpersonal Psychologies* (New York: Harper & Row, 1975).

12   See also Jochen Volz's essay in the present catalogue.

public spaces such as the Rio de Janeiro airport. The actions were incomprehensible and opaque to outsiders. Durkheim distinguished between positive and negative rites; rituals, he argued, played a pivotal part in establishing and reaffirming the boundary between the sacred and the profane. In his view, any successful ritual requires four components: symbols, or sacred objects that signify membership; a sense of identification with the group; emotional energy in the individual, which is to say, confidence in and enthusiasm for the goals that have been set; and lastly, standards regarding right and wrong that also underpin the sanctions imposed for deviation from the values of the group.[13] On this basis, rituals contribute to the cohesion and reproduction of groups and entire societies.[14]

Mauss addressed this point at length, drawing a rigorous distinction between magic and religion by emphasizing the private and secret as well as individual character of the former: "A magical rite is any rite which does not play a part in organized cults—it is private, secret, mysterious and approaches the limit of a prohibited rite."[15] Religion, by contrast, is defined by its collective quality; it constitutes a community of believers tied together by shared convictions, rites, and rules of membership. By Mauss's criterion, secret societies are ultimately hybrid in nature. They evince the collective elements that are characteristic of religions, but due to their clandestine operation, they typically also feature elements of magic. *RhR* portrays the mimetic aspect of a secret cult in which the members are bound together by defined codes. Language, dress, symbols, and rituals are shared points of reference and constitute the basis for the formation of a "collective body" that continually reinvents itself through its actions. As Greenwood emphasizes, rituals in secret groups also serve the communal attempt to establish contact with the "otherworld"; such contact or the induction of "magical experiences" it facilitates enables the group to potentiate its powers.

Rituals help create a space that transcends the individuals and allows for the mobilization of energies. They thus lay the foundation for the procurement of information from the "otherworld" that may then be circulated in the profane world: the "otherworld" also functions as an ample storehouse of knowledge.[16] As an interpretation

---

13 See Collins, "The Four M's of Religion," p. 6.
14 Durkheim, *Elementary Forms,* p. 360.
15 Marcel Mauss, *A General Theory of Magic* (London: Routledge & Kegan Paul, 1972), p. 24.
16 Greenwood, *Magic, Witchcraft and the Otherworld,* pp. 33–34.

of *RhR,* these observations are no doubt speculative, since Lima has steadfastly refused to reveal the code and mission of her society. Based on these tentative assumptions, the question arises: What is reality, what is part of an artistic project (even if the artist denies it was art)? And where and to what extent does a genuine dissolution of boundaries occur? In Taussig's terms, the mimesis involved in the practices of a secret society may be so successful that they can actually collect and transform energy that becomes real in the performative process. It is interesting and indicative to note the environment in which Lima has her group act: the contemporary reality of the modern world with its distinctively purposive structures in airports and public spaces. In these places, rites and magic are uncommon and in fact seem disconcerting and eccentric. Most importantly, they lack the symbolically protected framework of *The Naked Magician*'s closed studio situation, which exposes the magical aspect.

Another work that touches on the theme of the secret cult and the energy of groups, in addition to the idea of mimesis as discussed by Taussig, is *Nômades* (*Nomads,* 2007). For this piece, Lima created masks out of copies of European landscape paintings from the sixteenth through the eighteenth centuries. A professional copyist painted the works on canvas. Pieces were cut from the copies, seemingly at random, and then folded to make masks, with holes for the eyes and nose. The masks were mounted on a wall in the exhibition setting—they were not to be used, but contemplated as relics of a past ritual use whose meaning and purpose remained opaque to the beholder. The impression that these masks represent some "sacred and pure nature" is powerful, even though Lima used perfectly ordinary landscape paintings. It may also be described as a sort of halo effect, where the realities do not truly correlate with the qualities attributed to them, as when, in the case of the masks, their apparent magical properties are metonymically ascribed to the wearer. At the same time, the mask conceals the identity of the person and his or her self in favor of the mobilization of collective energy and action in the group, a mimetic impulse because, even though the landscapes are European, seeing the mask on a wearer charges it with paradisiacal symbolism; it is endowed with mystical energy and animated by woodland spirits. The mask undergoes a symbolic transformation into a sacred object. In contact with the wearer, it lets energies flow; its effect is heightened in the group setting of the collective ritual. A paradise of this sort functions as a place of refuge. As Susan Greenwood has argued, it may be experienced as a space of resistance, as an oasis that is created when a small group congregates, wearing masks, for the shared ritual.

Lima's most important work to date in the field of mimesis or object transformation is *Galinhas de Gala e Galinheiro de Gala (Gala Chickens and Gala Coop,* 2004). A structure in the shape of a crystal made of wood and chicken wire forms a spacious birdcage used to house chickens the artist has adorned with paradisiacally colorful feathers. In their new magnificent plumage in luminous pink, blue, green, and yellow, the birds seem to carry themselves with the majestic pride of peacocks. This form of travesty triggers novel reactive behaviors among the congeners. Lima reports that the pecking order has shifted, with those animals that have the most striking equipment rising in the hierarchy. As "quasi-sacred objects," the colorful plumes raise the standing of their wearers, functioning as "insignia of power" based on nothing but the perception and recognition of the members of the group. Mimesis, in this instance, implies the ease of seeming to be not a chicken but a bird of paradise.

Another work that addresses the balance between different energies is *Bar Restaurante (Bar Restaurant,* 2010), which will reach its full size for the first time at the Migros Museum für Gegenwartskunst in Zurich. It is a peculiar sort of bar: the patrons occupying the tables and chairs scattered throughout the room are not humans but things. Stacks of paper, cylindrical shapes, and rectangular solids in various colors have been set on the chairs as actants. Glasses of beer sit in front of these patrons, gradually emptying as though invisible drinkers were sipping from them. A waiter, dressed for the part, continually refills the glasses. The situation seems absurd, but also meditative and focused. The formal vocabulary suggests a reference to late-1950s Brazilian art, when Concrete Art started to integrate time and the human body into the works in a challenge to the era's ascetic geometry and its association with industry and progress. In Lygia Clark and Hélio Oiticica, it metamorphosed into an organic movement. Lygia Pape worked on these ideas as well, developing a Neo-Concrete ballet in 1958 in which cylinders and cubes floated across the stage. The figures in *Bar Restaurant* now give the impression of a colorful posse of descendants of Pape's geometric ballet figures sitting down for a drink. Is this a play with the animist idea of things possessed of a soul and agency? Or does the work conjure the spirits of art history?

It is as though the bodies Lima arranges in *Bar Restaurant* playfully blend the invocation of the spirits of Neo-Concrete art with aspects of magic. Interestingly, she manages to bring all these themes together in a syncretistic whole, for example referring to the animal as well as the human body and drawing no fundamental distinction between the two. The animal body is not regarded as a legitimate part of the rational world; it is assigned to the natural cosmos. That holds even for domesticated animals such as cows or chickens. All participants, be they human or animal, act as extras who, in keeping with the idea of mimesis as laid out by Taussig, enable a translocation to a different reality such as appears in *Gala Chickens*. The body serves various functions in this context. It may, for instance, become the scene on which forces and energies of the "otherworld," to take up Greenwood's concept, are enacted. The body is the energy field with the potential to "channel" such forces. Like *The Naked Magician* abiding in the "intermediary world," the server in *Bar Restaurant* is charged with maintaining contact with the "otherworld" of magical objects and determining the volume of energies to be deployed and extracted.

The *Gala Chickens* may likewise be read as representatives of a divine travesty. Lima reduces the bodies to flesh—without individual qualities—and focuses on the energy of the collective body. In the perspective of magic, this means that, for moments in works such as *The Naked Magician* and *Bar Restaurant,* she liberates the human being who has volunteered as a channel to the "otherworld" from his or her self, clearing a path for energetic transmissions; things and bodies become equals insofar as they act as extras in this liberation. In light of Taussig's idea of mimesis, the mimetic extras in Lima's imitative practice may even be sustained by such strong forces that they are capable of surpassing the copy. In Greenwood's interpretation, the extras have one foot in reality, but their energy is supplied by higher powers. So they belong to both spheres and do not draw strength from one world alone. This allows them to repossess the bodies banished from the rationalized world (Weber). That is where Lima's recourse to the magical appears to be of fundamental relevance to the present moment. Her actions extend out into the mundane world, where notions of rationality reign supreme. Her actors and actants manage in matter-of-fact ways to maintain a tense relation to the magical and ineffable amid the banality of everyday life. We should hardly expect that Lima's approach will be able to influence the rules and mechanisms of a society at large. On the individual level, however, her inspiration may prove contagious, spurring an ever larger number of people to offer resistance to the "overarching process."

Gala Chickens and
Gala Coop

Galinhas de Gala e
Galinheiro de Gala

Carnival feathers and plumes are attached to the tips of the feathers of live chickens using
the same hair extension technique as used by humans. Adorned in this fashion,
the chickens remain inside a specially constructed coop for the duration of the exhibition.

Gala Chickens and Gala Coop / Galinhas de Gala e Galinheiro de Gala, 2004 / 2007 / 2011
Live chickens, special technique for feather extension, water,
food, wood, iron, feathers, plumes
Dimensions variable (a comfortable coop for at least forty chickens)

Courtesy of the artist, Photography: Cadu d'Oliveira
Views: Centro Cultural Banco do Brasil gardens, Brasilia

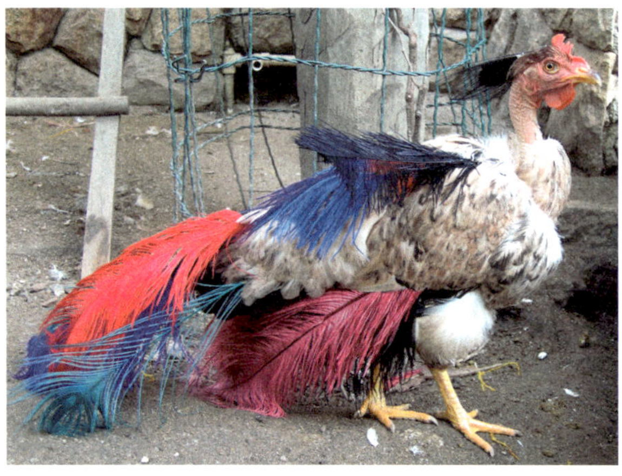

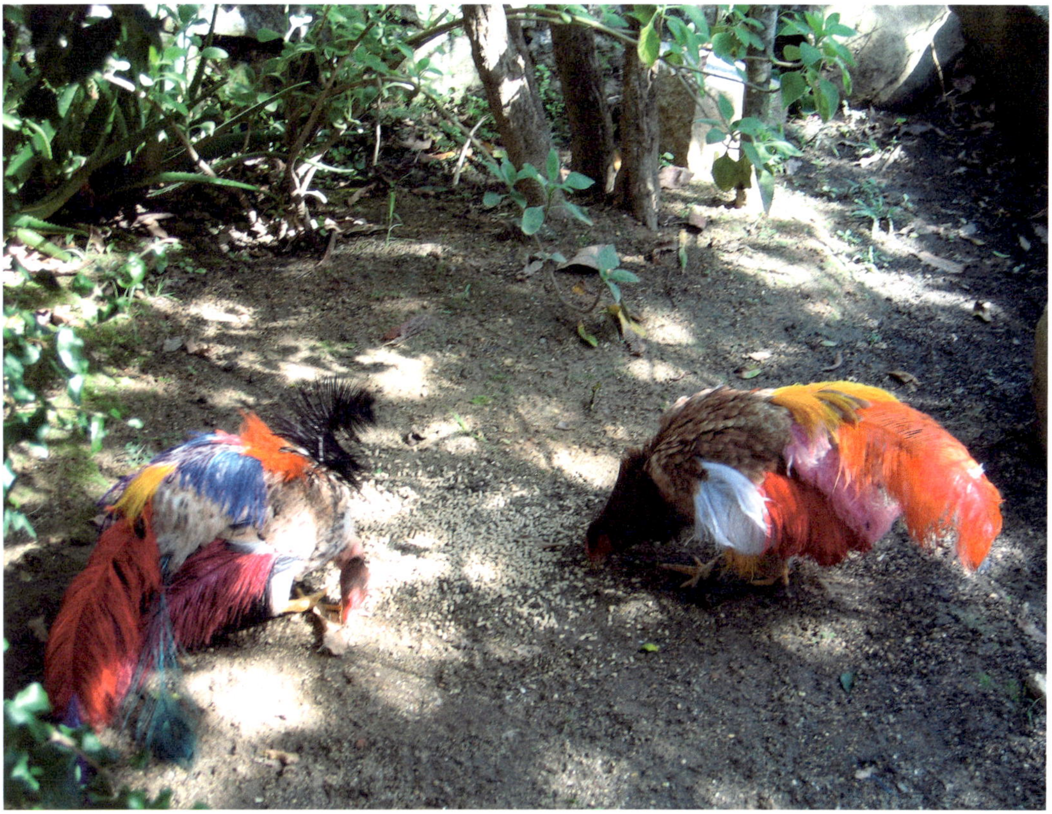

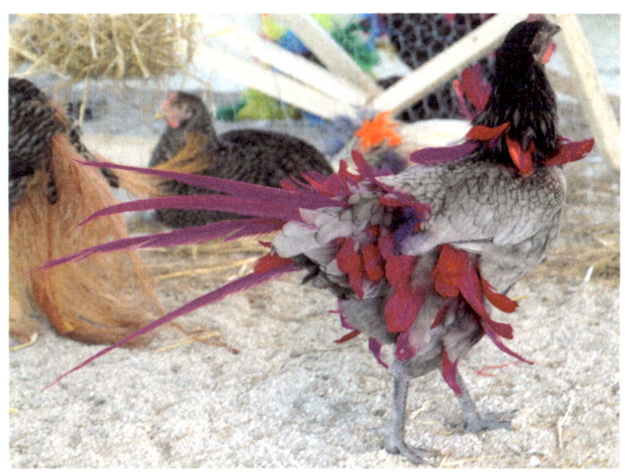

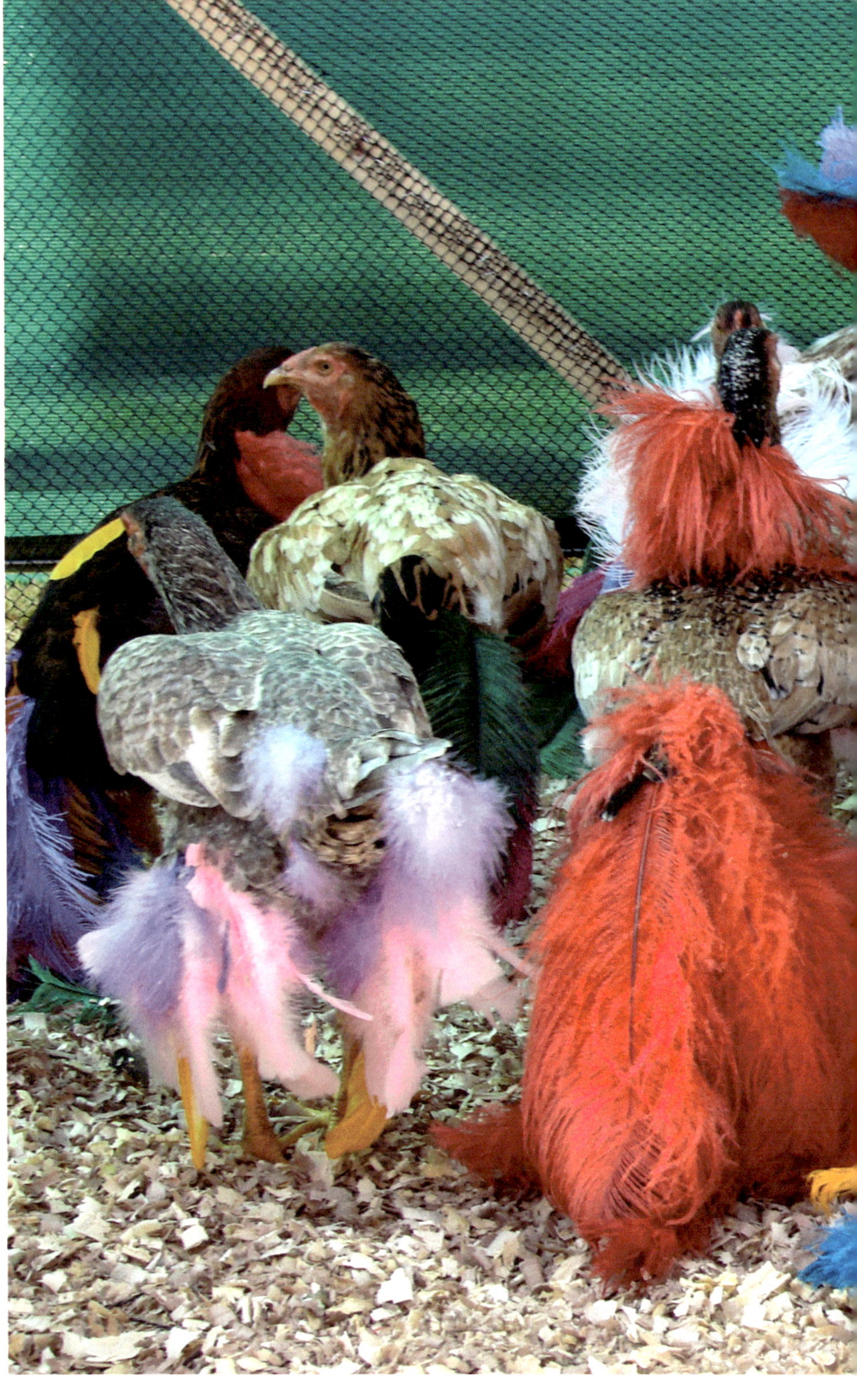

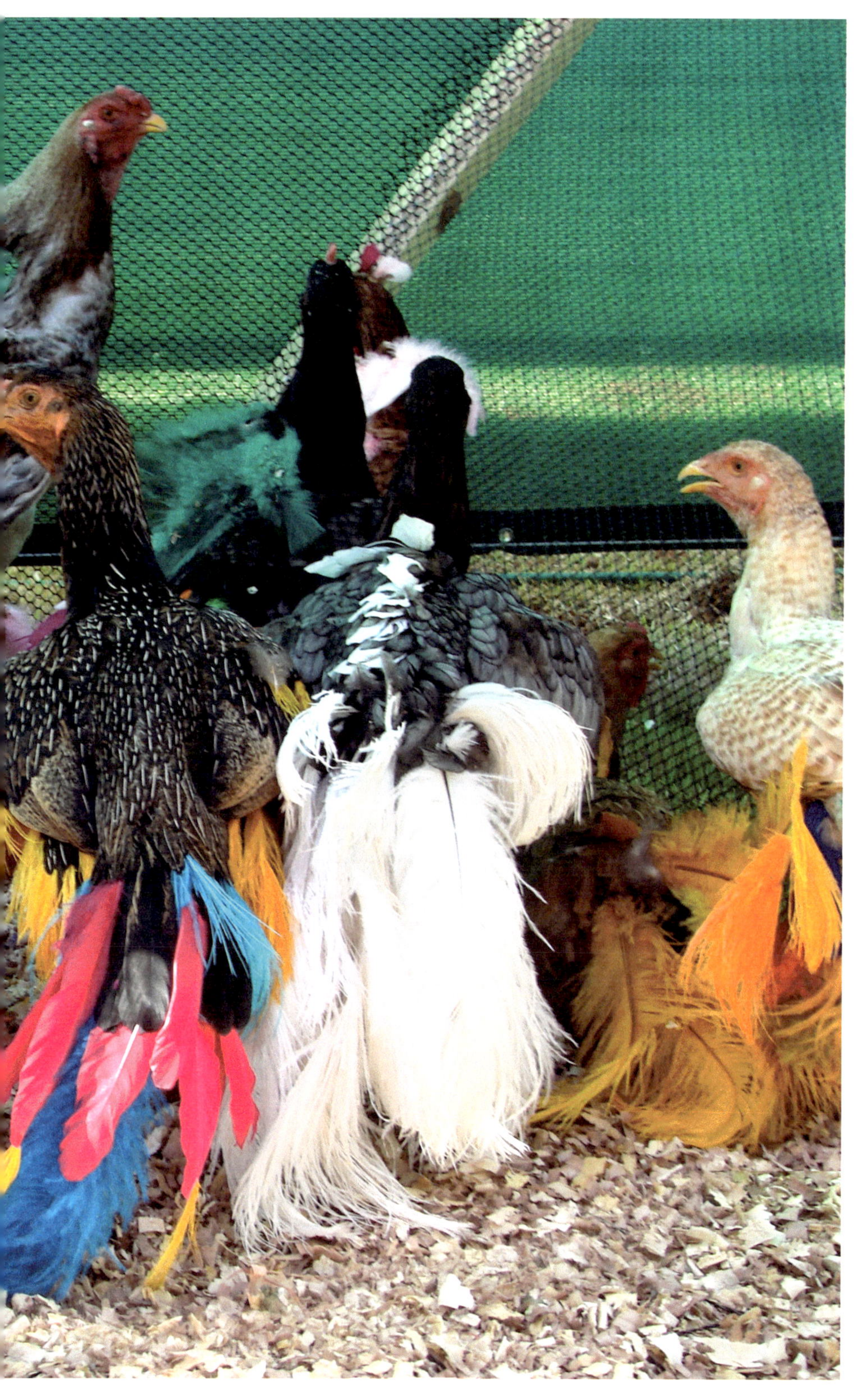

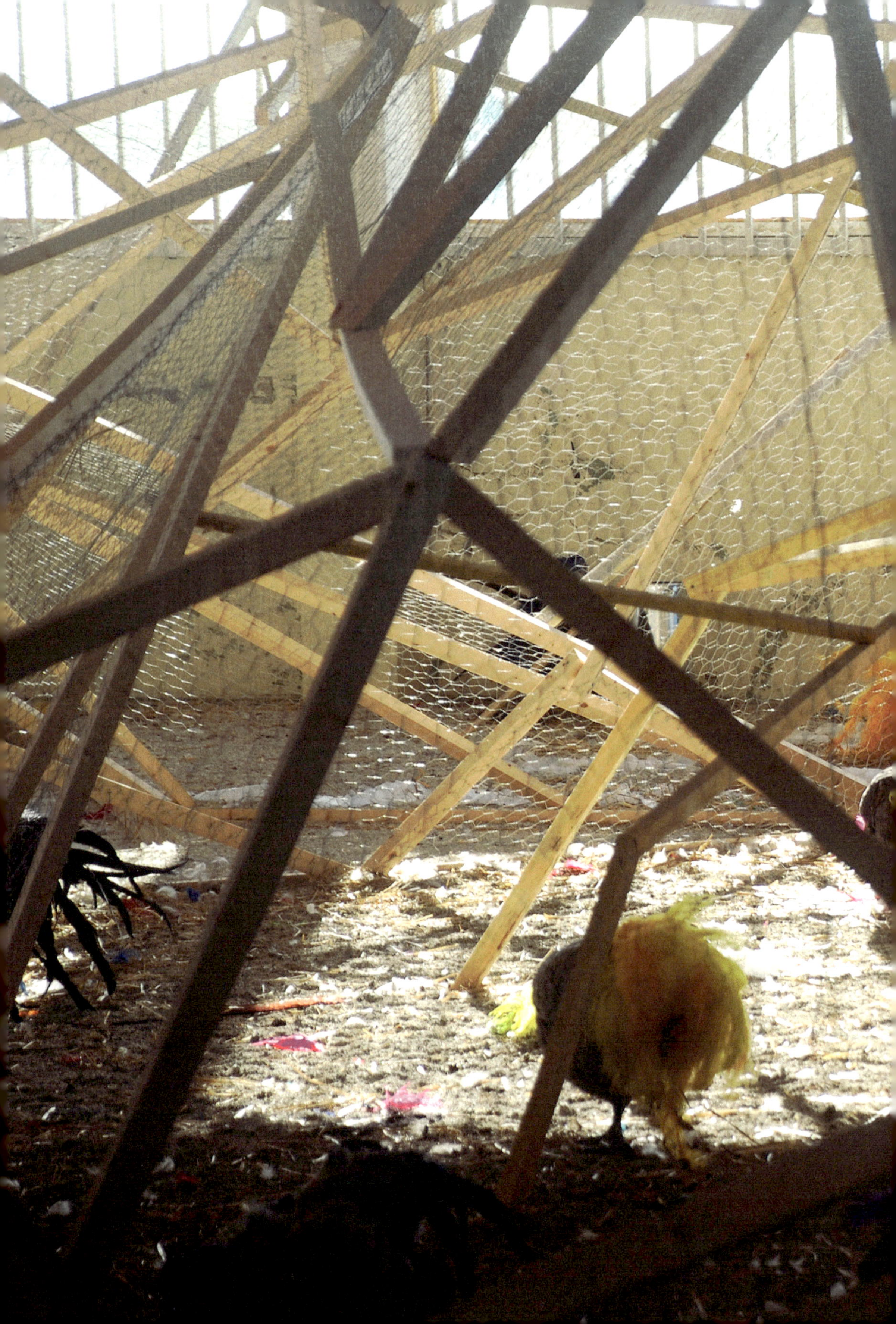

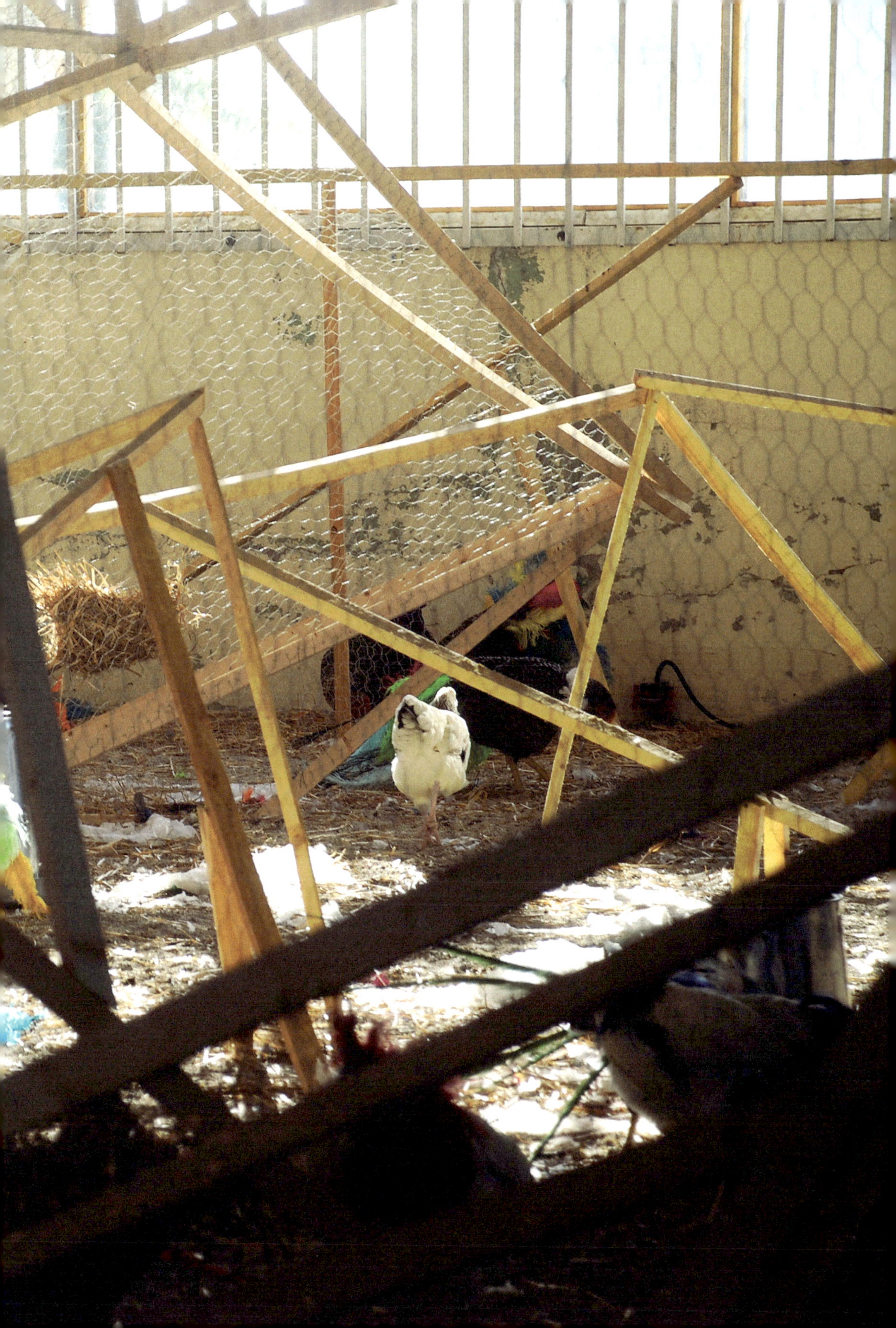

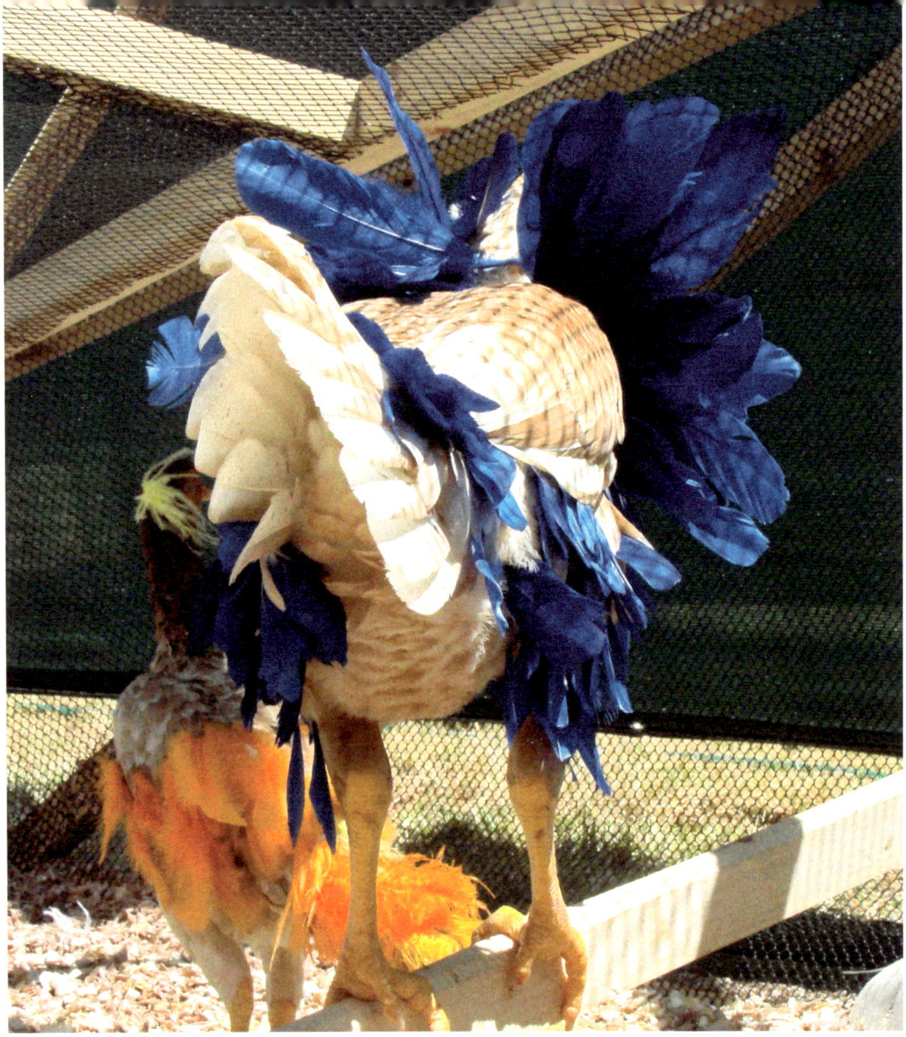

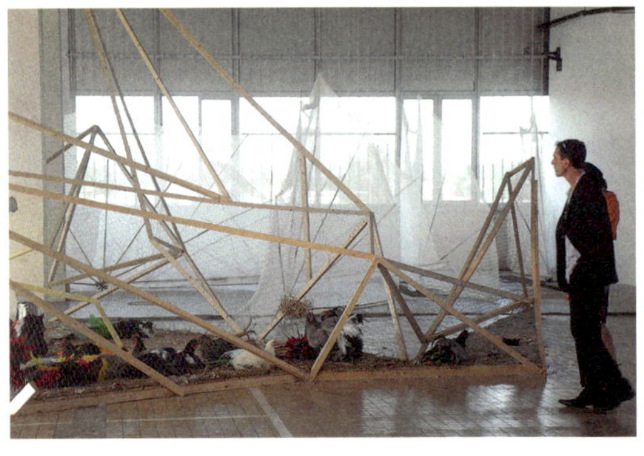

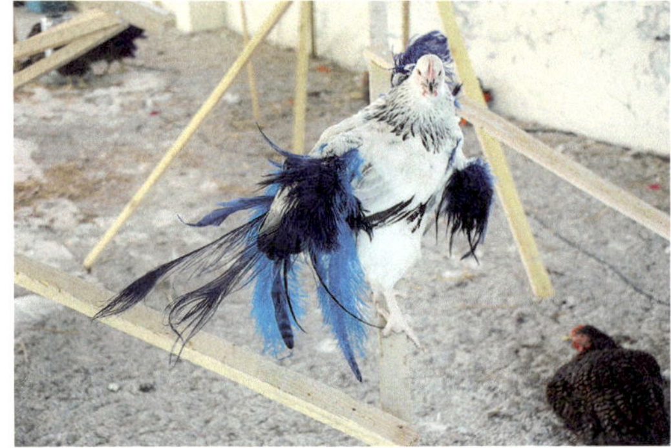

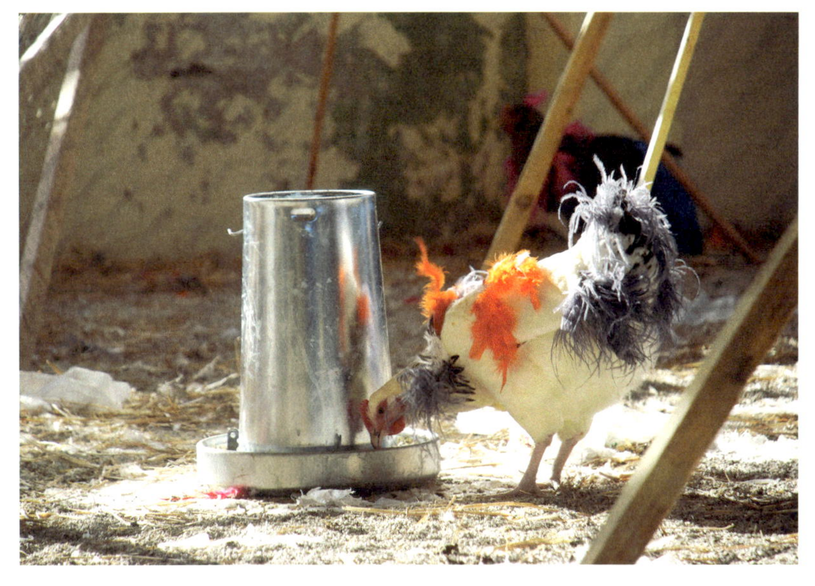

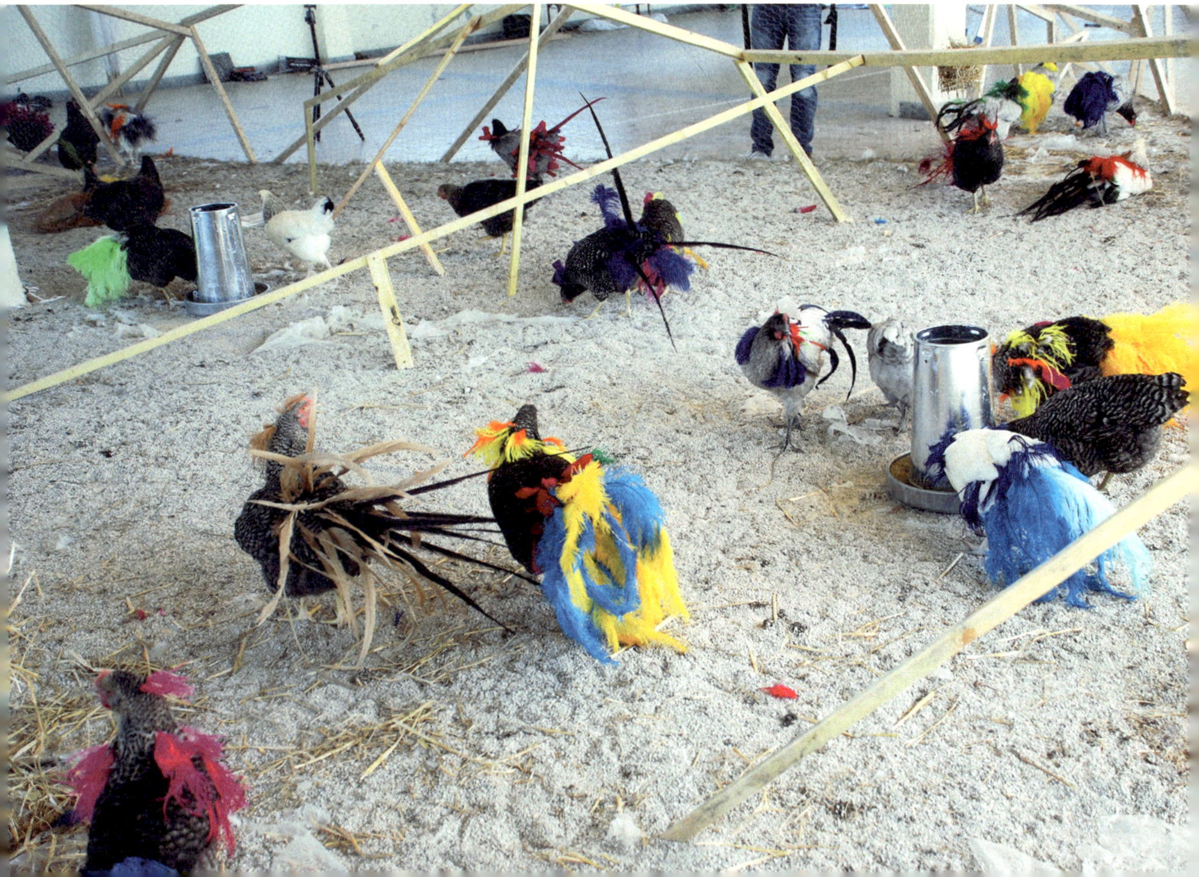

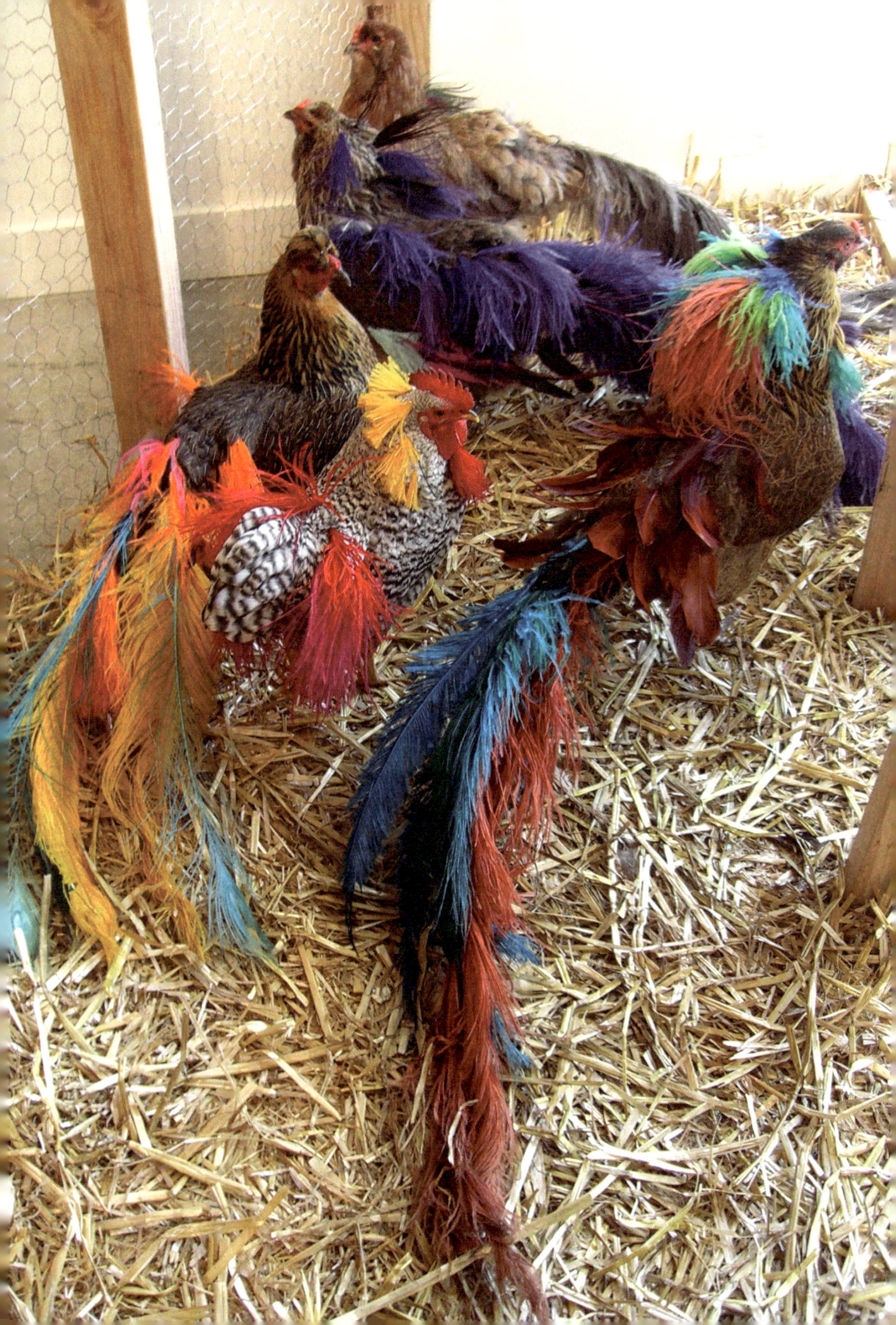

Victoria Noorthoorn

*Laura Lima's
Ornamental Philosophy*

43

In 1994, Laura Lima was studying art and philosophy at the Escola de Artes Visuais do Parque Lage and at the Universidade do Estado do Rio de Janeiro, when fellow art students organized an exhibition in the urban beach of Praia do Arpoador. Lima contributed to the show with an unusual action: she brought a cow from the surrounding *morros* of Rio de Janeiro to the beach, and with this gesture she initiated a personal philosophy and a way of being in the world and in art. She recalls her interest in creating "a landscape of estrangement, by incorporating elements where they do not belong." Lima was creating a new imagery for the world according to which the crucial terms that we have just referred to—exhibition, action, gesture, philosophy, world, and art—need to be considered anew. Her universe, a system of images and signifiers, is an approach to existence that is constituted in the crossover between her artistic proposals—to be situated always in the borders of the territory of the visual arts—and a very personal artistic *glossary* of terms in which she redefines the meaning of the words that may characterize her practice. By this I mean that Lima demands us to look *again* at what is before us in order to rethink our relationship to what we see, and to name or invent new words in order to be able to address the new experiences that she proposes. It is a practice that destabilizes and subverts a given order and behavior, and the subversion at stake is one to happen both at the level of the objects of the world, and at the level of the bodies both individual and social that occupy the world. The body—be it a human body or the body of an animal—undergoes a specific manipulation or treatment: an "ornamental philosophy," either real or imaginary, proposed by the artist. The act of ornamentation as applied to the living, existing bodies or to the potential, imaginary ones, implies the infiltration of the artistic gesture in diverse scenarios of daily life—including the exhibition space. All of which gives place to an experience of estrangement, absurdity, at times monstrosity or, very simply, of a rediscovery of the given.

Let's go step by step. There is, first of all, the question of the body. In the project that Lima initiated in 1994 *Homem = carne/ Mulher=carne (Man = flesh / Woman = flesh)*, she envisioned the human body realizing a series of fantasy-based actions in which the artist proposes an absurd and potentially traumatic relationship to an object. To name a few: Her *HcMc – O Puxador Arquitetura (The Architecture Puller)* could potentially pull an entire building out into the landscape or, vice versa, could bring the landscape into the building! Her *HcMc – Marra (Fighting)* would see two naked men, their heads united by one sole hood bringing them together despite their exhausting intent to fight each other and liberate themselves from each other. The woman in her *HcMc–Dopada (Doped)* would sleep beautifully for hours, her body being extended by a knitted head-piece that would continue to delineate the figure beyond itself in the context of an exhibition space. Her *HcMc–Pelos+Rede (Hair +Hammock)* would extend, with stark black soft-sculpted lines, the pubic hair of a female figure and the eyebrows of a male figure lying over a *chaise-longue.* All are images of a surreal bent that pave the way, irresistibly, to the experience of rediscovery. As time went by, Lima's noted drawings became actions (as when she enacted her *Puller* for the Museu da Pampulha in 2002), and the actions immersed the viewer in a feeling of estrangement. Indeed, Lima's work has the ability to point to the ways in which we experience the overwhelming power of art and to propose alternatives to our ways of life and to the ways in which we understand our current existences as human beings and human bodies. We become conscious of the domination that we experience in our daily lives: the homogeneity of behaviors that rules contemporary society, the homogeneity of aesthetics that rules the acts of dressing up and presenting ourselves to the world, and the homogeneity of norms that governs the use of both public and outdoor and interior spaces, both urban and architectural.

But how has the universe of her proposals in regards to the body unfolded? Another decisive moment, beyond the early notes in which Lima visualized the series *Man/flesh = Woman/flesh* for the first time, was the year 1997 in which she designed her series of *Dimensional Tattoos.* These instructions intended to improve bodily movements by suggesting precise transformations of the body: e.g. to remove three fingers from one hand and insert them in the other, creating an eight-finger hand to ensure a better performance of sports such as tennis, or, in another tattoo (borrowing a description by Zaya), "the bones of the leg under the knee must be cut. At the place of entry, eight joints are attached to enable new movement of the leg. A rubber and metal instrument must be inserted in the place of the tendons." [1] The *tattoos* were accompanied by a "Doctor's Note" so as to ensure that the action is carried out as envisioned by the artist. In these works, the notion of the body is subjected to imaginary alterations that allow us to free the body from usual social

---

1   Octavio Zaya, "Laura Lima," in *Fresh Cream* (London: Phaidon, 2000).

and individual behaviors. They also invite us to admit, in the understanding of the body, a dose of absurdity or of delirium that itself, in promoting the need to endorse the acts of the imagination and creation of alternative ways of being in the world, implies the design of a macro-system that is, contrary to what we might first imagine, utterly political.

The political nature of this, at first sight, seemingly apolitical work, could be the subject of an extended essay on *RhR* (1999), an "instance" (in Lima's glossary) or secret society of complex characterization whose title derives from the Portuguese *Representativo-hífen-Representativo* that highlights the notion of the *in-between*. Bringing together numerous members over a period of three years, *RhR* promoted the getting together of its members in diverse places—in Lima's apartment in Rio, in an airport, in a park—and their *dislocation* toward special landscapes (beaches, deserts, the jungle, or distant mountains). It also entailed the administration of its bureaucracy and rituals—the construction of a specific glossary of terms, the archive of the members's correspondence—and this task was assumed, during the first years of *RhR,* by Lima herself. The members would follow specific instructions in order to guarantee the cohesion of the group (such as the use of the Lima-designed *Uniforme-Desenhos (Drawing Uniforms),* or the orchestration of specific modes to greet each other or depart from each other). The *Instance* was created with no specific aim or purpose other than to live a social experience without norms that would nonetheless be united by a common desire to *belong* and *exchange* ideas and visions of the world, or simply to live the experience of *being* a social entity or organization. Since its inception, *RhR* has seen its members disseminate into the world, and today there might exist other administrators that we do not know about. *RhR* was born to outlive the artist and the art world, and to resist them both. (Such was the case that, at a certain point, when the Museo Nacional Centro de Arte Reina Sofía–MNCARS in Madrid invited members of *RhR* to participate in one of the museum's programs, *RhR* accepted the invitation to *be* there, yet in order to be coherent with its premises, it couldn't submit itself to an outside norm and therefore it was not actually visible by what we may assume to be the "public" of a museum.) It is important to note, in regards to our text, that *RhR* already enacted what we here call Lima's "ornamental philosophy," for the only feature that did distinguish and identify its participants was their use of Lima's *Drawing Uniforms* that anchored their existence as an artistic creation of sorts. With *RhR* Lima was, for the first time, addressing the alteration of a social body and was positioning her interests one step beyond the questions posed by the artistic system as such. As Felipe Scovino has brilliantly described, "clothing in Lima's work appears as a mutation, a glossary of absurdities and strangeness, decodified languages, a synthesis of fragmented identities and moving in a world made of accelerated identities and times."[2]

But why does Lima repeatedly underscore the need to change visuality, to alter a given being's exteriority or "skin"? Why is it so crucial to intervene on the surfaces of the world? The artist has previously stated: "People that participated in those images, to whom I gave instructions to be followed, weren't more important than the apparatuses that I constructed to realize the image." Lima's practice, above all, underscores both the need to rethink the role of images in the world, and the need to propose new, subversive images that have the potential to alter the status quo of a given mode of communication, to alter a given set of behaviors, and to alter a given set of social values. The alteration of the given social system is enacted through the construction of an alternative system of images and by means of the transformation of the surfaces of the world: "I create a system, but I know it is rigorous with rigorousness; I admit unfathomable things, constructive paradoxes, life as the wave in an impetuous sea." Lima's "ornamental philosophy" is an applied practice: it involves the application—as in the applied and decorative arts—of a logic of creating that will always be at odds with what is strictly necessary, or expected, or rationally predicted. Lima's universe, rather, borrows methodological twists from the realms of the absurd, the territory of dreams, the clash of opposites, and the enrichment of ideas provided by paradox and contradiction. In her images, lines are invited to navigate a surface for no specific purpose other than to destabilize a given imagery—as in the delicate drawings she has been creating since 2005 *Ouro Flexíveis (Flexible Gold),* in which Lima draws with golden ink over reproductions of images of Old Master European paintings. And previously unknown forms enter the stage and alter the functionality and logic of a set of given objects and beings—of matter, both living and inert—creating the need to approach each in its own terms rather than with preconceived ideas about how they should function in

---

2   Felipe Scovino, "Arquitectura da Pele" (Rio de Janeiro: Casa França-Brasil, 2010).

the world. Such is the case, for example, of the imaginary clay landscapes that she constructs for her *Faisões com Comida (Pheasants and Food,* 2005), in which biomorphic sculptures coexist with drawings delicately drawn or incised into the skin of the most diverse fruits, including pumpkins, coconuts, apples, and watermelons, as well as on grains and leaves. It is the case, as well, of the artist's more radical *Galinhas de Gala (Gala Chickens,* 2004), in which a group of chickens have been embellished by the artist with brightly colored natural feathers that have been attached to them like hair extensions, and in so doing she has created a new social scenario. Lima's ornamental practice establishes a rupture of the social order to the extent that the more timid animals become confident, even exuberant, and some even change their gender orientation. Inspired by the rupture of the social order that carnival manages enact, *Gala Chickens* proves that the creation of previously unimagined garments—or surfaces—for worldly items and beings may indeed give place to the creation of a new society.

In Lima's earlier *Costumes (Costume* in Portuguese means both costume and habit/tradition), the first series of which she created in 2001 in blue vinyl, the artist cut out, folded, and refolded the material, creating new applications for the body that would exceed more traditional notions of clothing. Beyond the garment, Lima's *Costumes* extend their functionality: "As a sort of unfolding of spontaneous generation, the vinyl itself is used to sustain the costume on a person's body, using straps and moorings, as if the material created, all by itself, the structure that holds it together. From there, a collective body springs, made of a single matter, only dismembered and disfigured."[3] Oliva's description signals toward a larger aim in the creation of these works: the collective body. Each of these pieces that propose either alterations of the body—as in her earlier *Tattoos*—or new possible functionalities and extensions for the body, enable the conceptualization of a new subject of unforeseen qualities and movements and possibilities of socialization. They allow for the birth of a new human subject, devoid of the contemporary illness of "normalization" and capable of embracing the infinite number of actions that the human being could potentially enact. Yet here, it is important to note how Lima radicalizes her own proposals by opening the door to the realm of the unfathomable, to that which will always exceed our expectations. Oliva continues, "From the start

---

3   Fernando Oliva, "Laura Lima Costumes," Revista Lápiz (Madrid), 2003.

there is something awkward in the piece's title: the garments are anti-utilitarian, uncomfortable to the point that wearing them habitually would prove very difficult. The 'Costumes' barely resemble any sort of conventional dress—so don't expect to find pants, shirts and jackets. Some, like the 'flat skirt,' to be used between the legs without enveloping the body, are almost impossible. Or, for that matter, a piece that encases the feet but projects itself backwards for six meters; or a glove that doesn't wrap the fingers but sits on the back of the hand as some sort of Cronenbergian protuberance. There are also masks, head pieces, shoulder pieces, waist pieces, and dozens of strange objects ... "

This feeling of estrangement is magically orchestrated in Lima's daringly silent project *To Age* (2001 / 2004) presented for the first time at the Chapter Art Center in Cardiff. The artist hired a professional make-up artist to alter the appearance of the art center employees (including the secretary, the curator, and the bar waiter) and make them look much older. A given spectator enters the gallery space. He or she is greeted by an employee who may or may not have been touched by the make-up artist. "Where is Lima's work?" he or she will probably inquire. In *To Age,* Lima challenges the notion of performance. Devoid of any specific programming or narrative, Lima's "ornamental philosophy" rather entails the act of touching the real to structurally alter any previous approach to the object or being to be transformed by her artistic proposals. In short, Lima demands us to change the lens of our gaze. This attitude finds historical antecedents in the beginning of the Romantic era around 1800, when several artists staged a doubtful and dubious relationship between the image and the viewer, causing increasing disquiet and discomfort. In Francisco de Goya, Caspar David Friedrich, William Blake, and Henry Fuseli, for example, we encounter a twist in the conception of the viewer-artwork relationship. In his recent essay on Dark Romanticism, Johannes Grave has noted how "Two motifs already occur ... that would become increasingly important after the turn of the nineteenth century: fear for the intactness of one's own gaze, and awareness of the fathomless power of images, which can seem to become the living counterpart of the viewer." [4] And indeed, before certain of Lima's works, the viewer takes the risk

---

4   Johannes Grave, "Uncanny Images: The 'Night Sides' of the Visual Arts around
     1800," in *Dark Romanticism: From Goya to Max Ernst* (Frankfurt am Main
     and Ostfildern: Städel Museum and Hatje Cantz, 2012), p. 31.

of getting lost in the relationship. The work—the subject touched by Lima's magical wand—turns around and confronts the viewer; it literally *touches* the viewer and in so doing vertiginously diminishes the distance that we are used to experiencing between ourselves and the work. The possibility of the analytical distance (and, with it, the voyeuristic distance) drops and what emerges is the presence of life in art. As a guest that was not previously invited, life intrudes in the scenario, calling attention to itself and its surroundings. Let us recall Grave's words in regards to Fuseli's *The Nightmare*: "The reality of the sleeping woman and her dream image fuse in a way that also causes the viewer to shudder. They may imagine themselves to be at a safe distance from the event depicted, but their gazes threaten to take on voyeuristic qualities, as suggested by the eyes of the incubus and the horse's head. The spookily empty and yet strangely luminous eyeballs of the horse illustrate that such gaze no longer testifies to rational control and mastery. The gaze itself seems to become a source of violence and horror. Fuseli's *Nightmare* thus does not simply illustrate the transgression of the boundary between reality and fiction characteristic of the dream image. Rather, the painting also makes clear that we can no longer find a secure, external standpoint from which we could view, as a supposedly uninvolved party, the inherent dynamic of dreamlike manifestations."[5] Lima's provocation is not very far away from Fuseli's. Her images confront the viewer. They confront either directly (when addressing the spectator as such) or indirectly (when articulating a new image for the viewer that does not necessarily recur to the gaze). They eradicate all distances and reach out, literally touching the viewer.

Furthermore, Lima's images are animated. They use the body as the ultimate living material and in so doing they alter a whole philosophy of knowledge. The image in Lima is no longer a sign that represents something other beyond the image, but, distant from any dynamics of representation, it *presents* an idea with full force. The real—the body—becomes the material to construct a new understanding of the image. In proposing an image that results from its ontological destiny—its *call to imagine*—Lima takes on the challenge of art. The body as live material is never predictable: formulas and rational control cannot be applied to a body whose nature is defined by movement and transformation. And further, if to the living

5   Johannes Grave, "Uncanny Images," p. 33.

organism we apply Lima's "ornamental philosophy"—one abundant in caprices, notes of delight for the sole joy of delight, nonsensical alterations destined to provoke estrangement, and lines that dress up life in unimagined ways—we arrive at a notion of image-making and image-construction that takes its force from the realms of delirium, fantasy, the absurd, and the paradoxical. For Lima's is a conception of the image that challenges all given discourses and art historical characterizations, demanding a new discursive approach with respect to images that will not stay at a distance and that are destined to stir profound, surprising emotions.

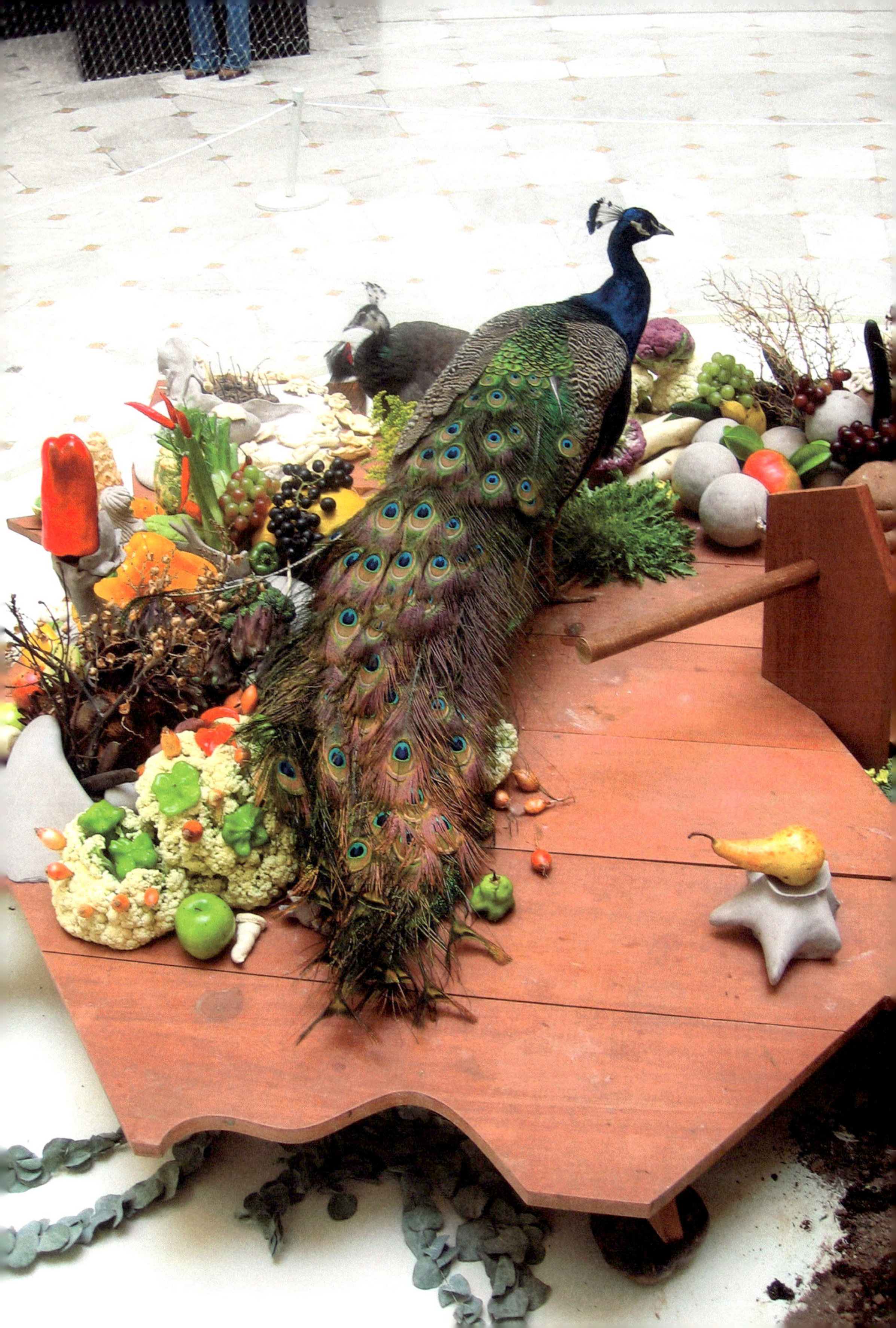

Pheasants with Food

Faisões com Comida

Based on the idea—once practiced by some members of the aristocracy—that one could
acquire beauty by eating beautiful birds, in *Pheasants with Food* the artist
turned the idea around and offered a banquet for the birds instead, creating a dreamlike
atmosphere. She constructed an intricate installation with sculpted ceramics
and a 22-meter-high aviary built from fishing net. A chef de cuisine came everyday to cook
an extraordinary meal for the birds, who were also fed plants with drawings
on them (so the birds could eat the drawings). The piece remained for fifty days and was
shown with a new banquet each day.

Pheasants with Food / Faisões com Comida, 2005
Live peacocks and pheasants, a chef de cuisine every morning, special clay for porcelain,
nuts and coconuts, grains, water, pastries, fruits, leaves, plants, gold ink, vanilla,
food coloring, soil, wood, fishing net
Dimensions variable

Courtesy of the artist, Photography: Paulo Innocêncio, Laura Lima
Views: Centro Cultural Banco do Brasil, Rio de Janeiro
Commissioned by the Goethe Institute and Banco do Brasil SA
Collaboration of Oicram Rama, chef de cuisine

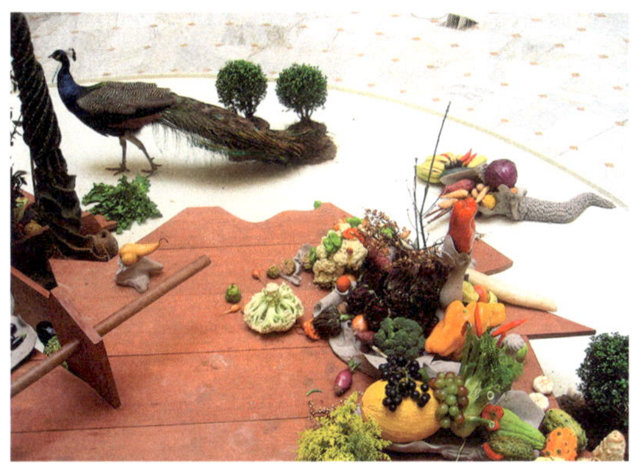
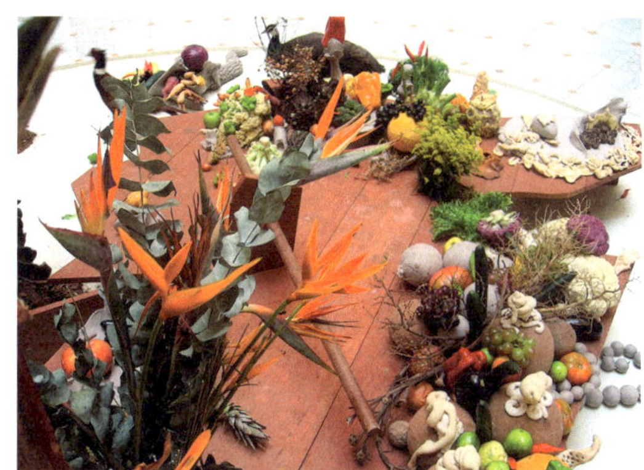
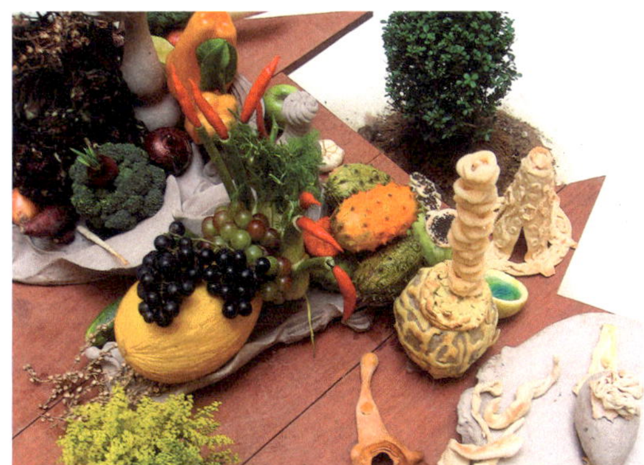
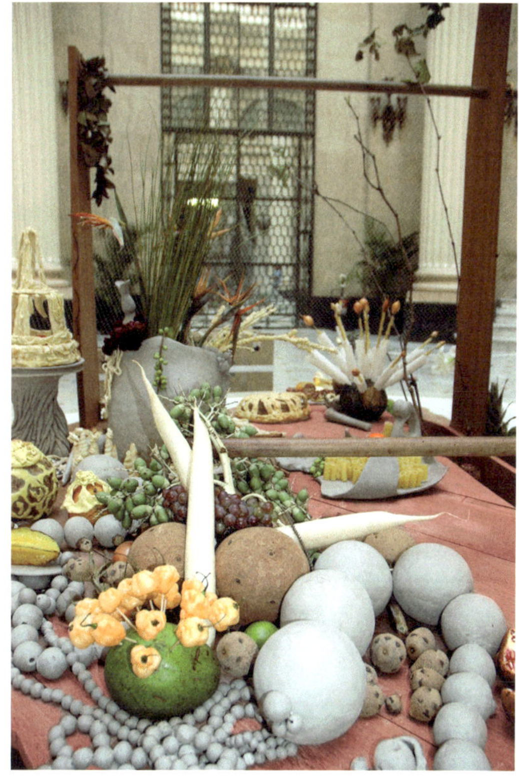
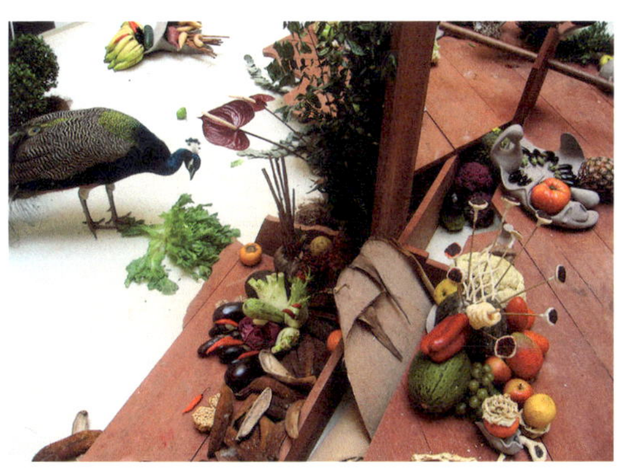
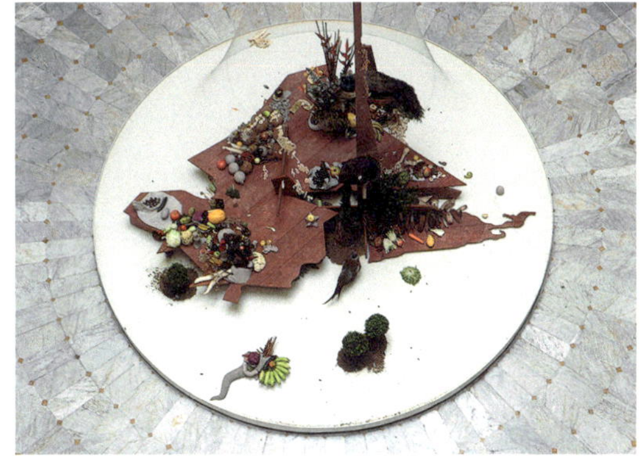
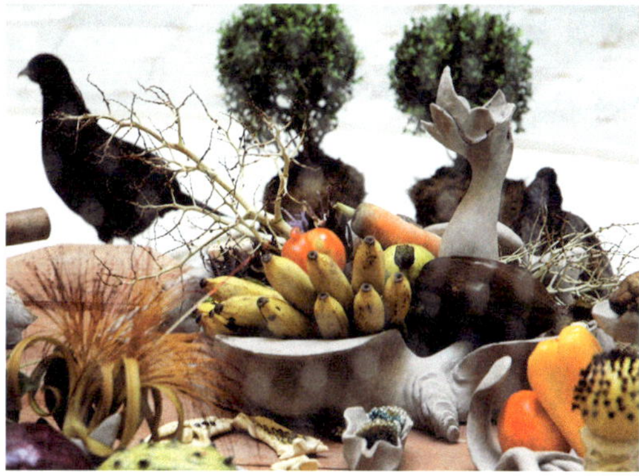

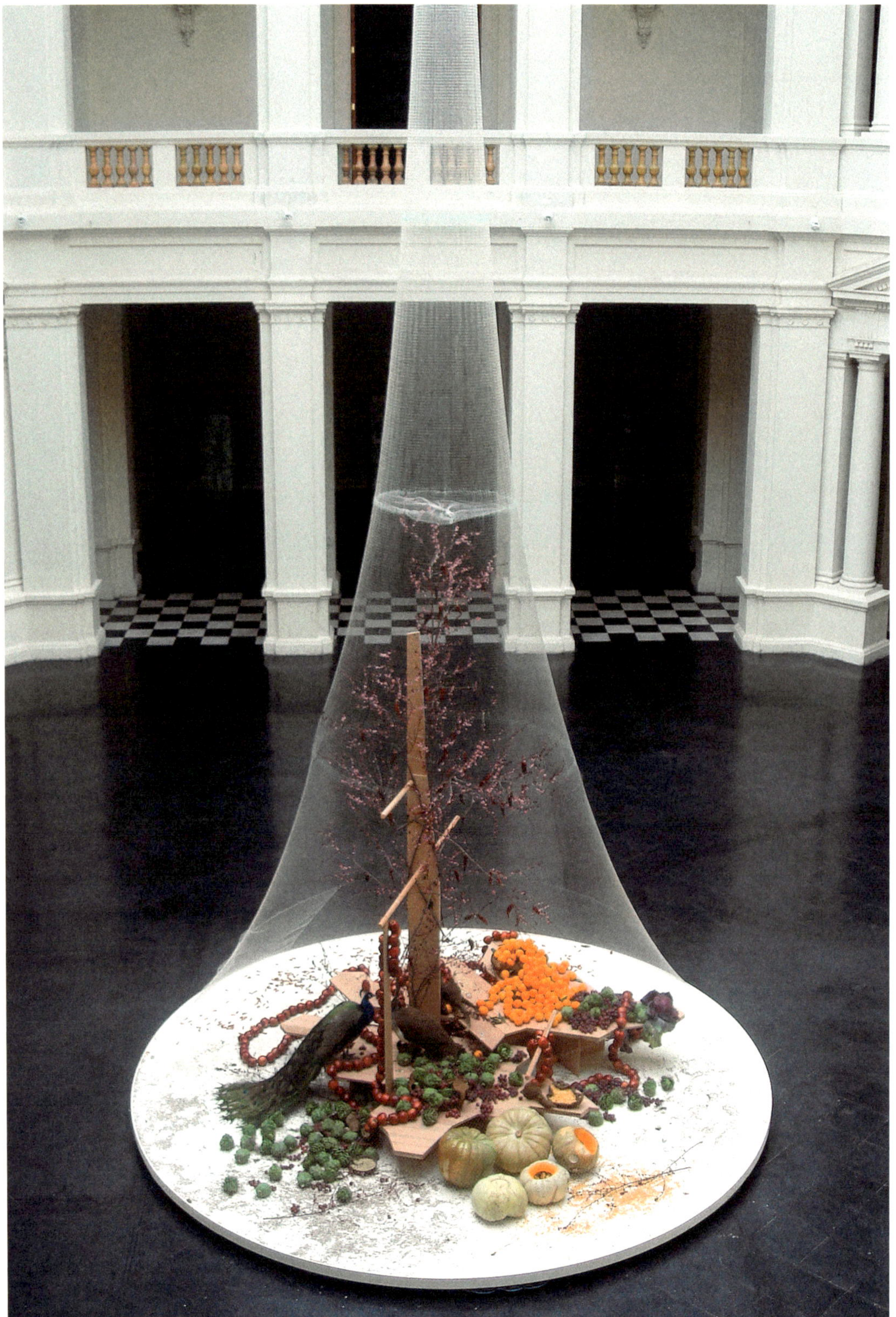

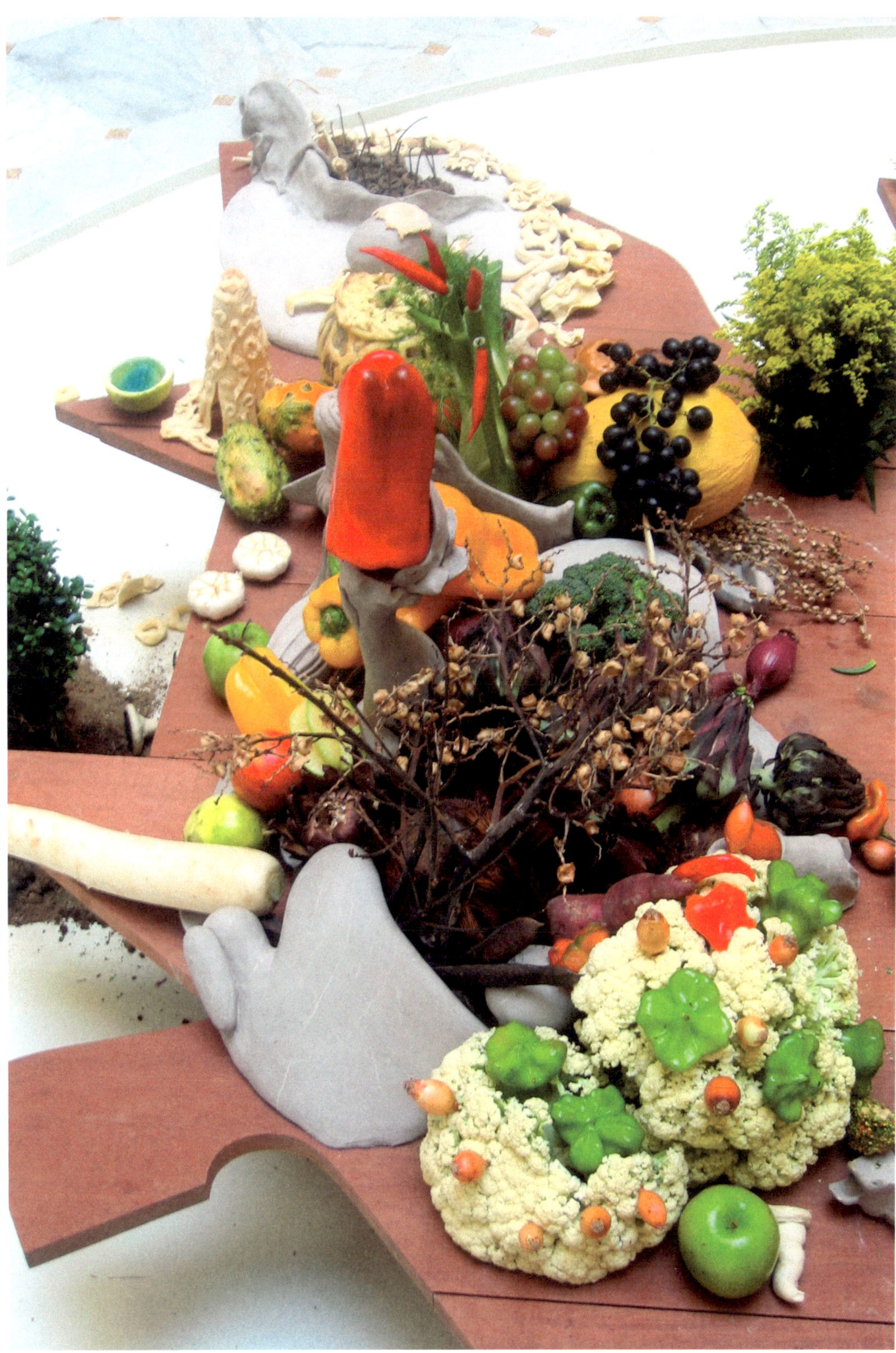

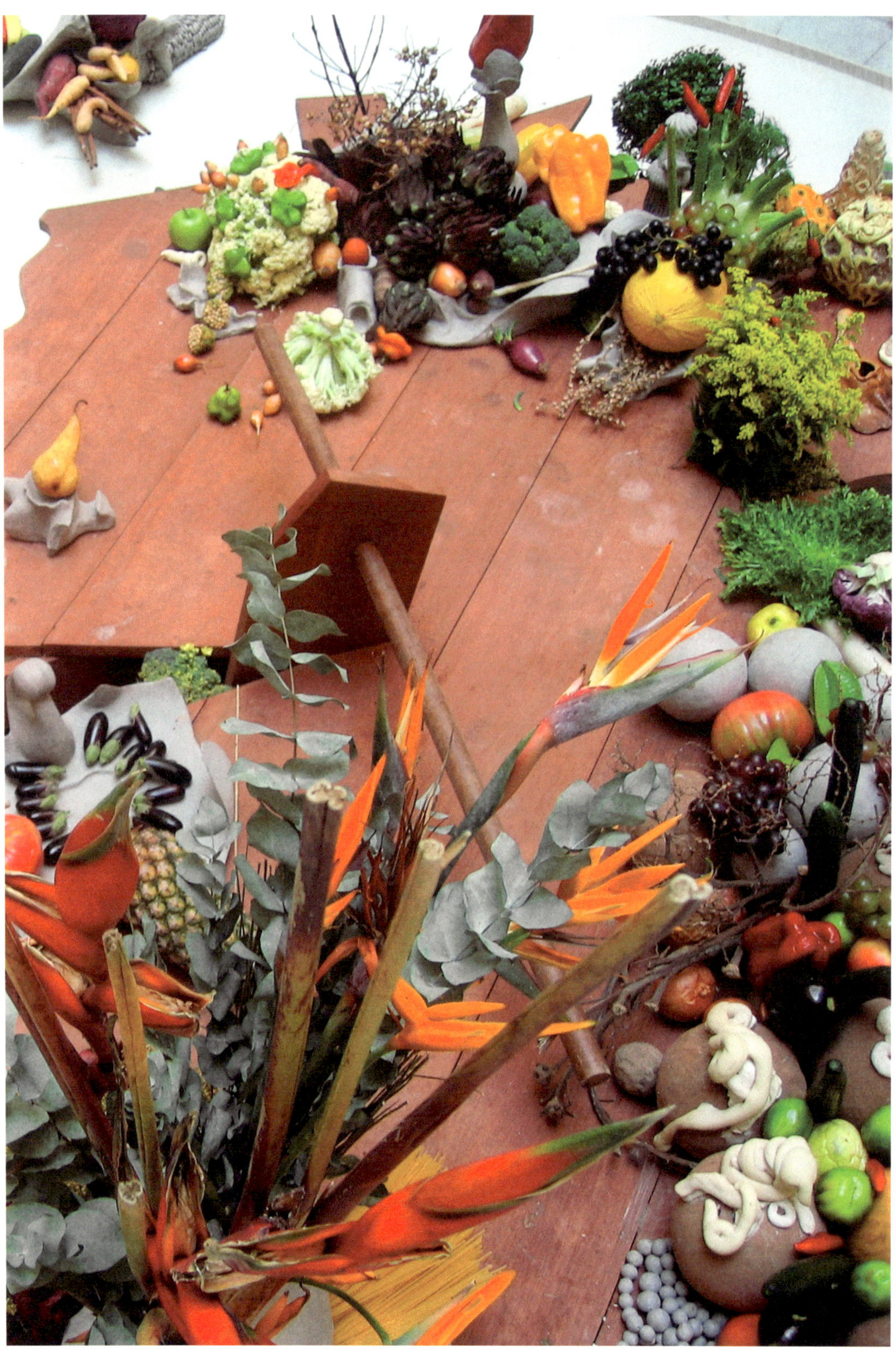

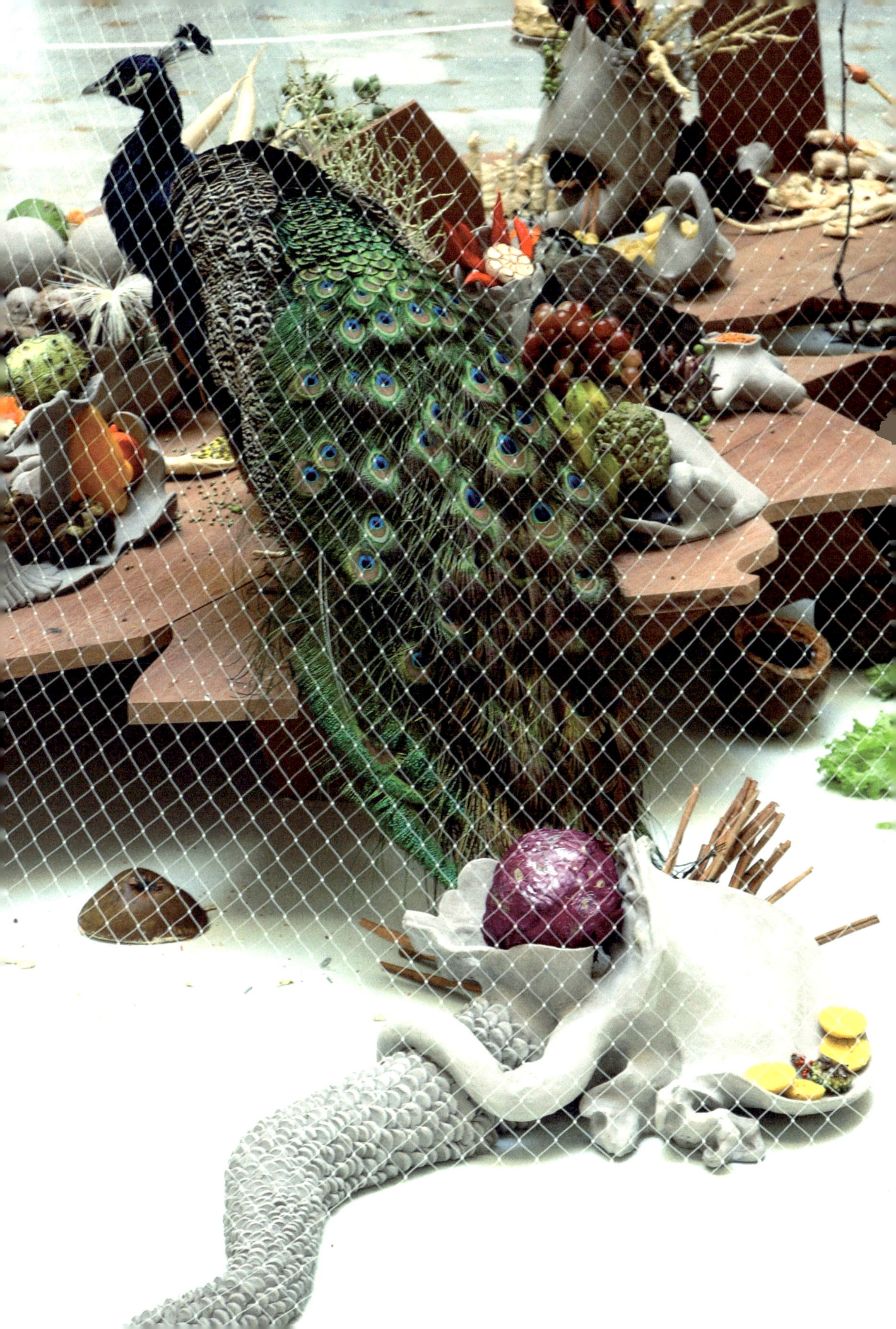

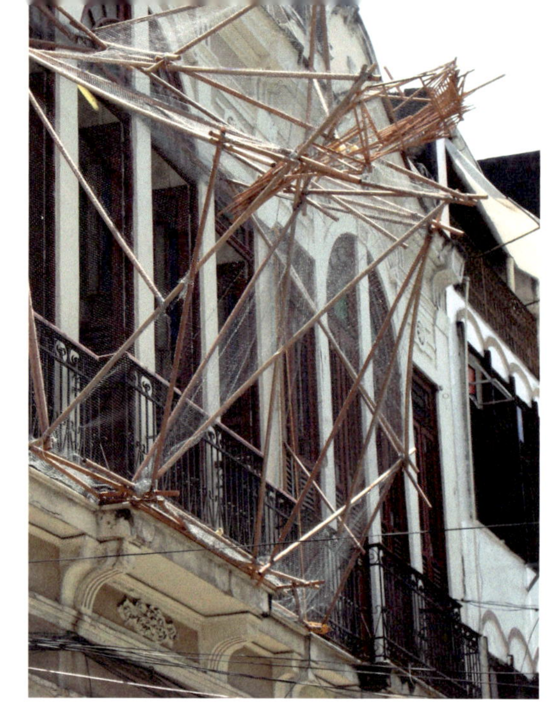

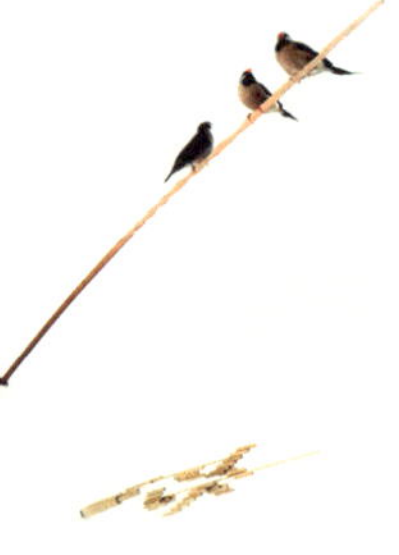

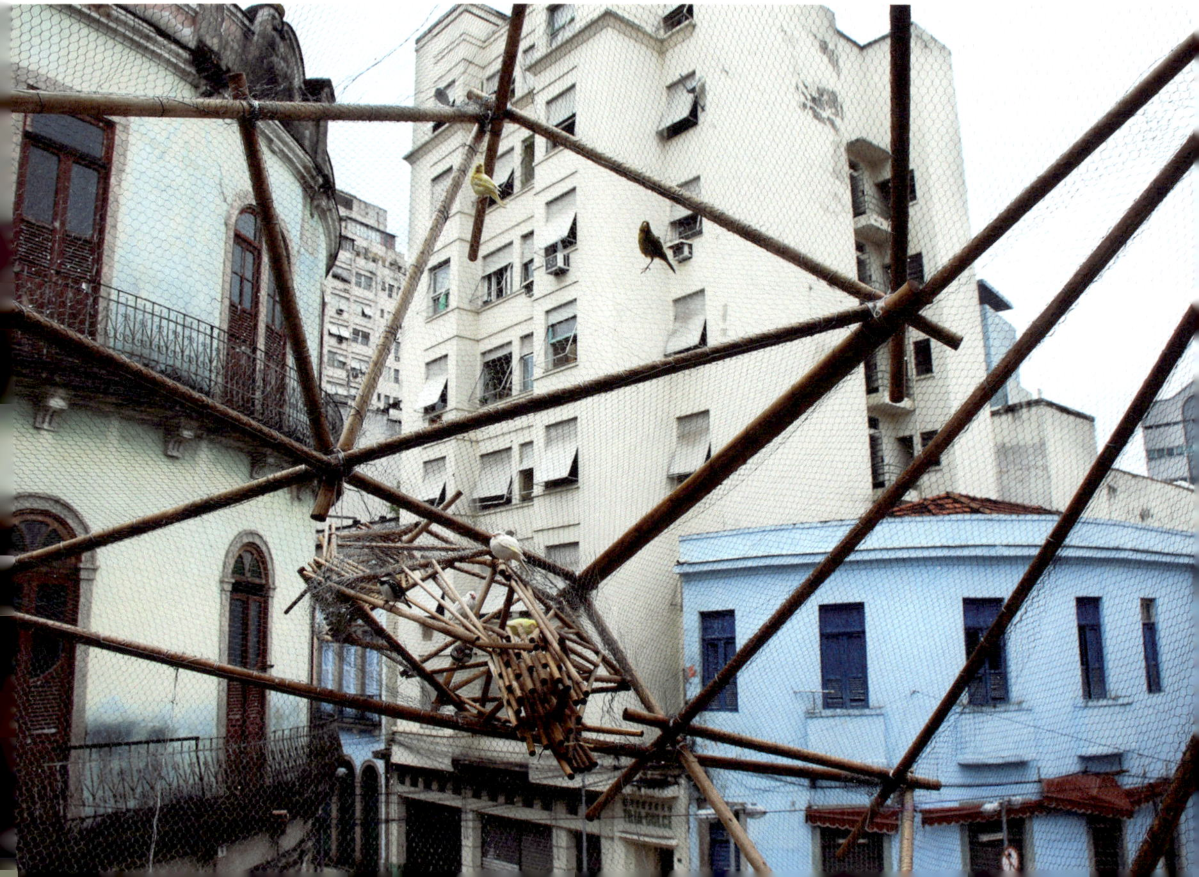

Escape

Fuga

A number of birds usually born in small cages were brought to a big aviary to relearn how to fly. With the advice of a bird specialist, the artist created a whole environment in which the birds could live, fly, and possibly escape. In her exhibition at A Gentil Carioca in Rio de Janeiro, she devoted the whole gallery to the birds, creating an atmosphere where the humans felt like strangers. The installation also included small copies of classical paintings with inclined horizons (suggesting the view the bird has of the landscape when it is flying), geometrically designed perches for the birds to rest after flying, a big nest and small houses made out of straw hats, a large-scale façade projection on wood and, finally, a small outlet for them to escape and fly away.

Escape / Fuga, 2008
Fifty live birds, bird food, water, paintings, wood, straw hats, ceramics, plants
Dimensions variable (enough space for the birds to fly around)

Courtesy of the artist, Photography: Laura Lima, Ana Torres
Views: A Gentil Carioca gallery space

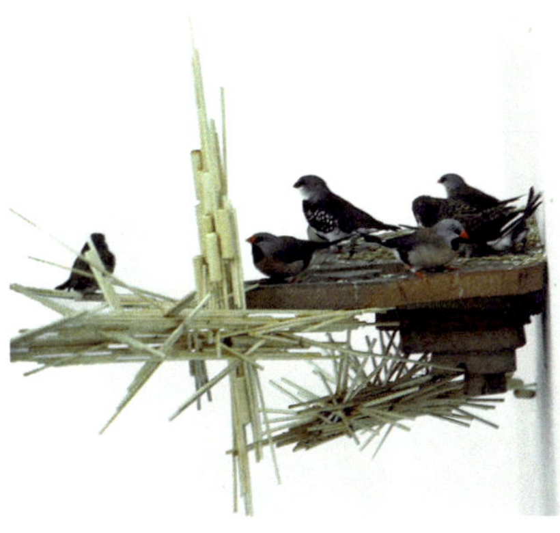

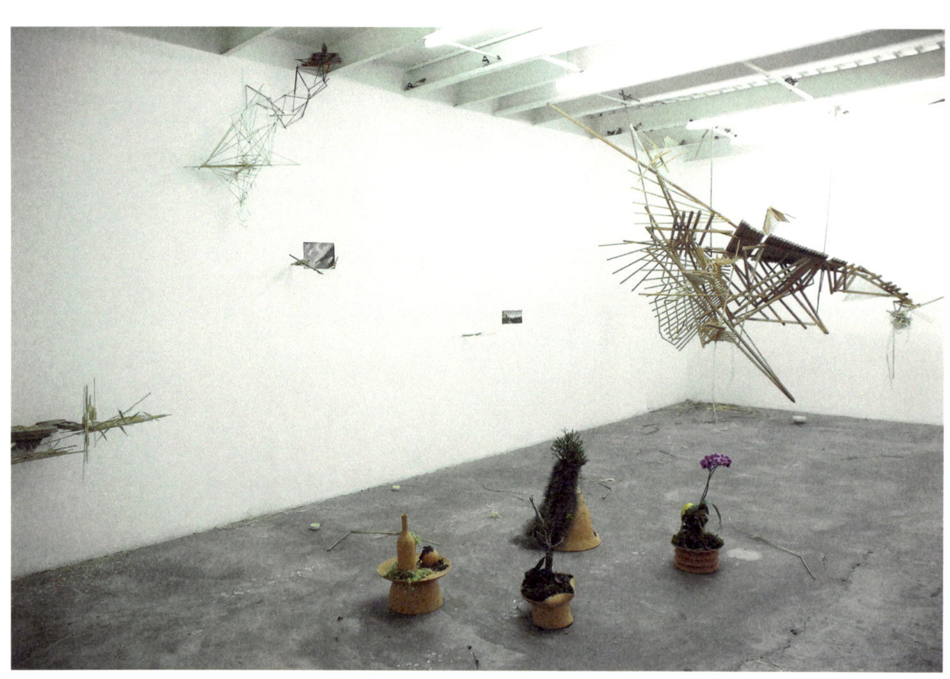

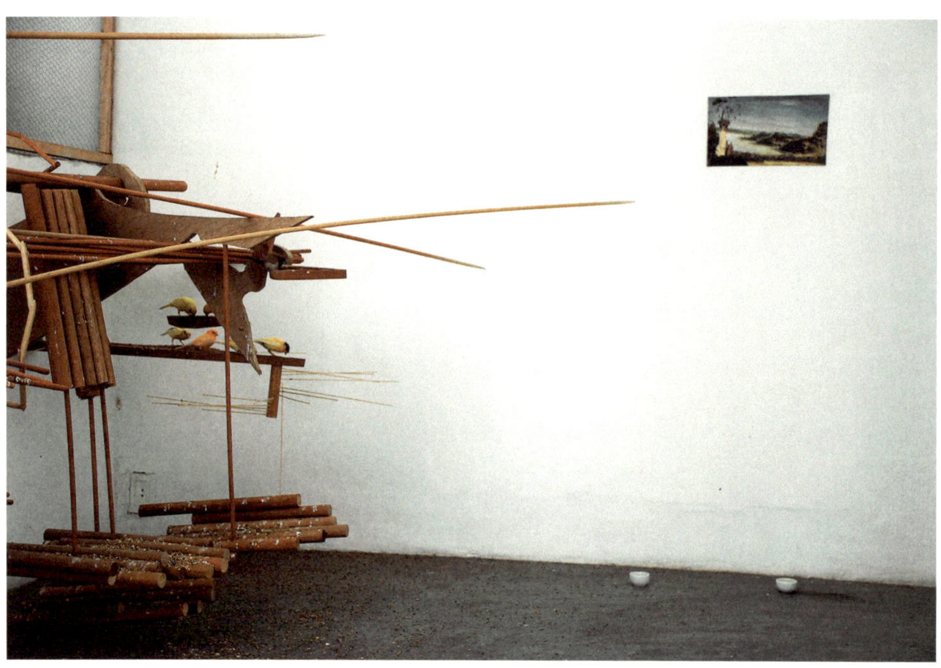

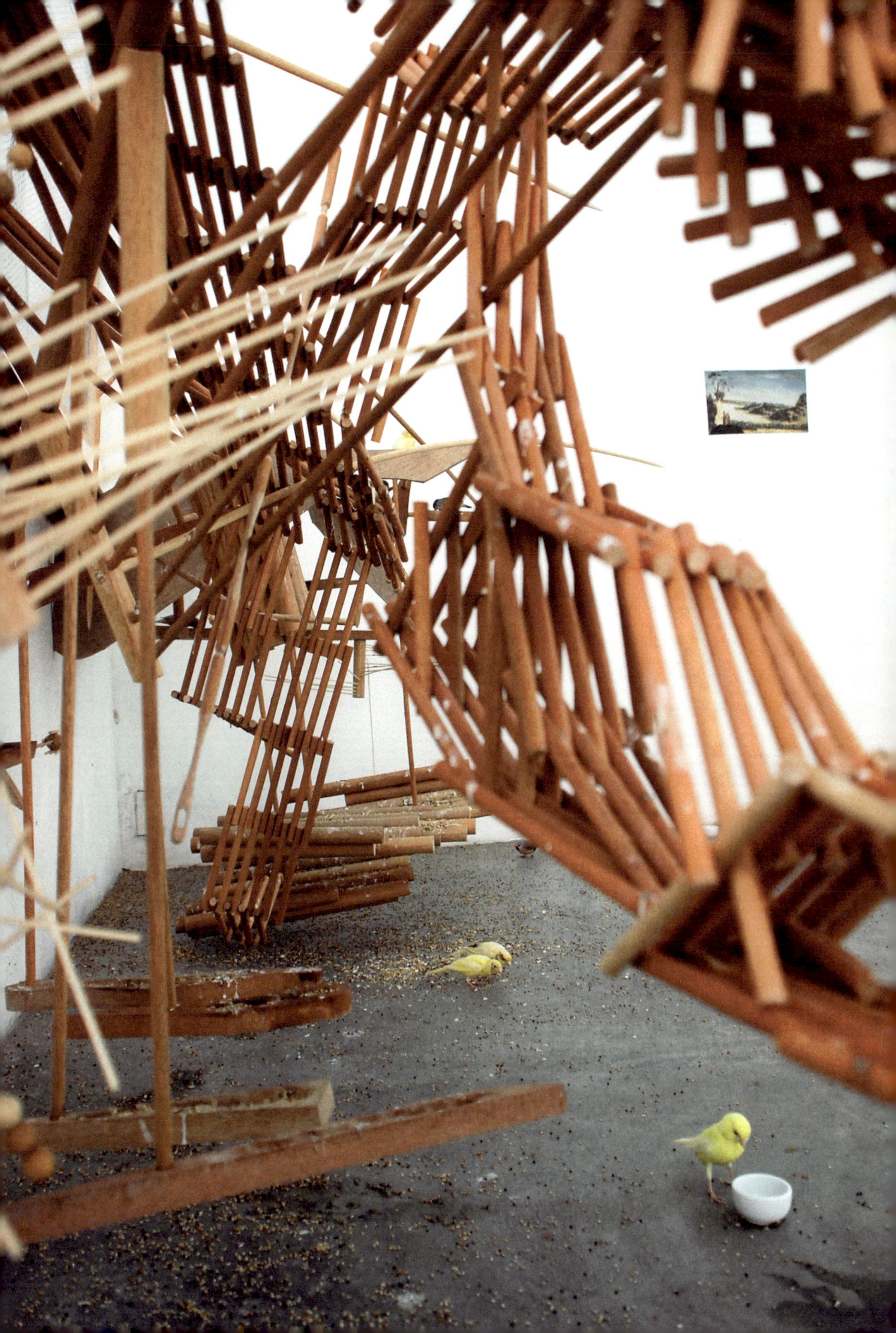

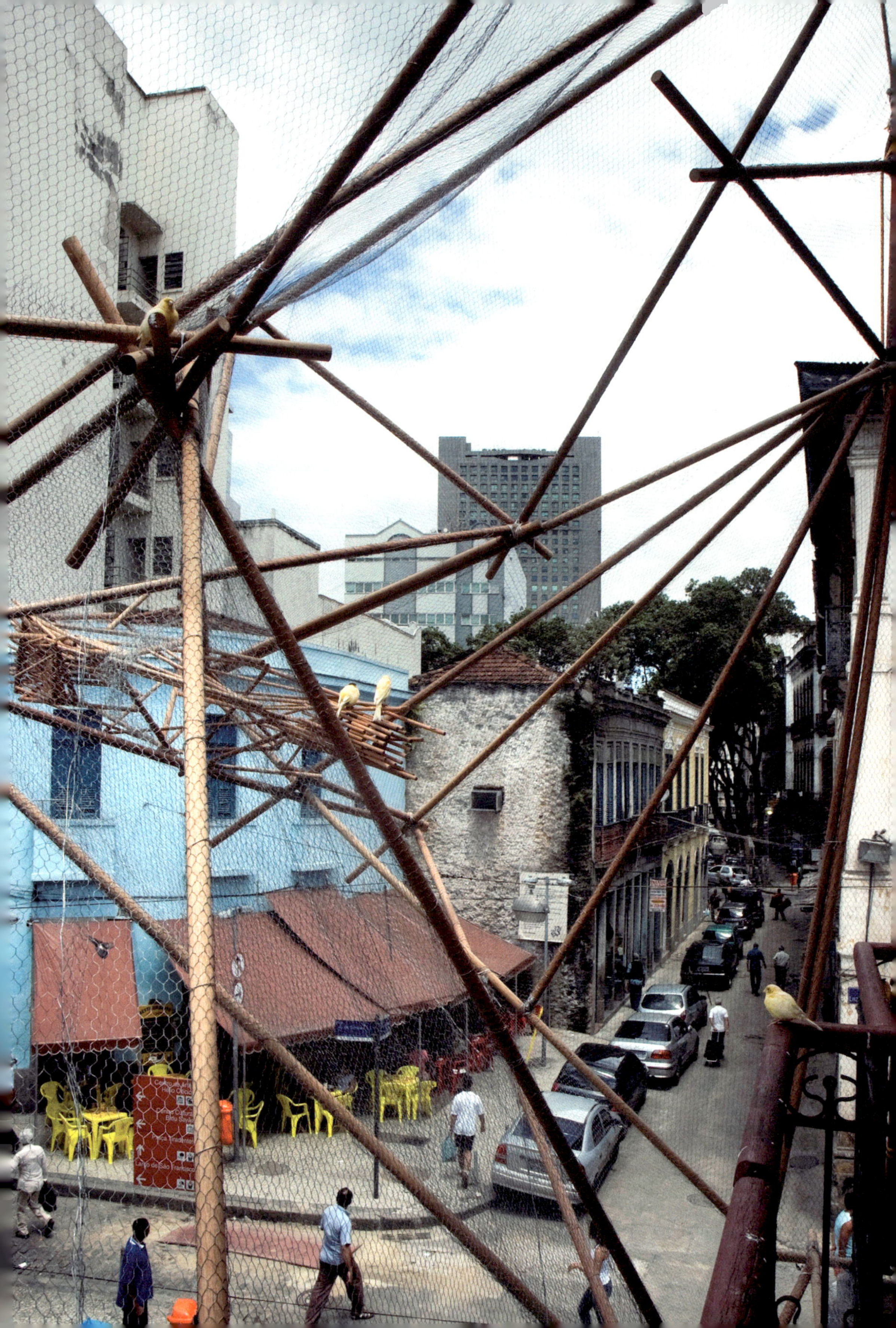

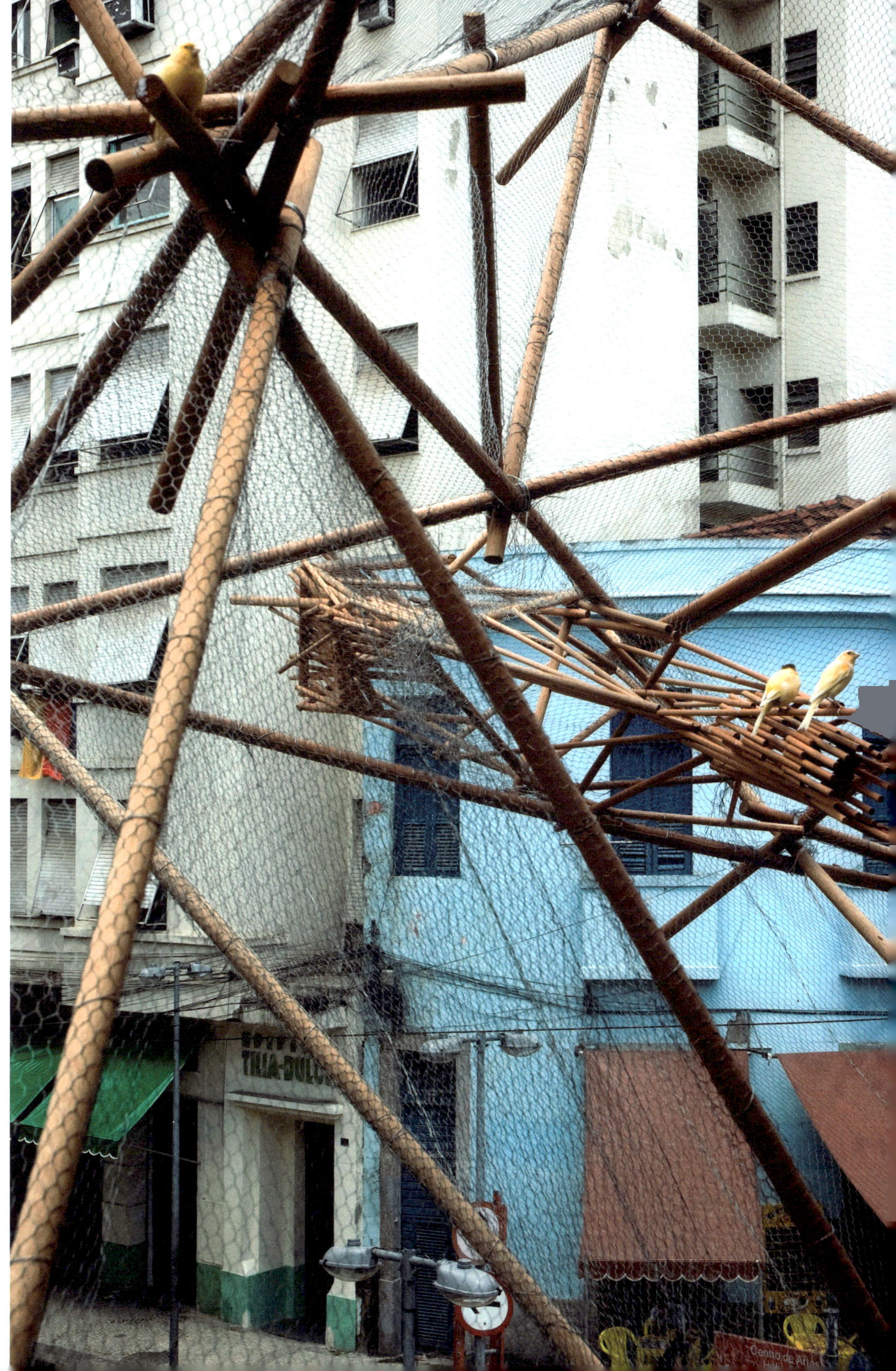

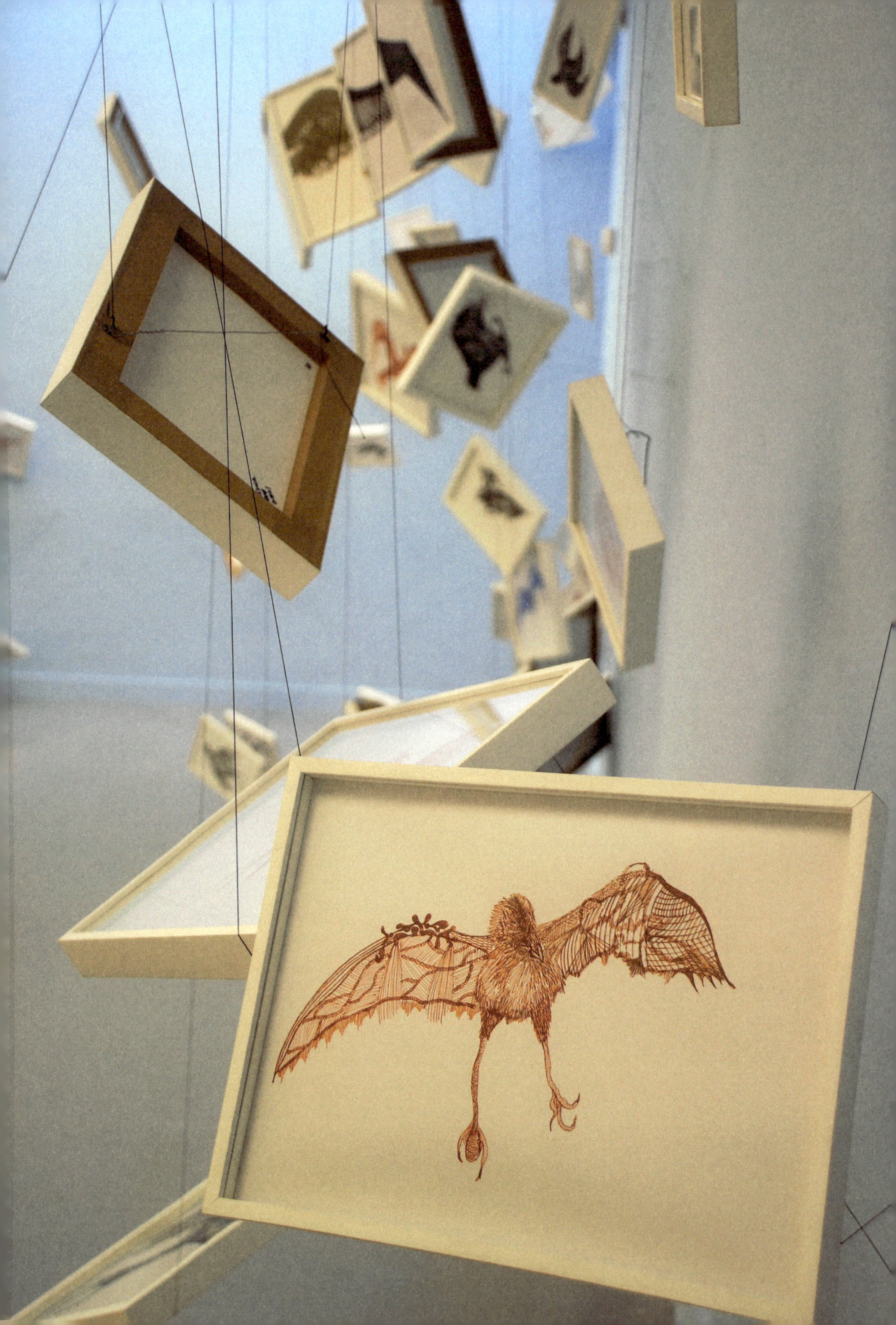

Birds

Pássaros

Modeling her work on encyclopedia representations of bird movements and on the
Hitchcock film *Birds,* Laura Lima draws flying birds on white paper with white frames,
some of them captured with wings spread. She hangs them like marionettes in
the space, where their thin black lines seem to freeze their wing strokes in mid-flight.

Birds / Pássaros, 2008 / 2010
Paper, glass, wood, line, black lines, special nails
Dimensions variable

Courtesy of the artist / Private collections, Photography: Laura Lima
Views: MuHKA, Antwerp

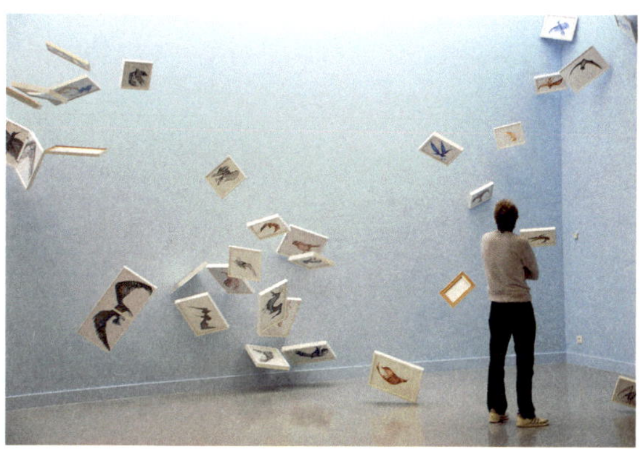

Nomads

Nômades

With the collaboration of a copyist, several landscapes from art books and plants
from a book of botanical gardens were copied, using oil and acrylic on canvas, except that,
in the process, the artist removed the humans and animals from the paintings.
She cut and folded the paintings and incorporated copies of the plants, making them
appear to emerge directly from the landscape and making the rivers appear to
flow out of the paintings onto the exhibition floor. Unlike the work *Costumes,* the *Nomads*
installation, in which the masks are presented for display rather than being worn,
evokes the world of museum ethnographics.

Nomads / Nômades, 2007 / 2008
Oil and acrylic on canvas, wood
Dimensions variable

Private collections / Collection of Instituto Inhotim
Photography: Laura Lima
Views: Museu da Republica, Brasilia
In collaboration with the copyist Adriana Ricardo

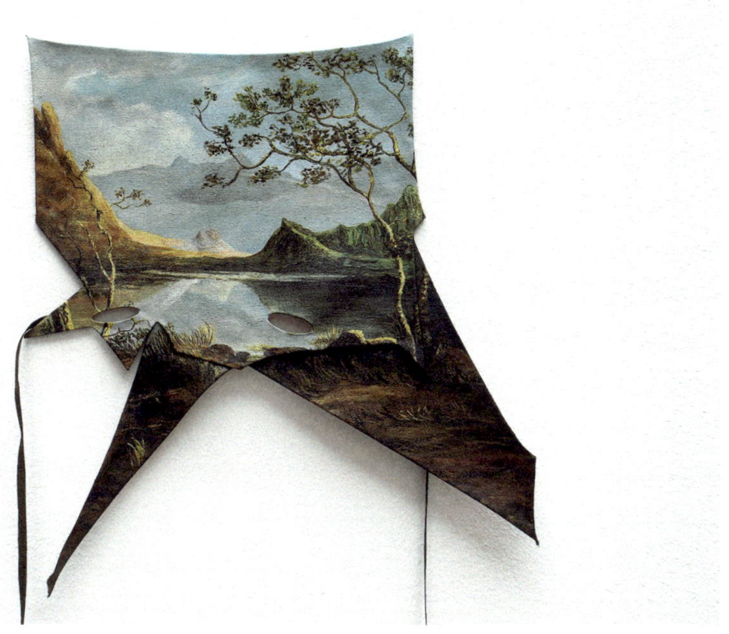

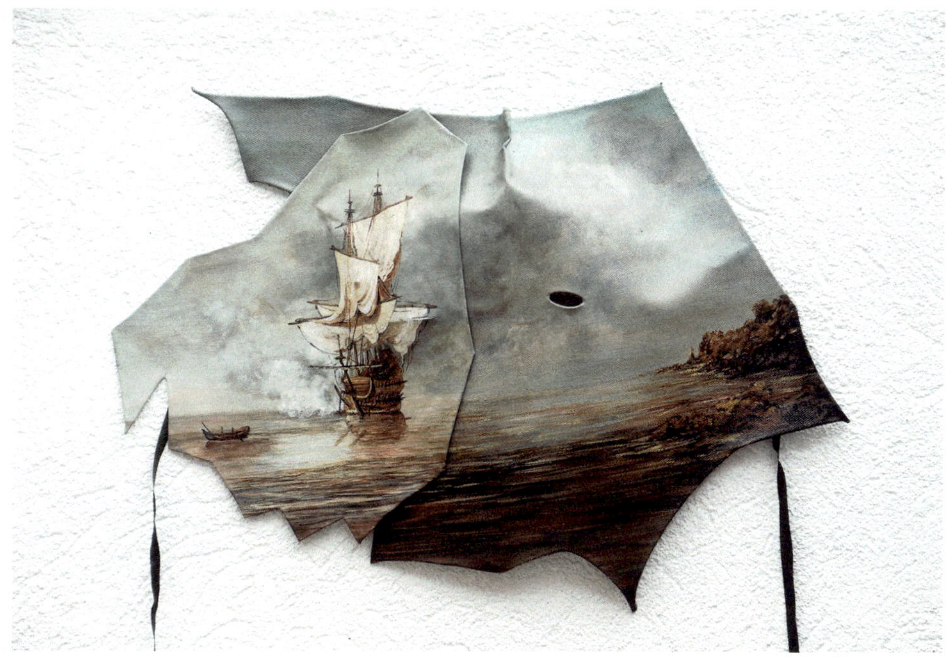

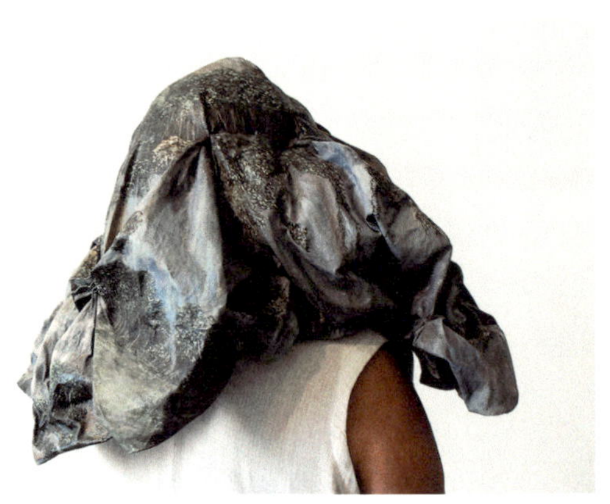

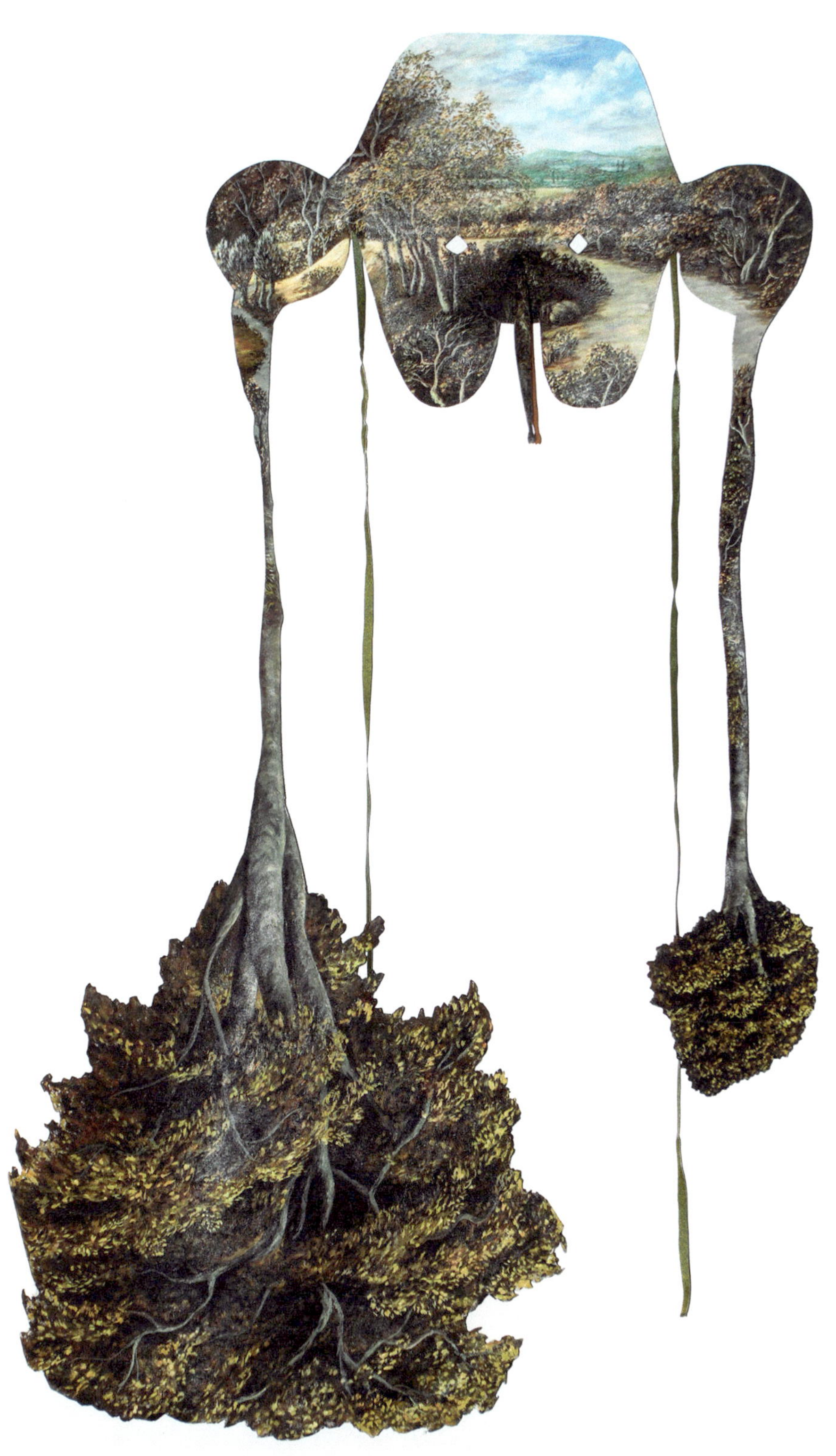

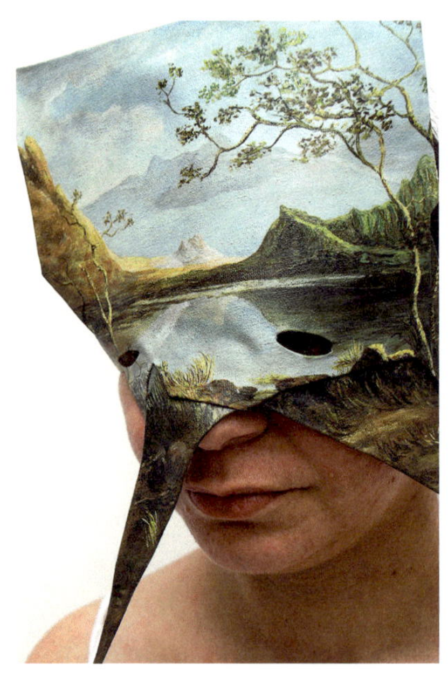

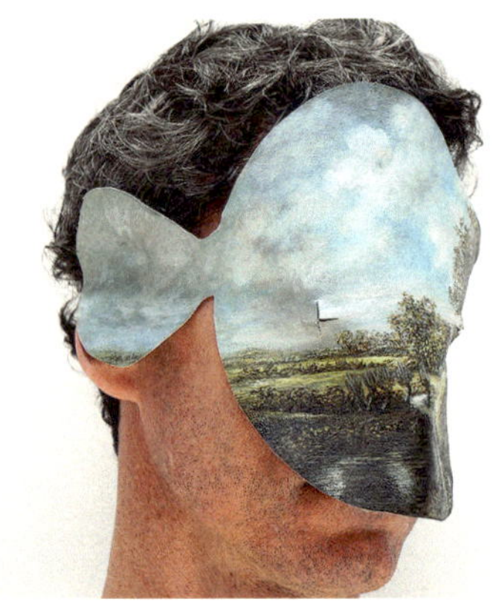

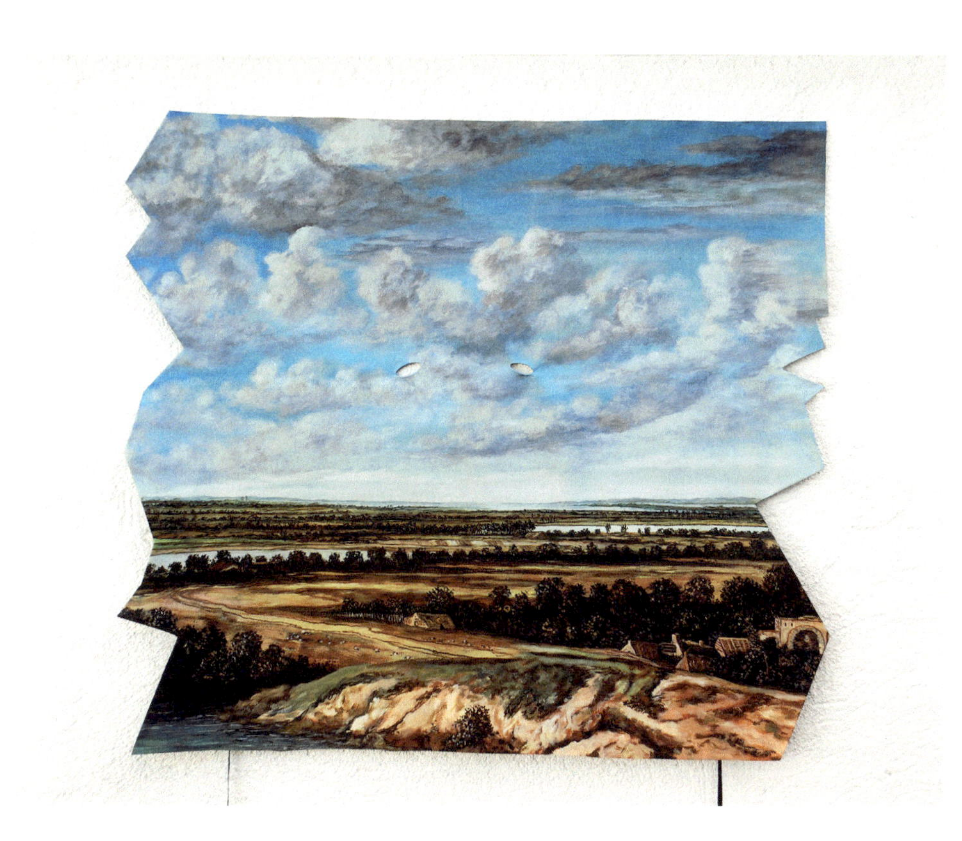

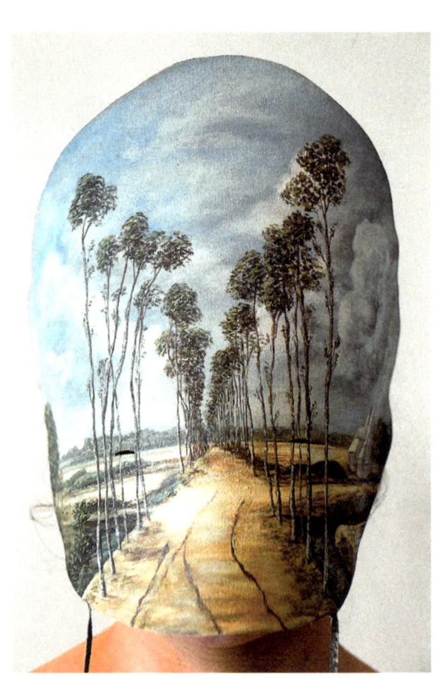

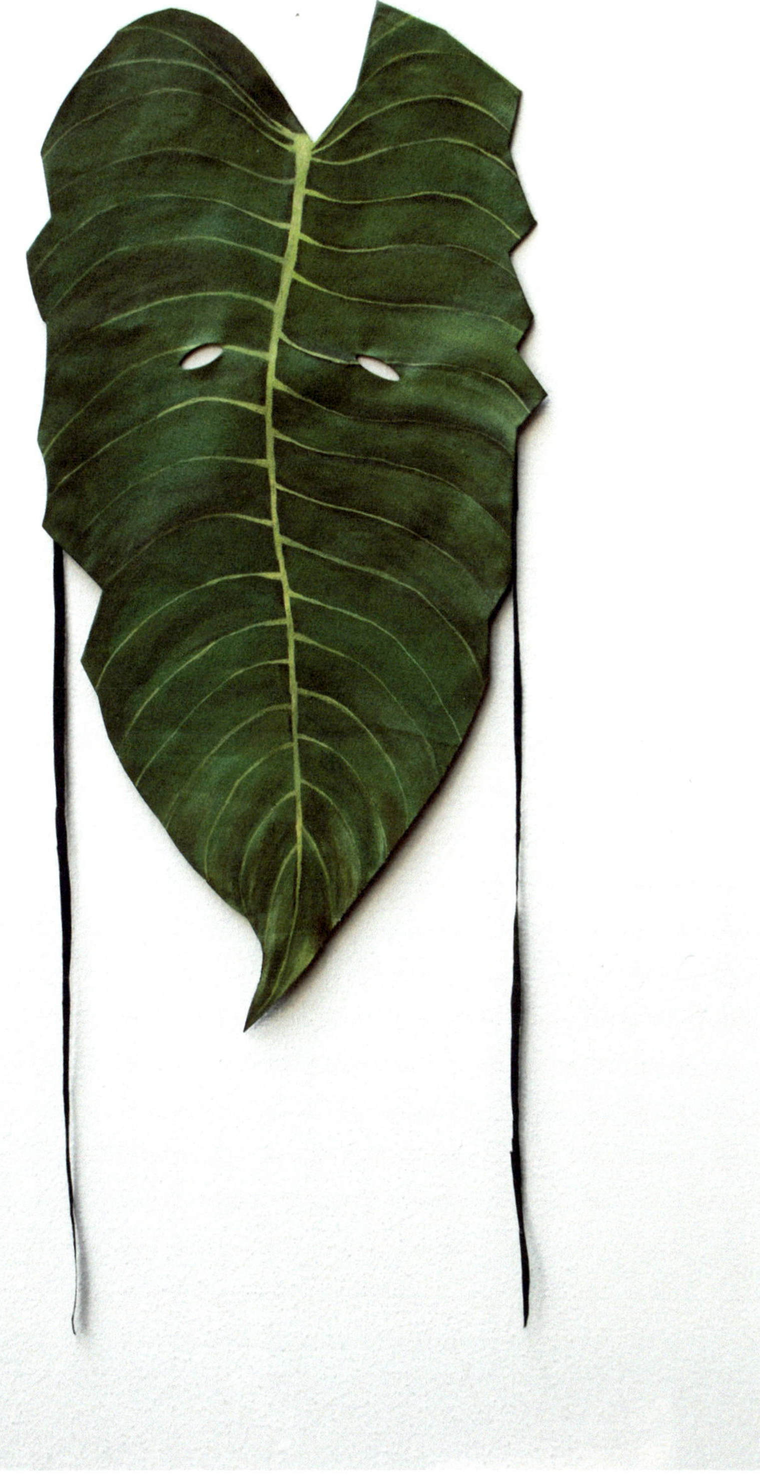

Flexible Gold

Ouro Flexível

Images of paintings from a certain period of art history are extracted from art books and then drawn over with gold ink pen. In the most of the cases, the frames are modified.

Flexible Gold / Ouro Flexível, 2005
Images from art books, gold ink, paper, glass, acrylic, wood
Dimensions variable

Courtesy of the artist / private collections
Photography: Ana Torres

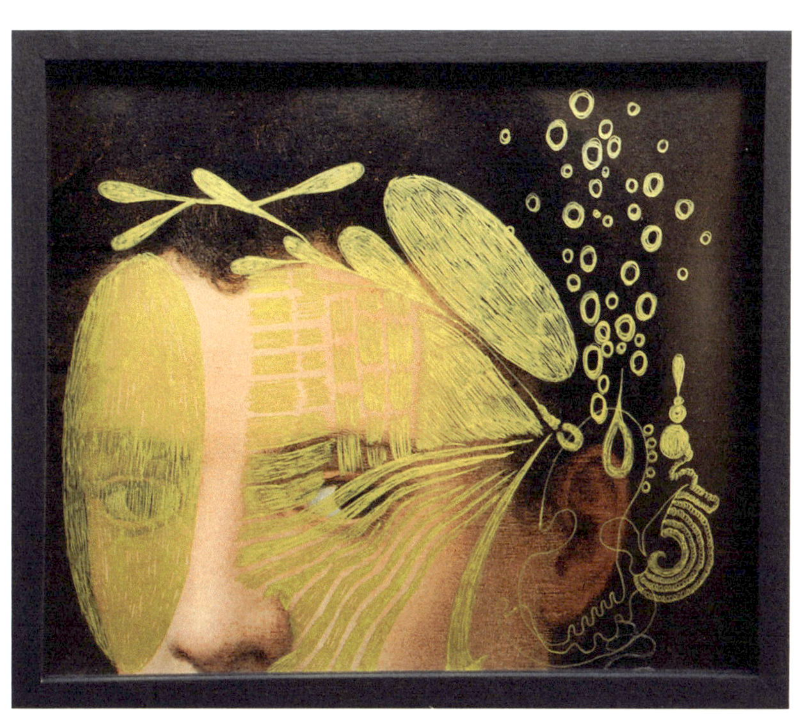

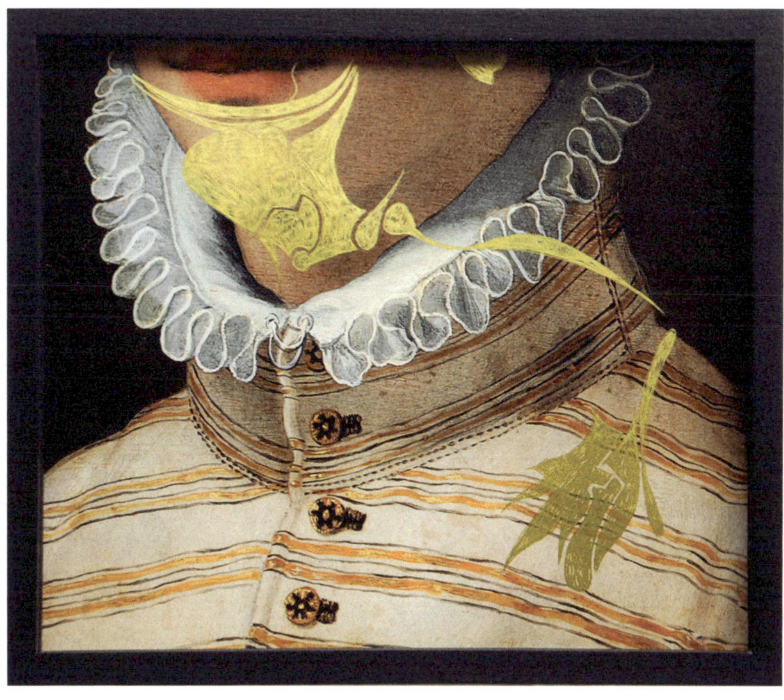

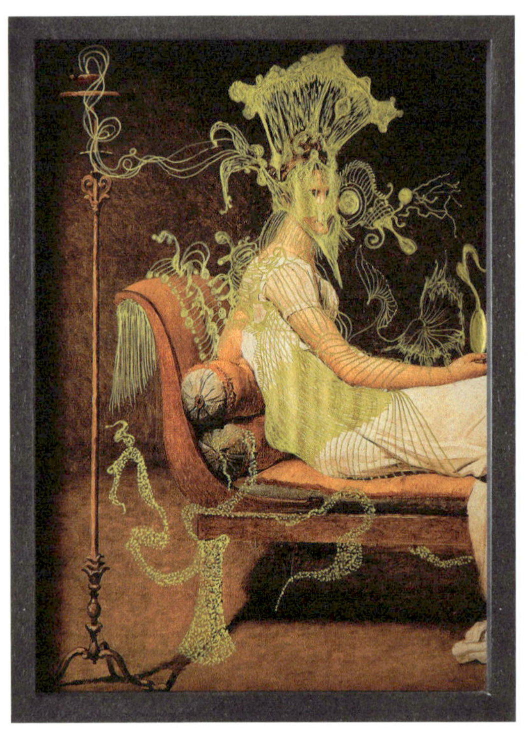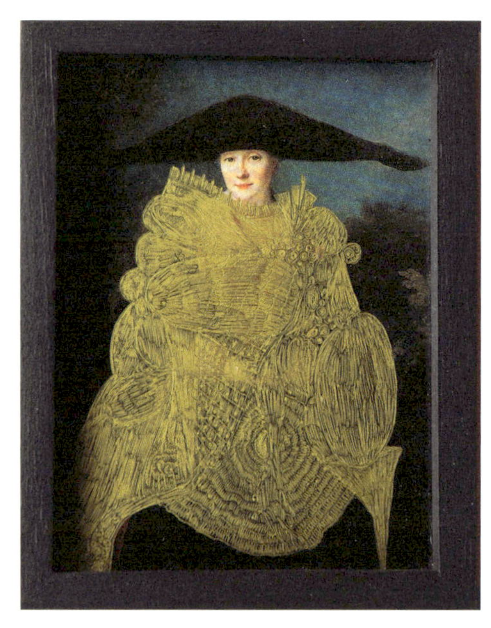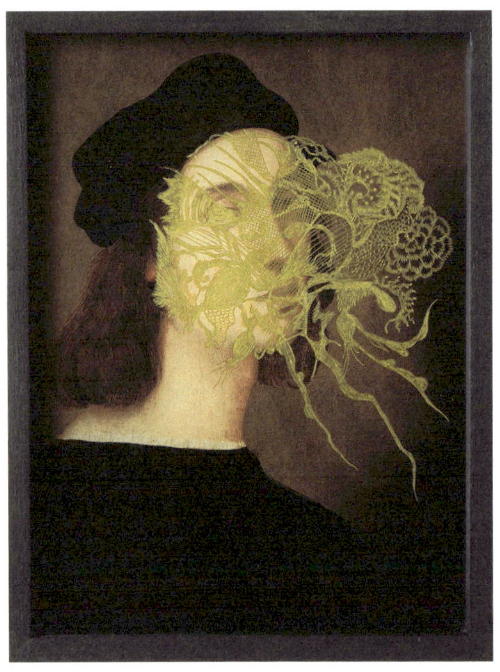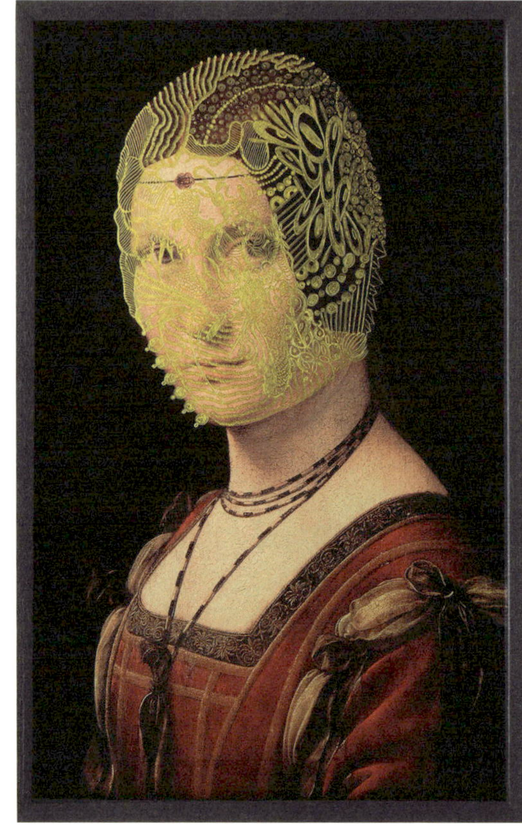

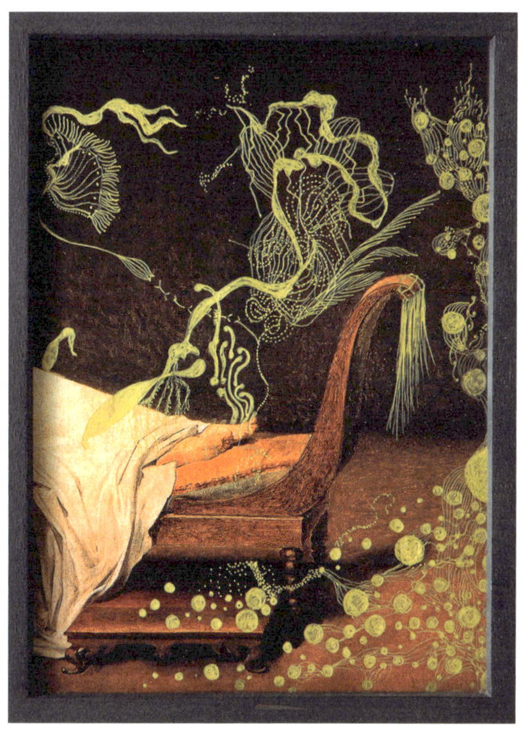
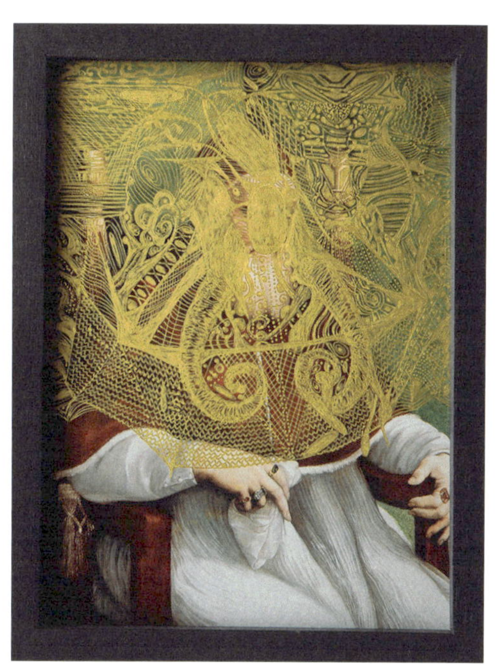
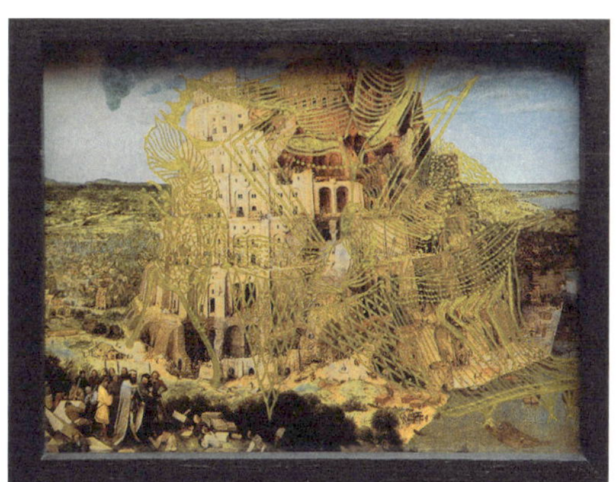
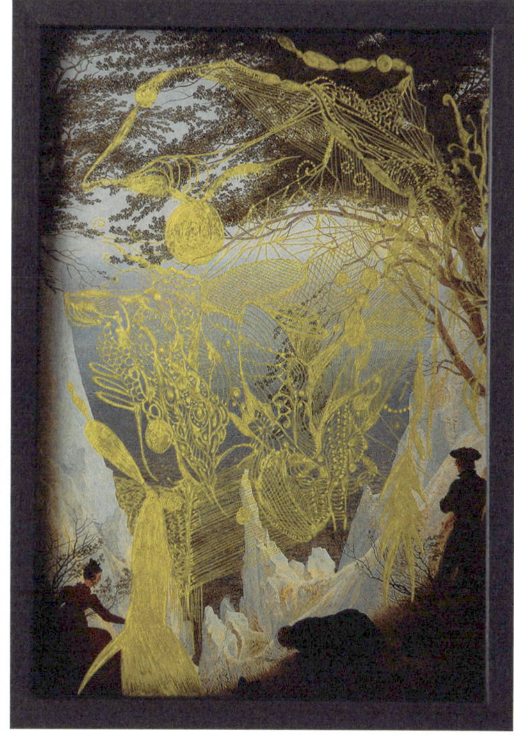

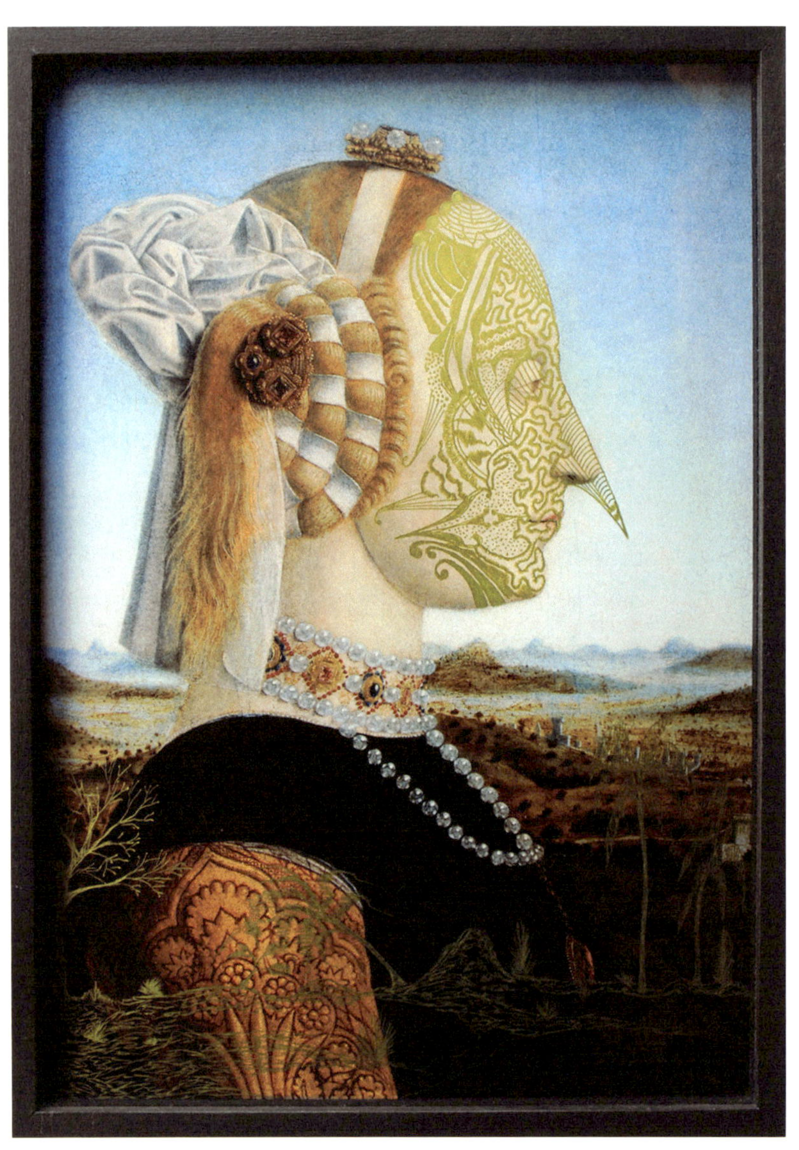

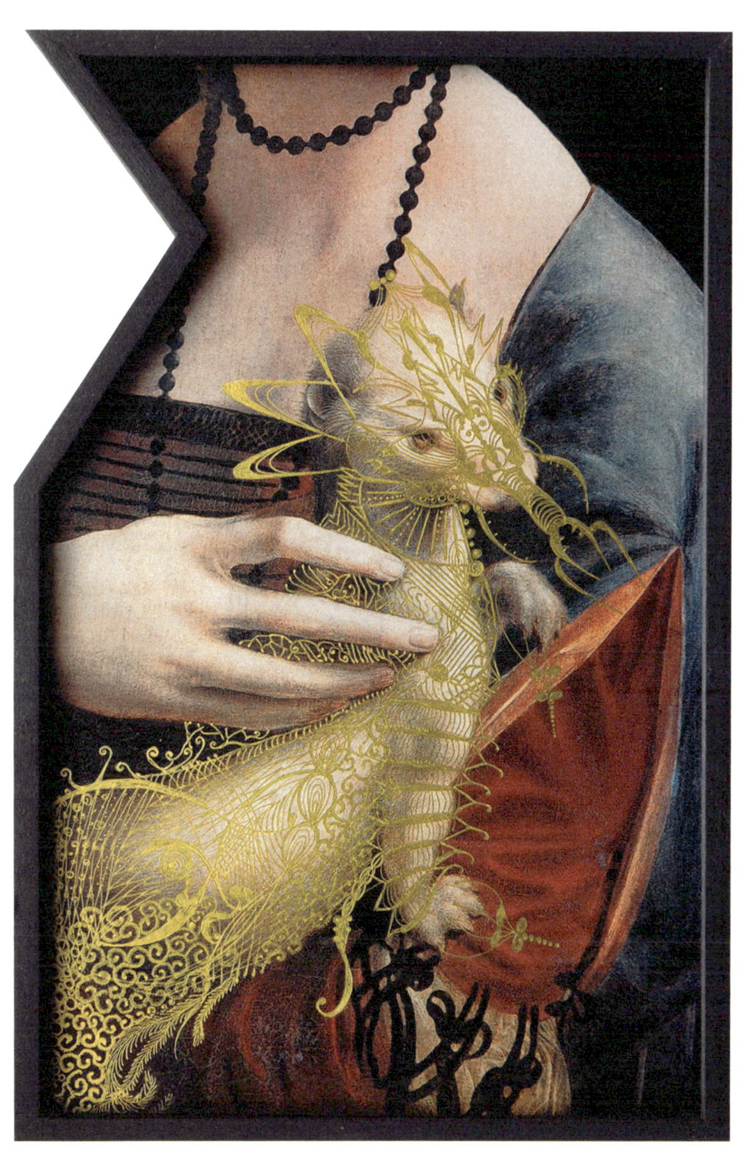

Ball

Baile

The reproduction of a painting (*Ball at the Court of Henry III,* 1581, anonymous) from the
Musée du Louvre was given to a carnival crew from Rio de Janeiro. The crew
was asked to re-create the wardrobe (fifty-five pieces) and accessories, bringing the
atmosphere of the painting to life. The work culminated in a restaging of the ball
itself. Many guests were invited to the party and asked to wear the costumes from the
sixteenth century. The entire room was decorated with fresh clay pots, plants
altered by scissors (Lima's *Vegetal Instance*), and Baroque-style frames done with the same
carnival technique. Chickens with bright and fanciful feather extensions *(Gala Chickens)*
walked freely through the space, and food, beverages, music, and dance were
offered. When presented at an exhibition, *Ball* starts with the rehearsal, as the musicians
begin to practice for the main event. This period of rehearsing and setting up the
ball is open to the public.

Ball / Baile, 2003 / 2004
People, fabric, bronze, wood, clay, foam, glass, gold ink, food, water, beverages,
alcoholic drinks, plastic, music, plants, feathers, paper
Dimensions variable

Courtesy of the artist, Photography: Paulo Innocêncio, Marcus Wagner
Views: Parque Lage, Rio de Janeiro

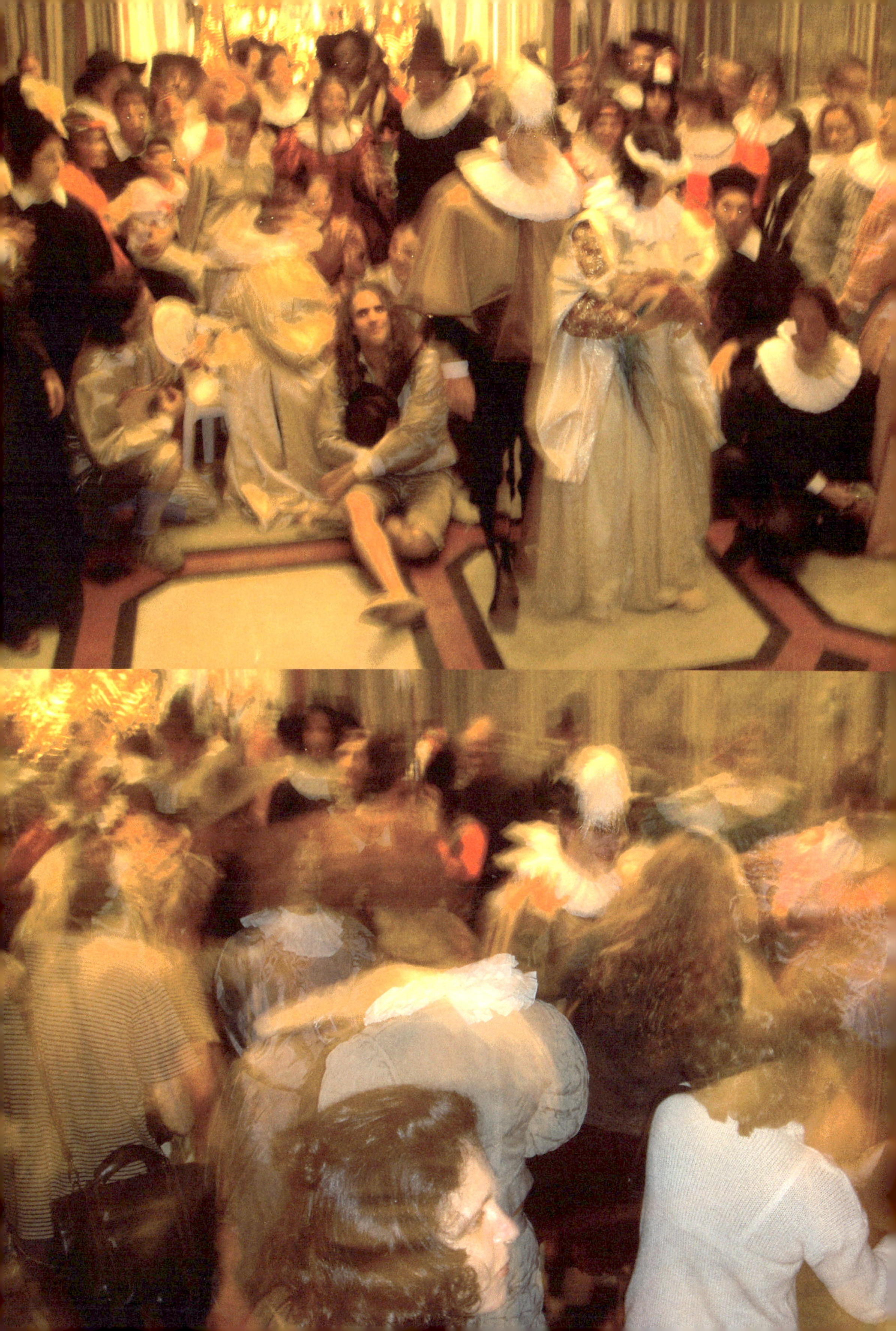

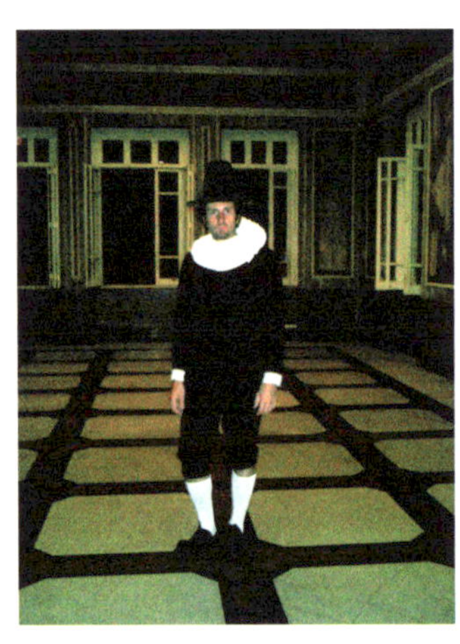

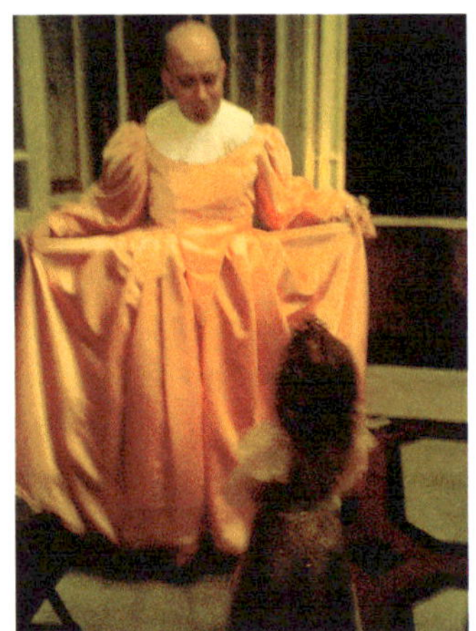

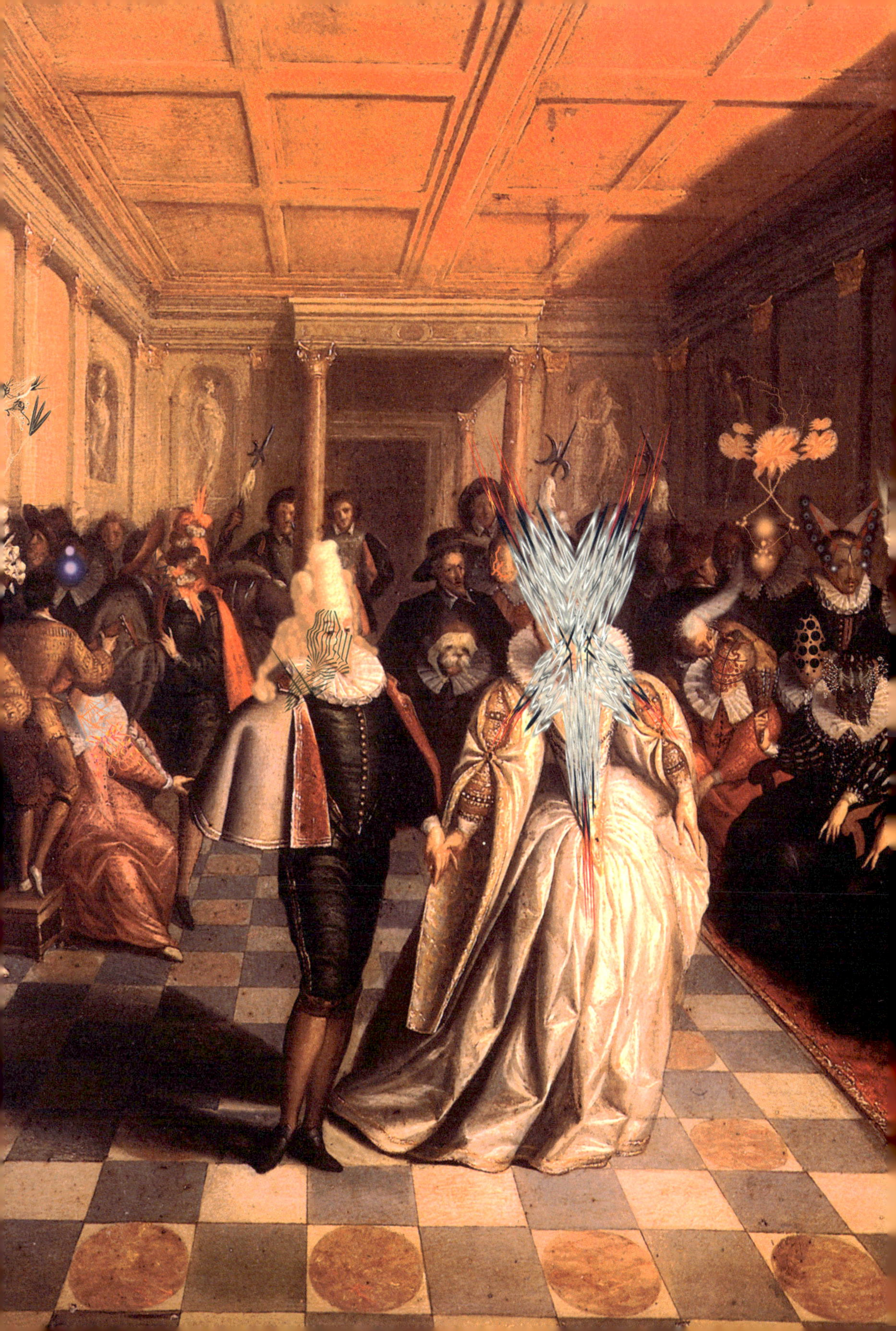

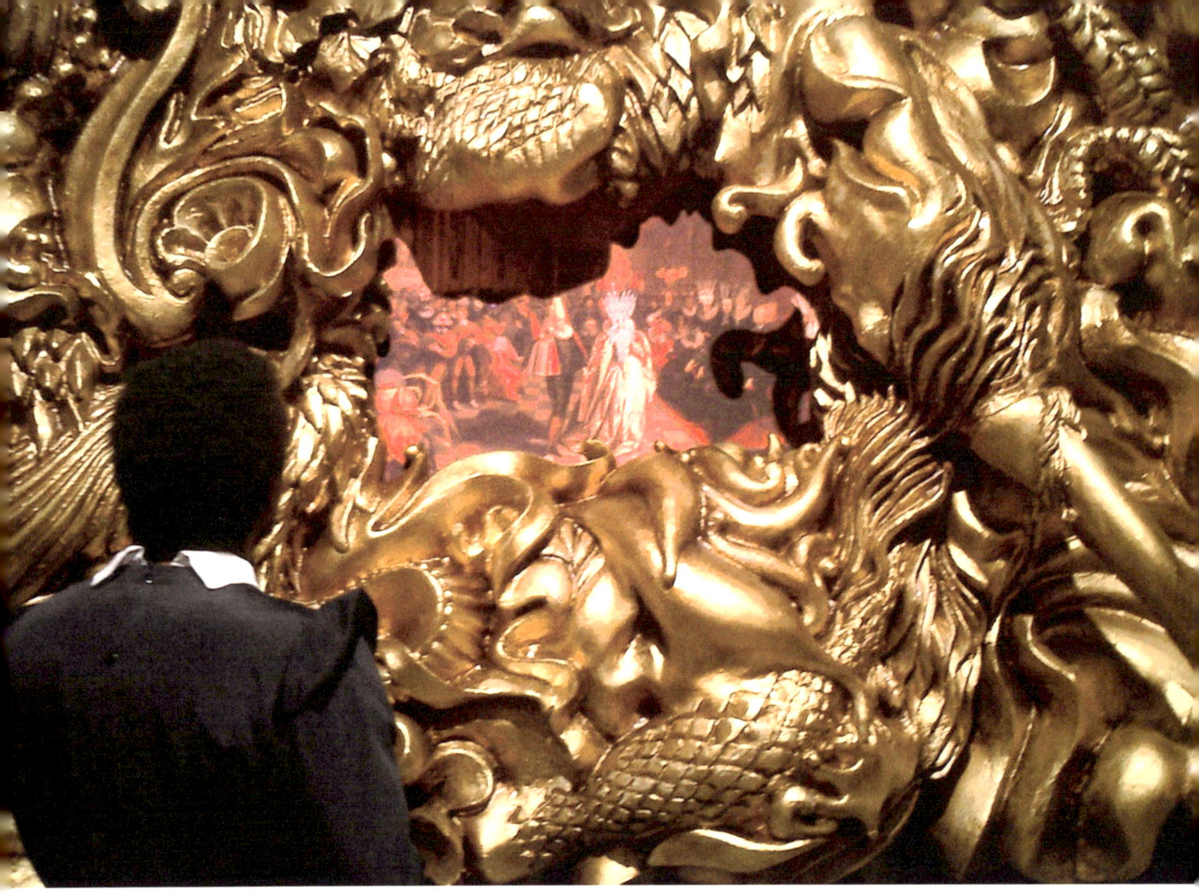

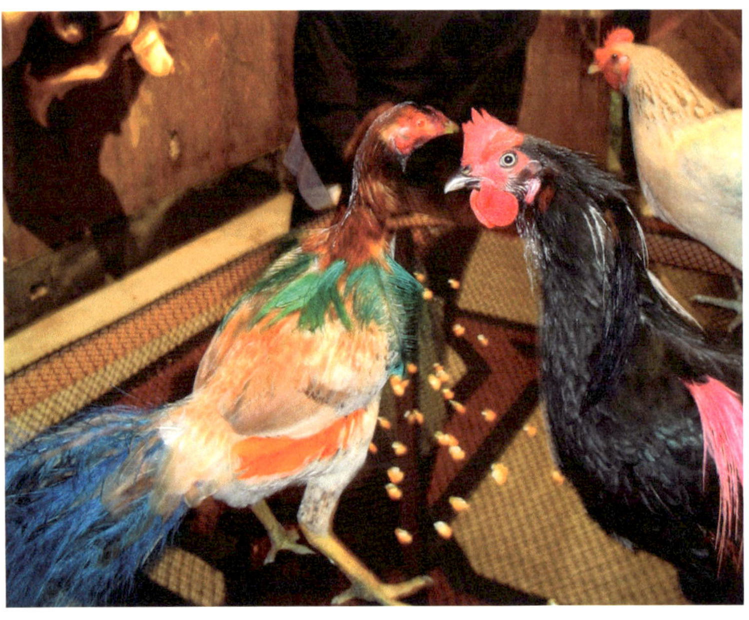

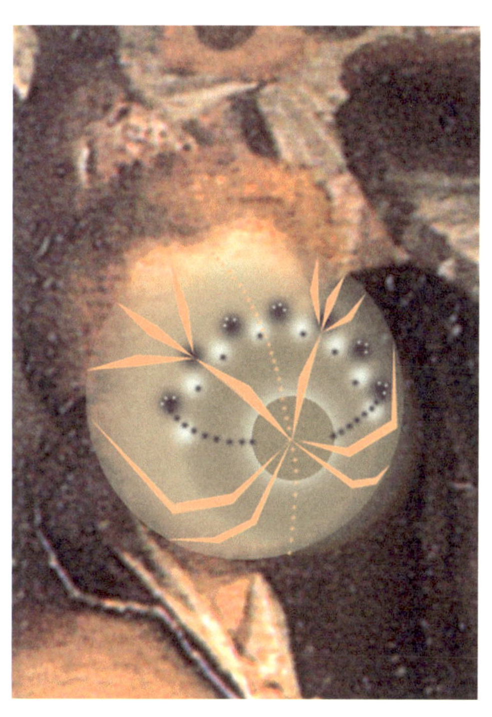

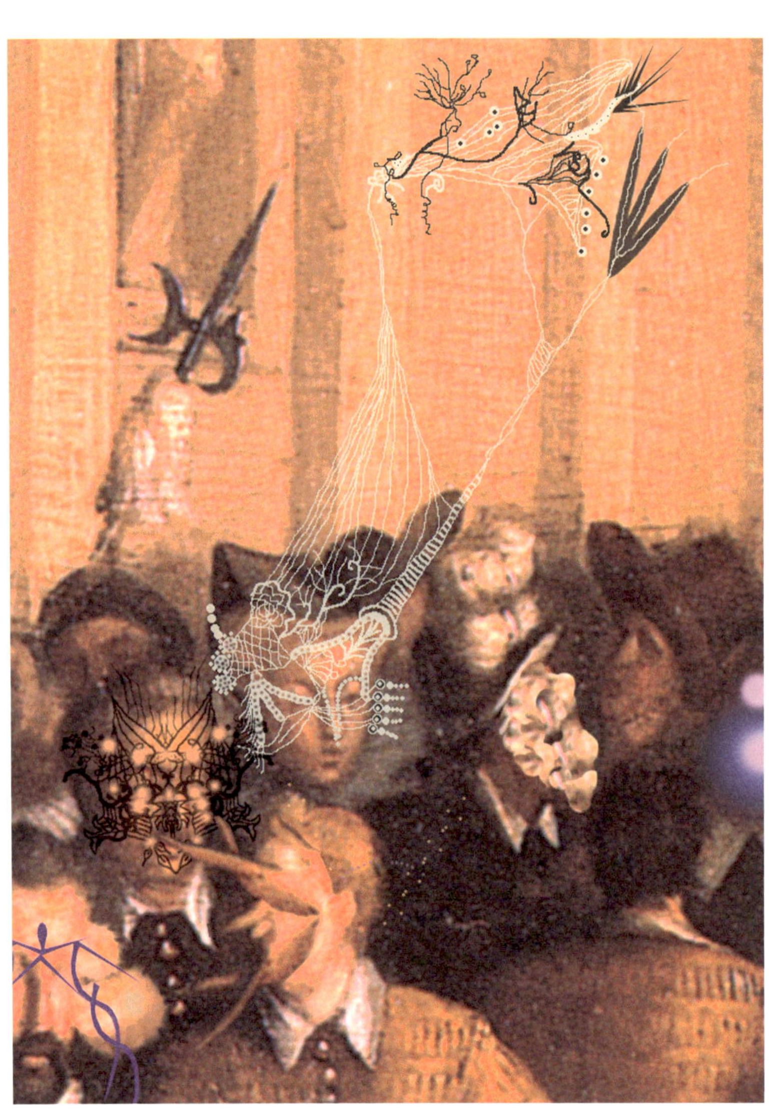

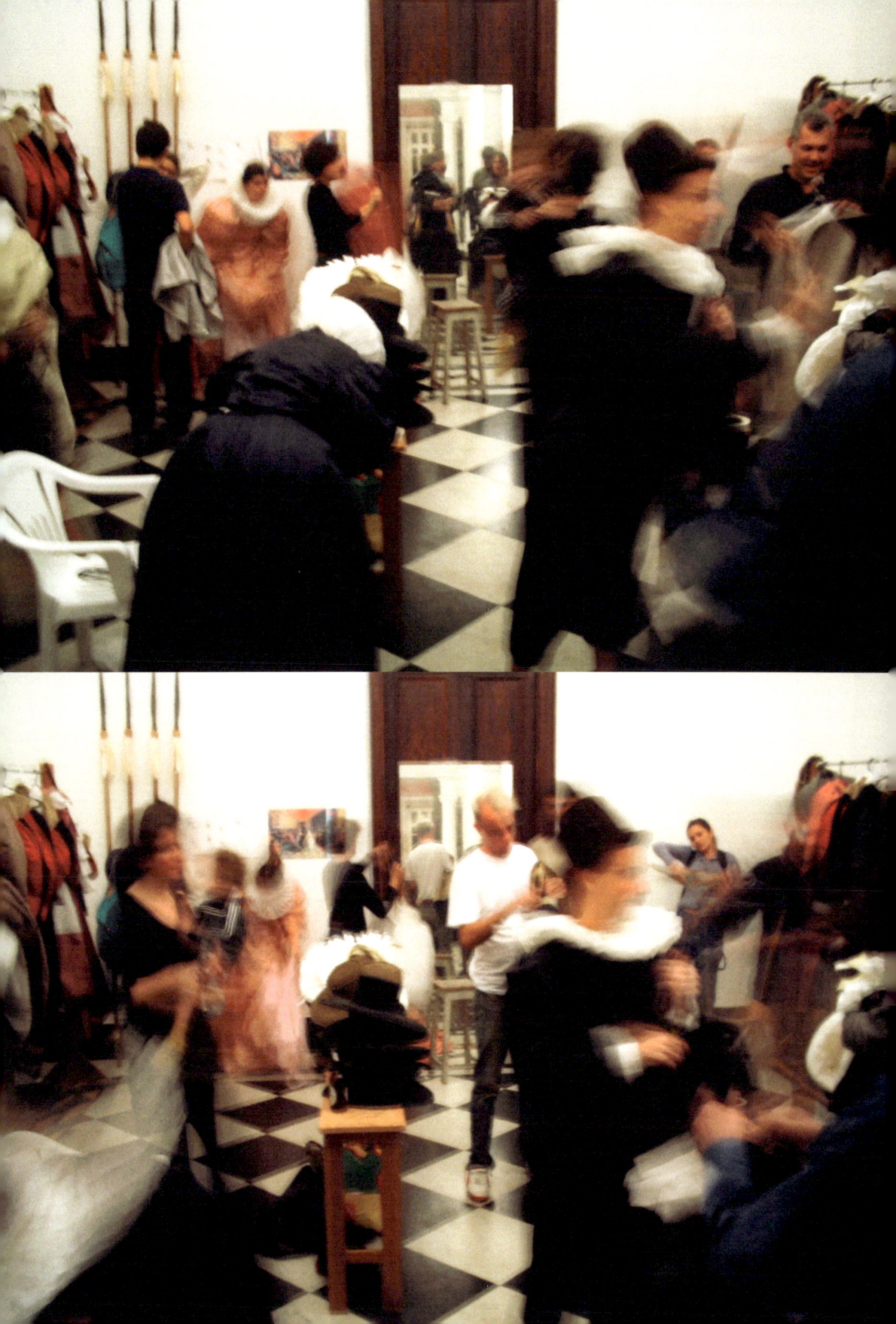

Costumes

Using scalpels and scissors, the artist constructed hundreds of "garments"—the *Costumes*
and *New Costumes*—by folding and carefully cutting out sections from a flat surface of
blue vinyl (*The First Collection,* 2001) and transparent vinyl (*The Second Collection,* 2006).
Made for humans and animals, the garments are designed to fit on the body and
offer new possibilities of adorning it. In the exhibition context, the pieces are offered to the
public in a storelike environment, with mirrors and attendants to help people try
on the garments as they wish. The *Costumes* extend the wearers' range of gesture, attaching
to various parts of the body or magnifying their movements and area. A profusion of
details, engravings, and drawings cover the surface of the *Costumes*. About three hundred
detailed pieces.

Costumes, 2001 / 2002 / 2003
Blue vinyl, special glue, wood, attendants (people), fabric, mirrors
Dimensions variable

Courtesy of the artist / private collections
Photography: Vivia 21, Ana Torres

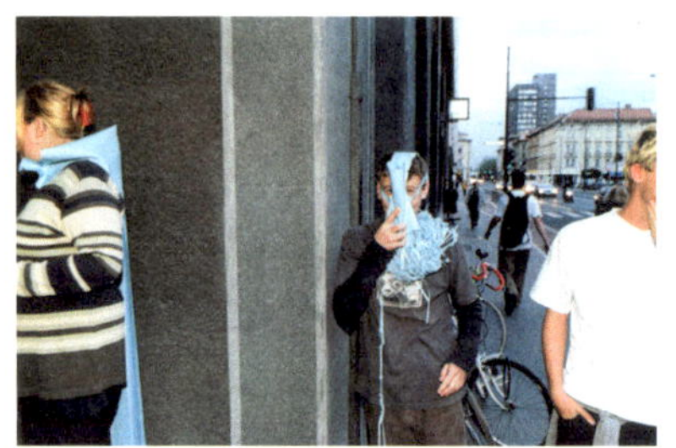

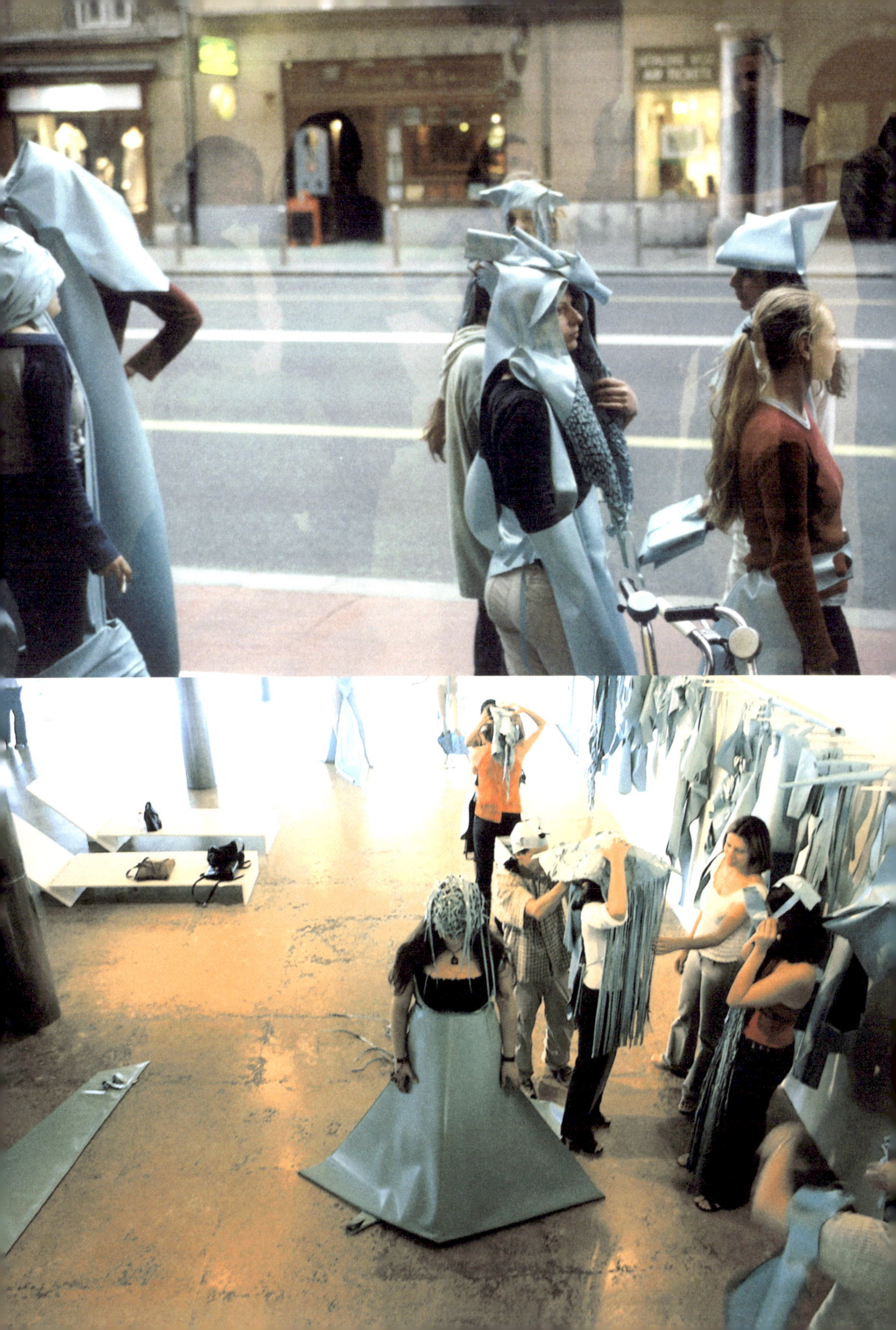

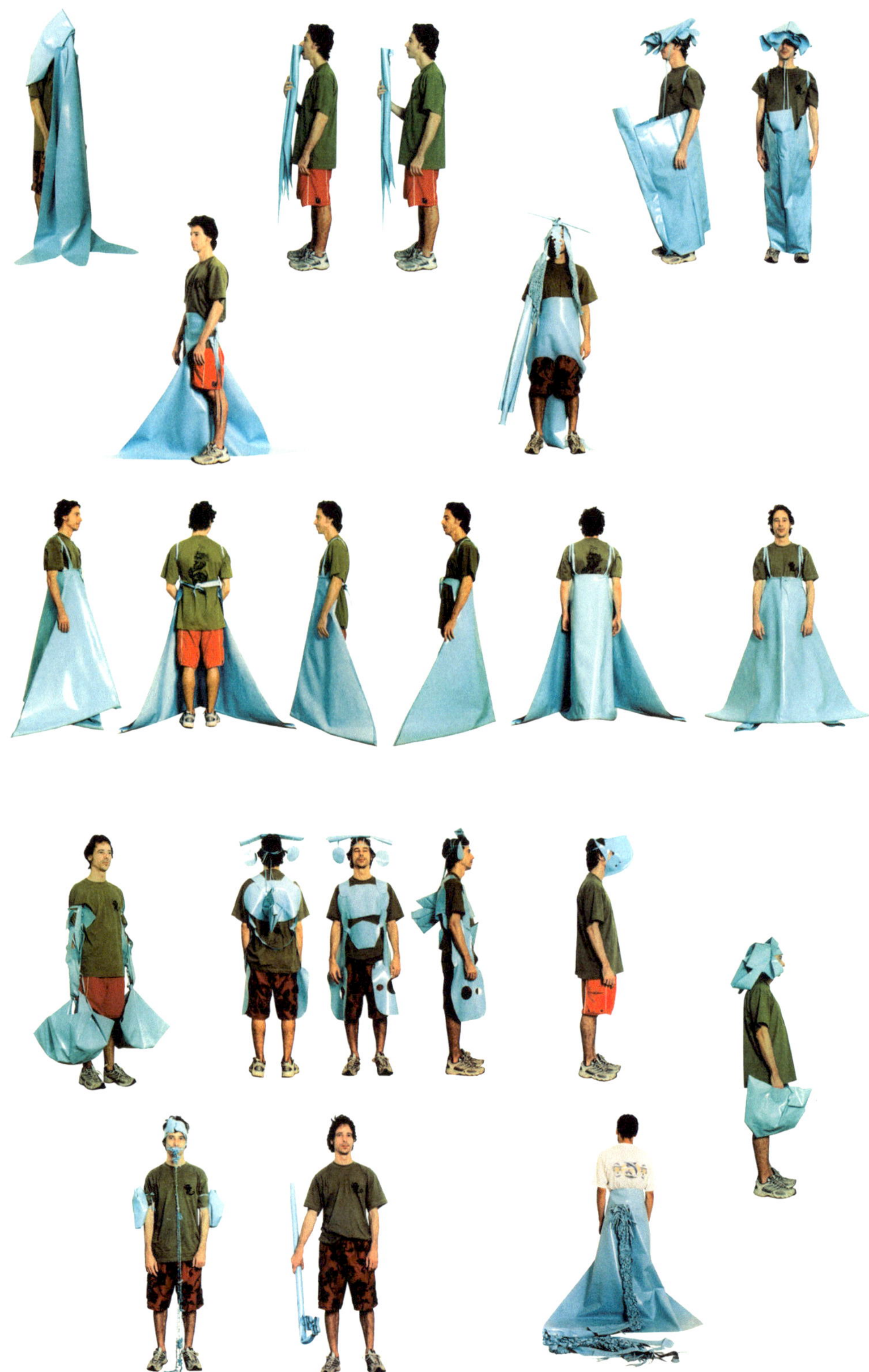

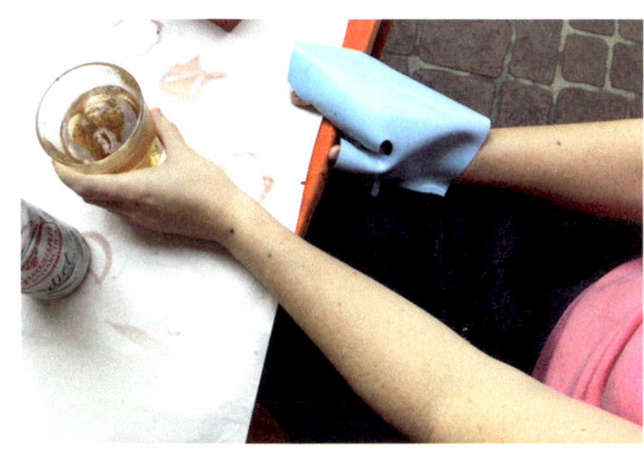
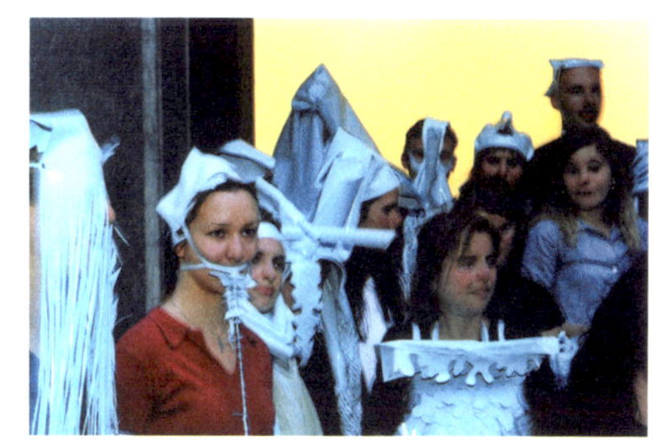
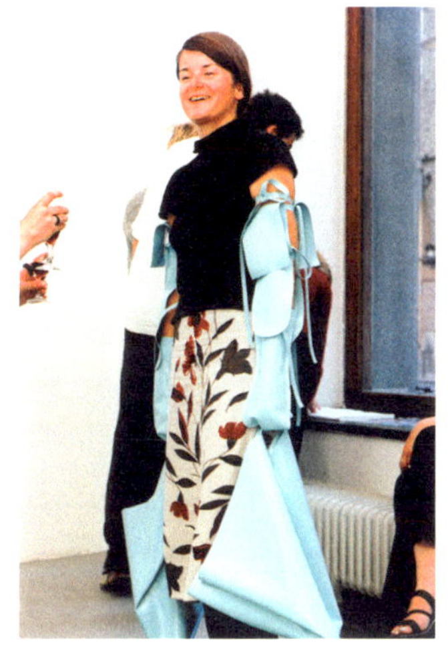
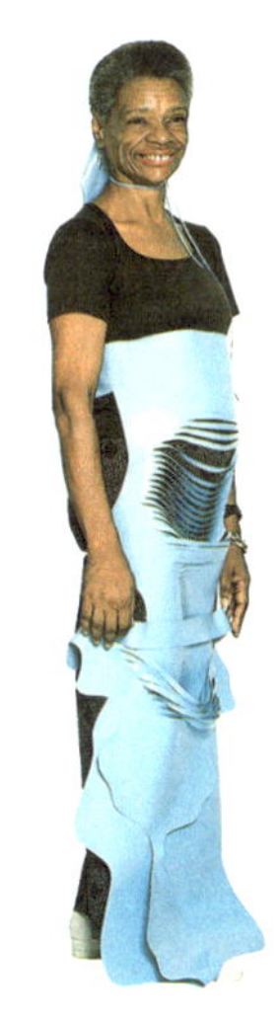
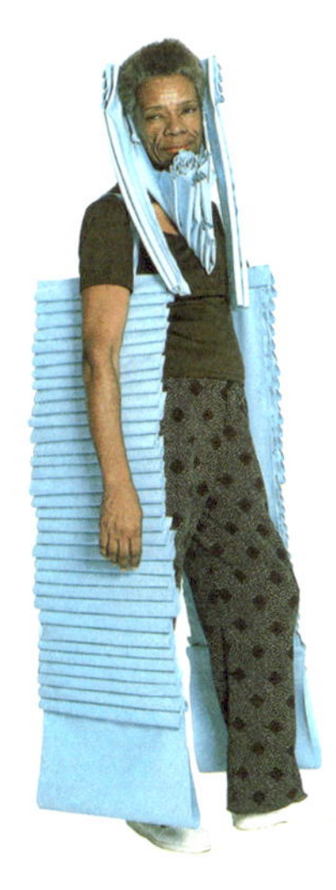
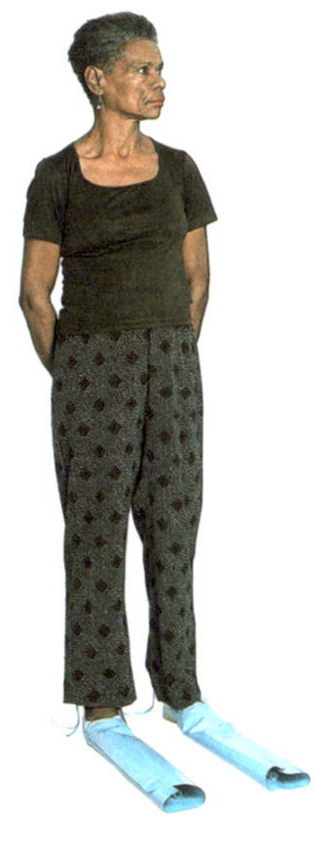
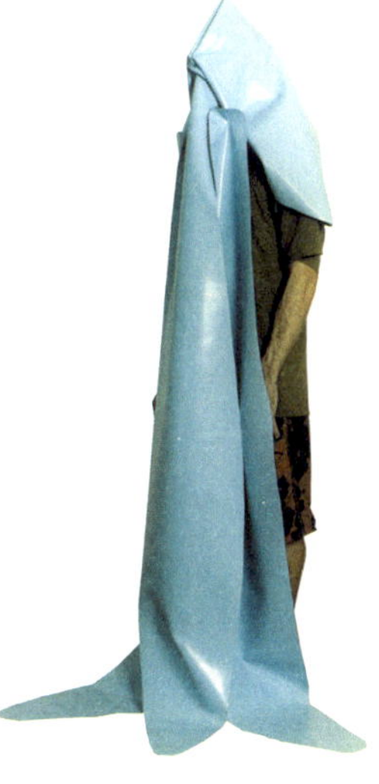
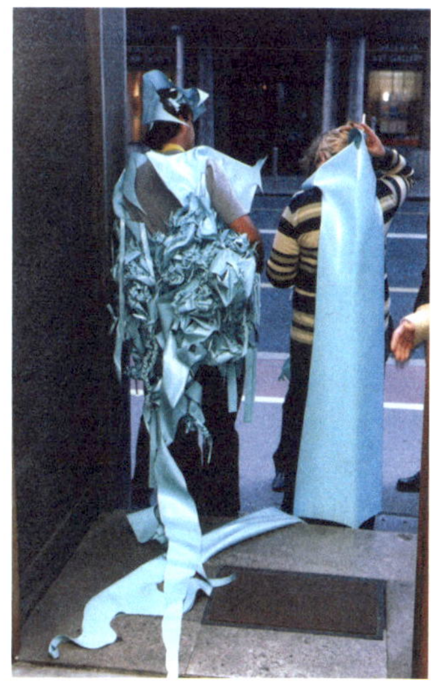

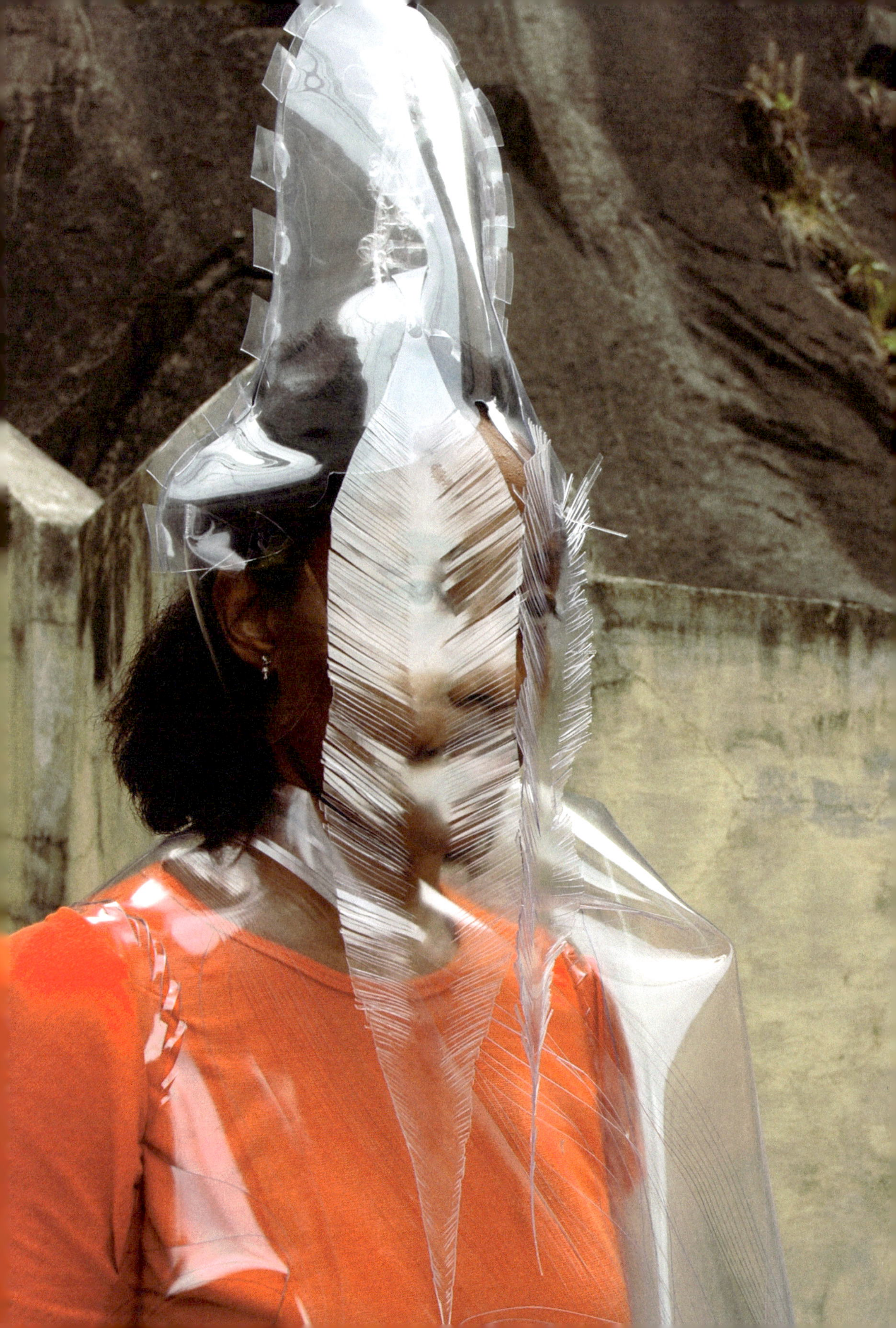

New Costumes

Novos Costumes

New Costumes / Novos Costumes, 2006 / 2007
Blue vinyl, special glue, wood, attendants (people), fabric, mirrors
Dimensions variable

Courtesy of the artist / Collection of Instituto Inhotim
Photography: Ana Torres, Vivia 21

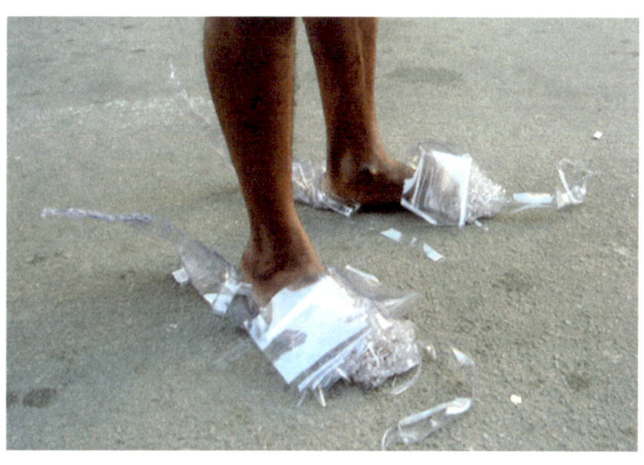

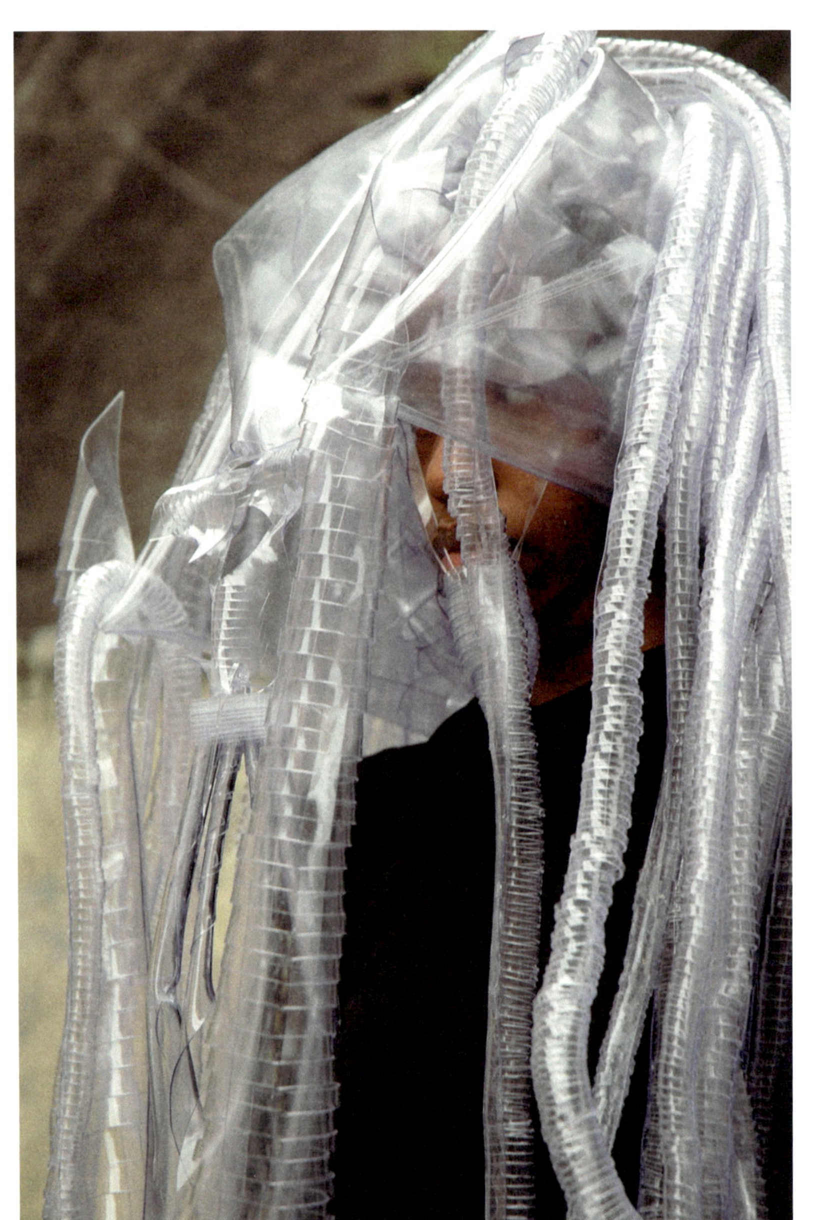

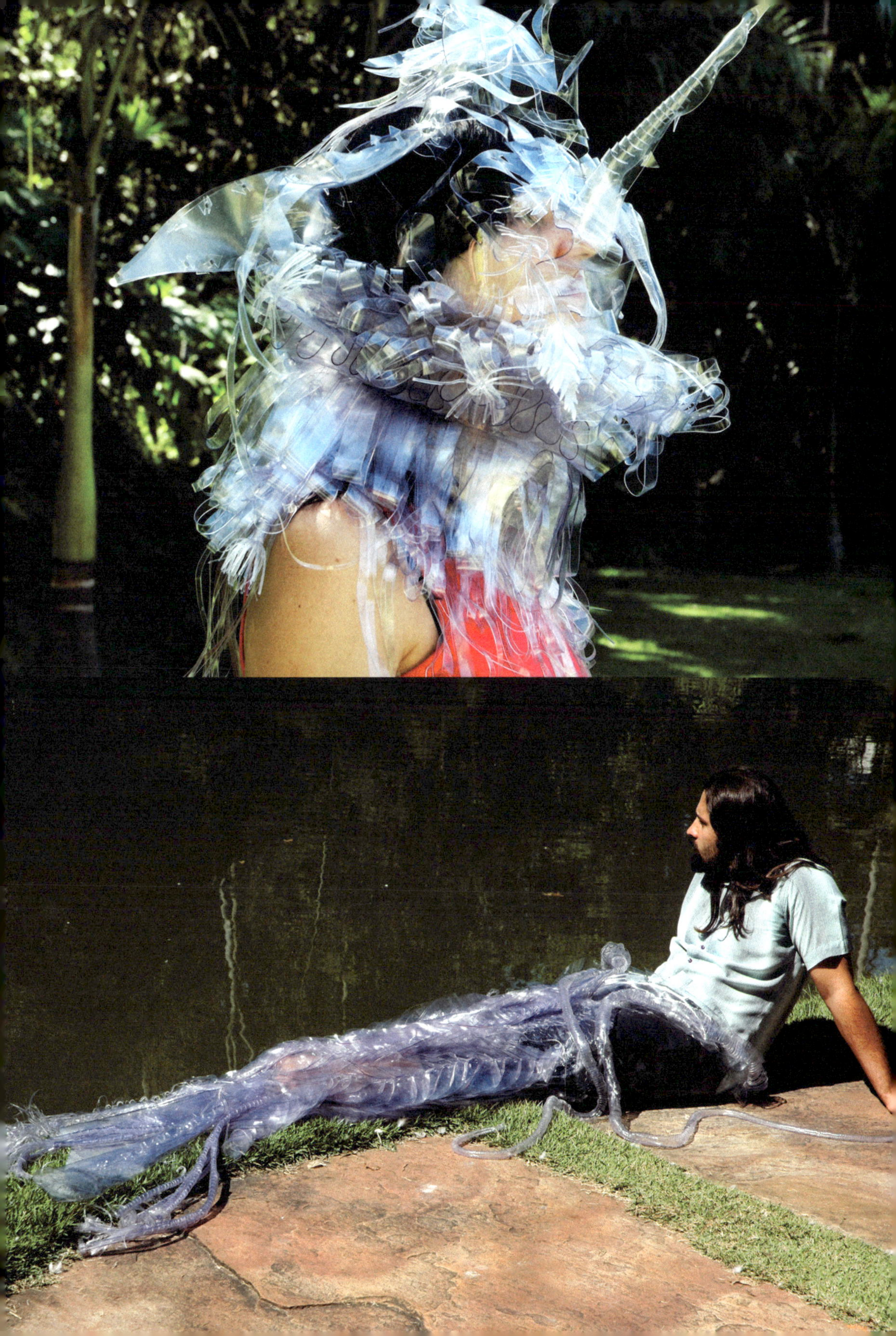

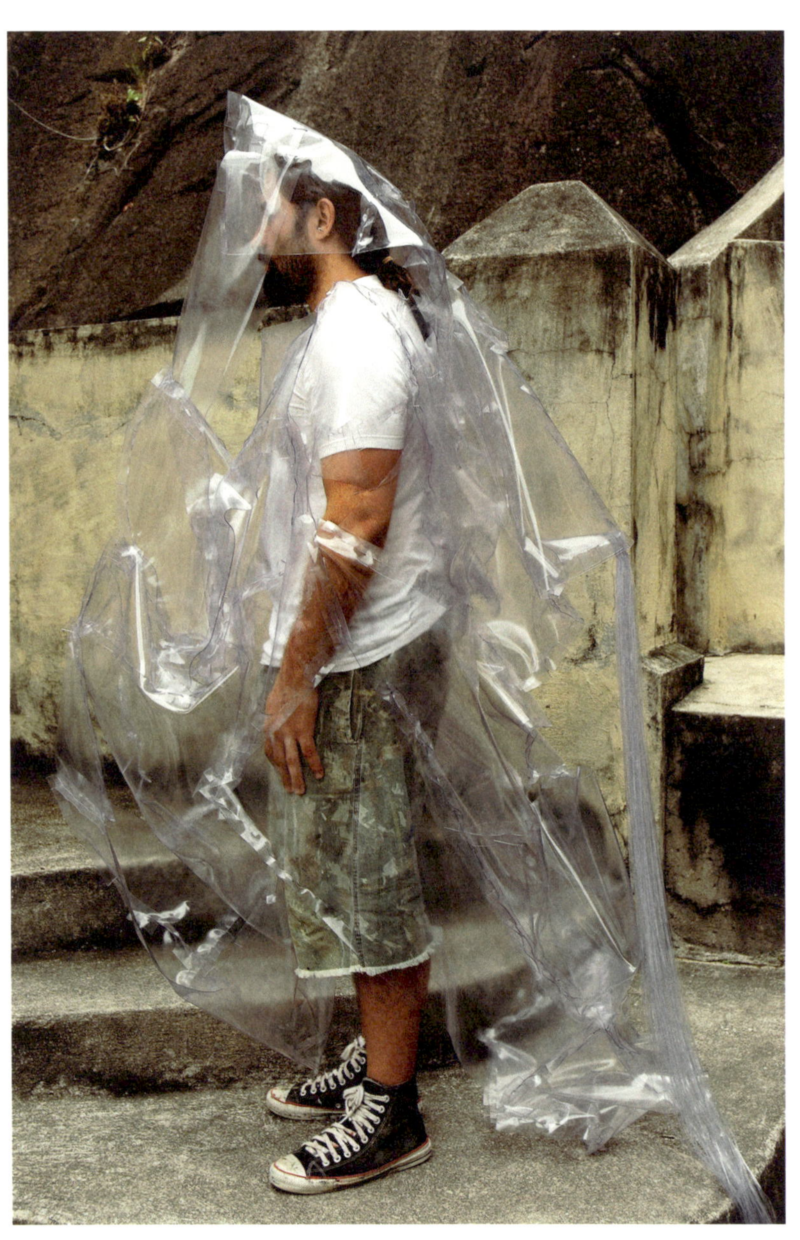

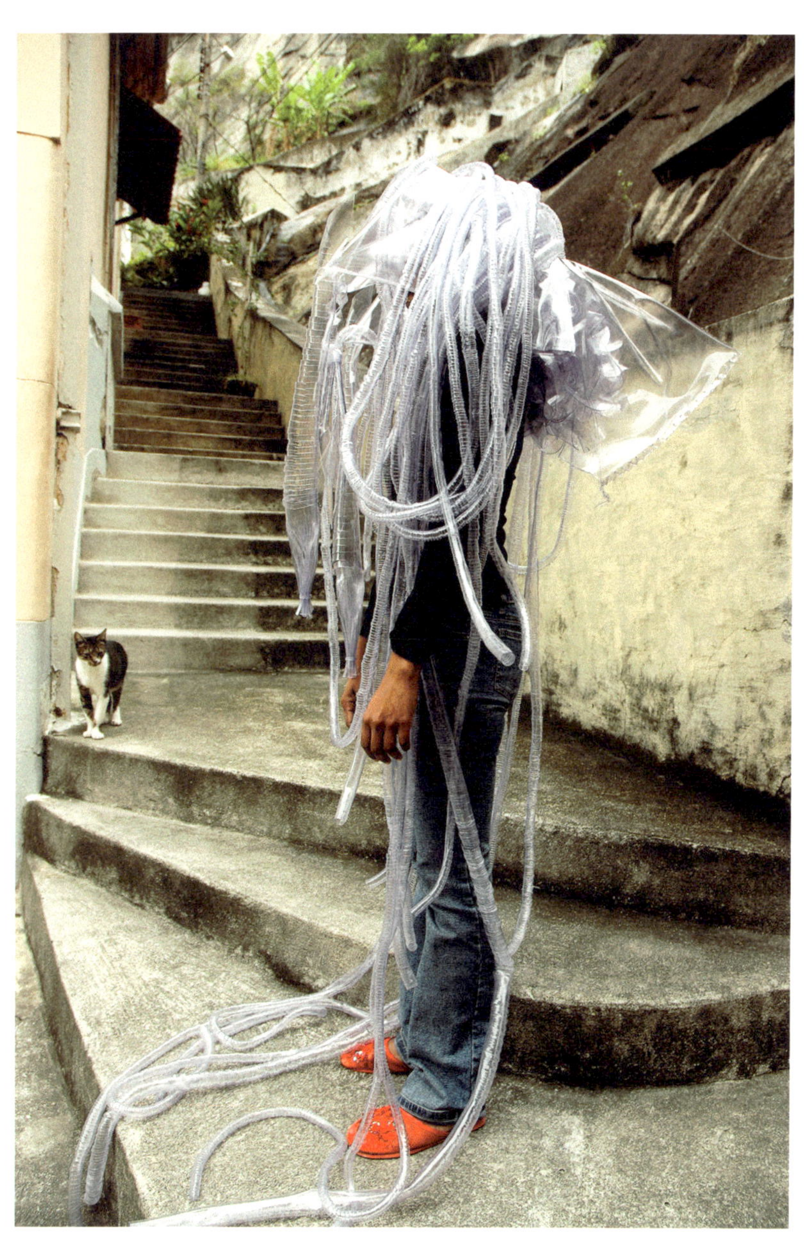

To Age

In 2001 / 2004, the artist "aged" the staff of an art center where she had been invited to exhibit—from the man at the reception desk to the director of the institution.
Over the course of several days, two make-up artists came during the morning and applied effects to artificially age the working staff. Some of them were office workers who then followed their normal routine for the rest of the day, going to work aged. Part of the idea was not telling the public what was happening, making the piece almost invisible.

To Age, 2001 / 2004
People, latex, makeup artists, powder, silver ink
Dimensions variable

Courtesy of the artist
Commissioned by Chapter Art Centre, Cardiff
Photography: Love's House, Rio de Janeiro, and Chapter Art Centre, Cardiff

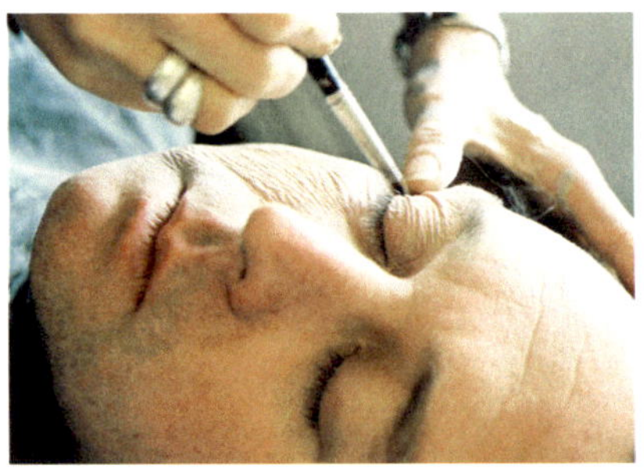

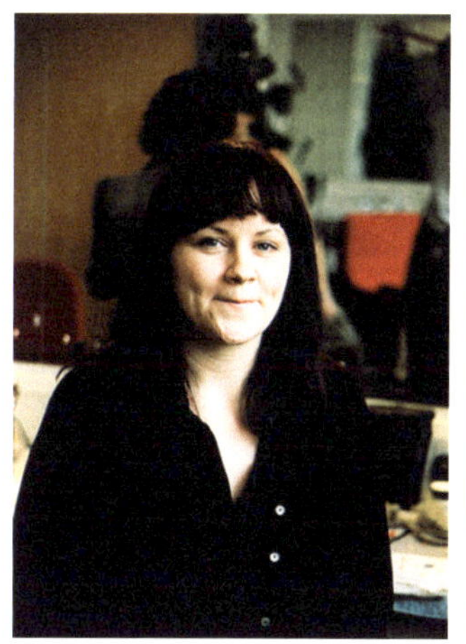
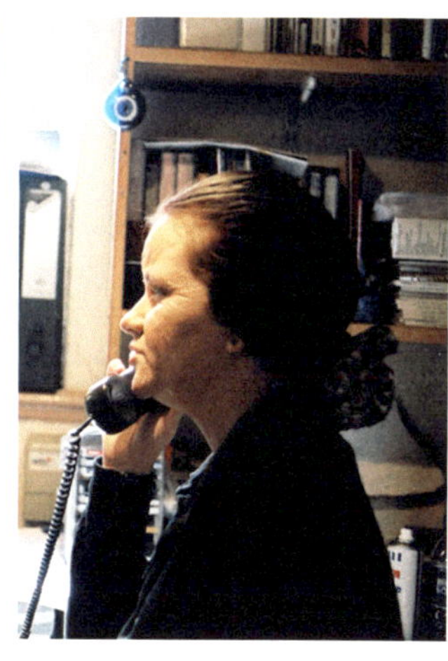
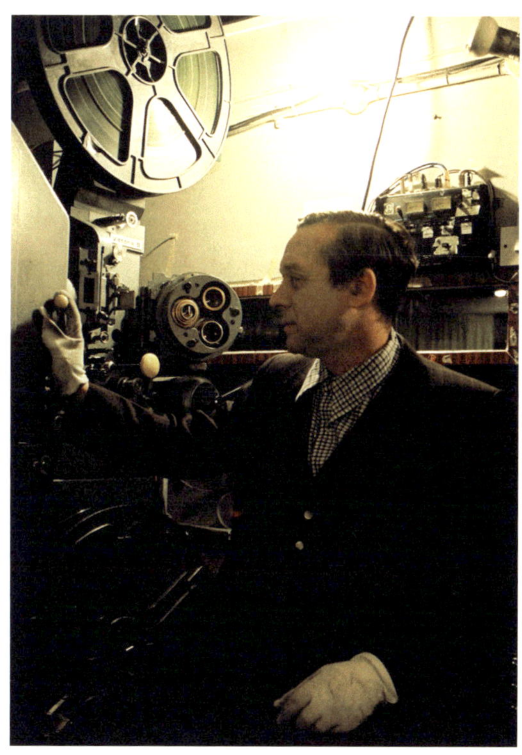
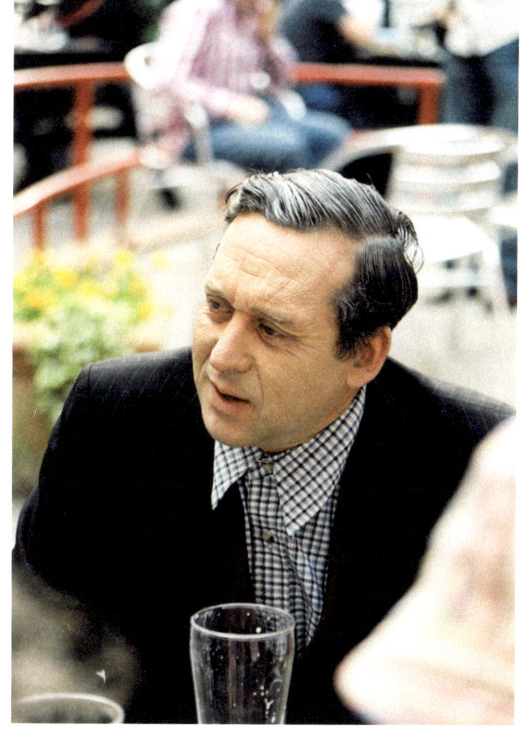

Jochen Volz

Matters of Equation

103

Homem = carne/Mulher = carne (Man = flesh/Woman = flesh) is the title of a body of works Laura Lima has been experimenting with since 1994. In these, often first conceived as drawings, Lima instructs humans to execute a certain action, mostly equipped with specific utensils or costumes, or shaped by architecture or devices. In *Marra (Fighting,* 1996), for example, two naked men push and shove each other with their hands and bodies, but their heads are stuck into one common hood. In *Dopada (Doped,* 1997), a woman in a white dress takes a strong soporific drug and sleeps for hours on the gallery floor, with her head connected to gallery architecture through a long woven net. In *Baixo (Flat,* 1997), a person with physical disabilities lies beneath a radically dropped ceiling next to a lamp, a body oppressed by the architectural space it inhabits. In *Gelatina (Jelly,* 1997), a child in white garments jumps rope in a basin filled with red gelatin. And in the subgroup of works titled *O Puxador (The Puller,* 1998), a nude man is bound tight into an armature, which is connected to long straps that multiply into bundles through the length of the space and which are tied to the trees on the backside of the gallery building or to the structural elements of the building itself; the man tries both to free himself from the armature and at the same time to pull it along with full physical effort.

The above-mentioned are only a few examples of a larger group of works operating under the same title, but these already clearly demonstrate the sculptural thought behind the *Man = flesh/ Woman = flesh* works. They have been described as living sculptures, a label which hardly grasps the complexity of Lima's operations. Each work consists of an instruction, a sculpted prop, an architectural or spatial frame, and humans.

The artist herself never performs in the *Man = flesh/Woman = flesh* group of works. These pieces can be realized by anyone, and no professional training is needed. Laura Lima selects her workers only on the criteria of gender, sometimes age, and occasionally in regard to physical stature: the woman, the child, the handicapped person, the man, two men—these are all generic categories. The artist explicitly prefers not to work with actors or dancers, but rather with people who have not developed a performative consciousness and therefore potentially execute her instructions with more immediacy. The preparatory process and the artist's directions for the works—strictly speaking, the brief she gives to the people working for her—have proven to play an important role, even if the instructions are simple. For *Fighting,* for example, the rules are pragmatic and clear: If the fighting men get tired, then they are to stop, rest, and start all over again with full energy. And it is preferable not to have the same men fight with each other repeatedly, allowing them to get used to one another. The fight should neither become a routine nor a dance.

Lima herself calls *Man=flesh/Woman=flesh* constructions of permanence with neither narratives, climaxes, nor evolution, even though some works do have a natural beginning and end, like *Bala* (*Candy,* 1996), which consists of a man with his mouth held open through a surgical device and a candy slowly dissolving on his tongue. This work naturally comes to an end, once the sweet has totally disappeared, and so does *Doped,* once the woman awakens from her sleep. But there is no choreography and no dramaturgy, not even a script. Also, the artist is not interested in the individuals who work in her pieces beyond the defined labor relationship between employer and employee, based on delivery and pay. And even though Lima could be said to be influenced by the strategies of Hélio Oiticica and Lygia Clark, yet in her work, quite unlike the performative practices of the latter two, the subjective experiences of the humans executing the works are not of interest at all. There is no transformative process at play, or at least it is not being examined.

Laura Lima's works are genuine investigations into a practice that operates between the conventional categories of sculpture, installation, and performance. To denominate her work, the term "instauração" ("instances," with the literal translation being "instauration") has been borrowed several times. It was Tunga who coined this term first, to describe certain works of his own production that are both installations and performances. Like Tunga, Lima activates a suspended state of the static and the variable. Whereas Tunga's use of performative elements in his work does lend fluidity to the sculptural form, *Man=flesh/Woman=flesh* seem to operate in the opposite direction: they are compositions of iconic images out of living material.

It is for this reason that Lima early on developed her own glossary to distinguish her practice. The formula *Man=flesh/ Woman= flesh* suggests an equation that turns living beings into one kind of raw material, flesh. According to Lisette Lagnado, "Laura Lima states the problem of representation with a disconcerting dryness of choice: any human being equals any other when kinship is reducible to the materiality of flesh."[1] Then again, an equation between

---

1   Lisette Lagnado, "The Task of Distance: In Laura Lima Project Rooms," poster for Casa Triângulo at ARCO Madrid 2000, trans. Stephen Berg (São Paulo, 2000).

variables, even if written in the form of a proposition, is by definition less a statement or an affirmation, but rather a problem consisting in finding the values, or solutions, that, when substituted to the variables, yields equal values of expression. Man=flesh/woman=flesh or even person=flesh, like any scientific equation, demands proof and provokes discussion and counter-argument.

Laura Lima's works are indeed not interested in the moral, spiritual, or social components—what the human individual who executes it is made of. But then again, it becomes evident, when seeing any human exposed in an exhibition context, executing any action, that the reduction of a person to flesh doesn't sustain itself. The viewers' urge to read and interpret turns the equation into a constant process of negotiation. This is where the strength of Lima's operation lies.

When entering *Grande,* Lima's 2010 exhibition at the Casa França-Brasil in Rio de Janeiro, one immediately found oneself approaching an apparently anarchic workspace from the back. Through awkwardly arranged shelves, erected between the building's Neoclassical Doric columns, a large number of work-in-progress situations could be identified. There were open books, paper rolls, boxes, maps, work gloves, bottles, pans, wood boards, files, rubber tires, paper objects, clay piles, textiles, half-finished ceramic sculptures, a large variety of tools, and many other objects, not only laid out on work benches and shelves but also suspended from the ceiling, floatingly occupying the space as if the laws of gravity didn't really apply here. And there was a man, dressed in a black, short-sleeved tuxedo and top hat; at times, he was sculpting in clay or building something and then moving on to arbitrarily arrange and rearrange other objects or simply wander through the space. His field of action seemed to be quite carefully organized in two zones, one of production, labor, and, to a certain degree, order, while the other one of chaos, madness, and decay. *O Mágico Nu (The Naked Magician,* 2008) clearly provoked a reading of the situation as a representation of an artistic process, balanced between creation and destruction, reflection and pause, affirmation and uncertainty. *The Naked Magician,* though, is part of the *Instances,* which represent another group of works as well as a methodology in Lima's oeuvre, even if rooted in similar strategies.

The exhibition's baffling beauty was constituted in dialogue with a second piece in the exhibition, *Homem=carne/Mulher=carne – Pelos+Rede (Man=flesh/Woman=flesh – Hair+Hammock,* 1996). In a giant hammock, a naked man and a naked woman recline. She has artificially lengthened pubic hair and he extended eyebrows. Both seem totally at ease with their unconventional forms of hair growth. The two occupy one common space, one hammock, but it would seem wrong to describe them as a couple. The man and woman are evidently told to either rest or observe the magician and visitors to the exhibition, with attentive but indifferent facial expressions. This directness is what one senses when wandering between the magician and the two nudes in the hammock, a void charged by non-verbal dialogue, which seems to embrace the visitor. Who is the creator? Who watches? Who is the object?

The equation proposed in the works' titles obviously counts on a third element, the spectator. The viewers' reactions, be it shyness, care, anticipation, pity, discomfort, surprise, or even prejudice, represent constituencies to the work itself. This is where the formula gains space for argument. Skillfully, Lima manages to draw scenarios, which address, on the one hand, matters of representation in the broadest terms and, on the other, strategies of subversion. As much as the artist defines the rules of the work itself, the viewers' reactions reveal subjective states of the individual and of society in many moral and ethical aspects. This is what can throw such a simple, but maybe provocative, equation as *Man = flesh / Woman = flesh* off-balance.

Here, one more important aspect comes into play, the circumstances of the works' presentations in galleries or museums. The institutional space operates as a frame for these pieces. Whereas Lima's protagonists would likely be perceived outside the gallery as vulnerable, the codes of behavior—guided by caution and a minimum of respect inside the institutional frame—do allow for more open-minded readings as sculptures or performance. In fact, thinking of *Doped* as maybe the most explicit example, it does need confidence in the audience's understanding to instruct someone to be sleeping for hours in a publicly accessible space.

This kind of provocative confidence is even more perceptible in the series of works that make up the group entitled *Nuvem (Cloud,* 2009). In an apparently classical gallery space, hands and ears come through holes in the walls, holding lamps, monitors, drawings, and jewelry and rolling and lighting cigars to offer to the public. In fact, fake walls are constructed to hide the staff, which is working at the exhibition by lending parts of their body as display devices. Though operating on a very different scale than *Man = flesh / Woman = flesh,* these works do illustrate the same aspect of Lima's artistic strategies. Reduced to sheer body parts stuck through museum walls, Lima's collaborators do not even share the same physical space with the audience: without any visual contact, the question of confidence becomes even more pressing.

And as much as the institutional space does serve as a protective space, it is also a viewing space, a space of individual observation and obsession. The desire to observe the flesh that makes up the works, but also the joy of watching other members of the audience react as they discover that the sculptures on display are living human beings, kicks off a series of sensations and uncertainties, rooted in curiosity and shame. The *Man=flesh/Woman=flesh* group of works qualifies as one of the most open-handed queries in recent decades into the nature of art because of an extraordinary precision that simultaneously questions the potentials of artistic form, the role of the viewer between co-creator, voyeur, and consumer, the limits of the illusion of the so-called white cube, and portraying moral states of society through simple matters of equation.

RhR

"RhR"—there is no correct way to articulate this sound. Read the word "RhR" as you see fit.
RhR is an organism that emerged with the *First Movement* (in 1999). It has no purpose,
no specific function, no hierarchy. Its existence is corruptible. It has members of different
nationalities and species (including animals).
Any person, of any nationality, creed, or ideology is already a potential member of *RhR*.
Members can be invited by other members; or offer their own participation;
or even just initiate their presence without this being disclosed to anybody or anyplace
pertaining to *RhR*. But, to be a member, for whatever period, long or short, it is
necessary to wear the *Uniform-Drawing* (a condition of passage and initiation up until the
present *Movement*).
RhR doesn't answer to any ideological content. Many times it witnesses the void that is
borne out of bureaucratic channels. A natural process of constant change can
already be observed in *RhR* as the relations between members, administrators, and
crossers take place. That is its disposition.
There is no party line whatsoever in *RhR*. It has a predisposition to change, and to erring
in facts and things. With this, any moral yoke is also broken.
Members contribute to the existence of *RhR,* participating in it, talking about it,
or administrating it, in any capacity. Wearing the *Uniform-Drawing* in the most simple
quotidian circumstances is a way of contributing to *RhR*. Writing a text with the
word/sound "RhR" is a way of contributing to *RhR*. We could call it an *RhR* administrative
moment. *RhR* can also just disappear for a period of time, long or short, and it can
even be rescued in the future. It isn't teleological and has no obligation or duty to win or
prosper. These things are alien to it since they come from a specific form of rationality.
RhR exists but, who knows, just for now.

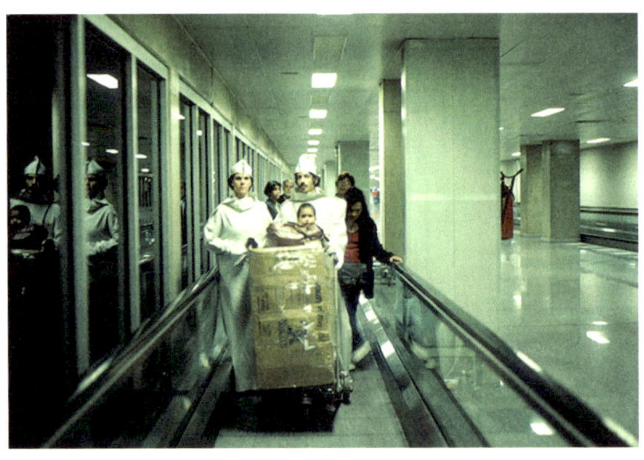

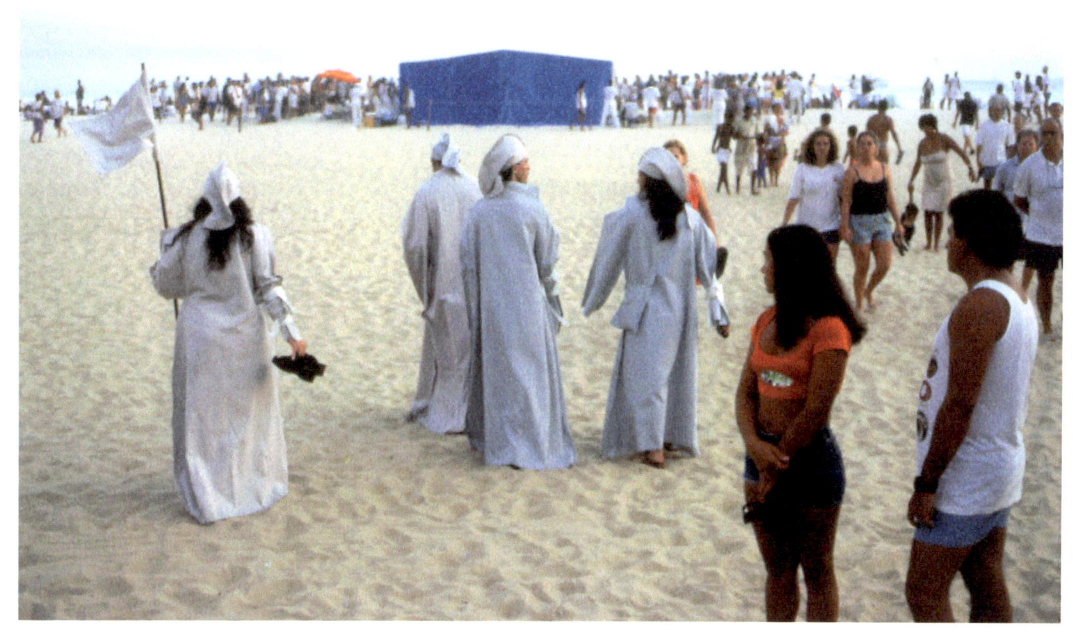

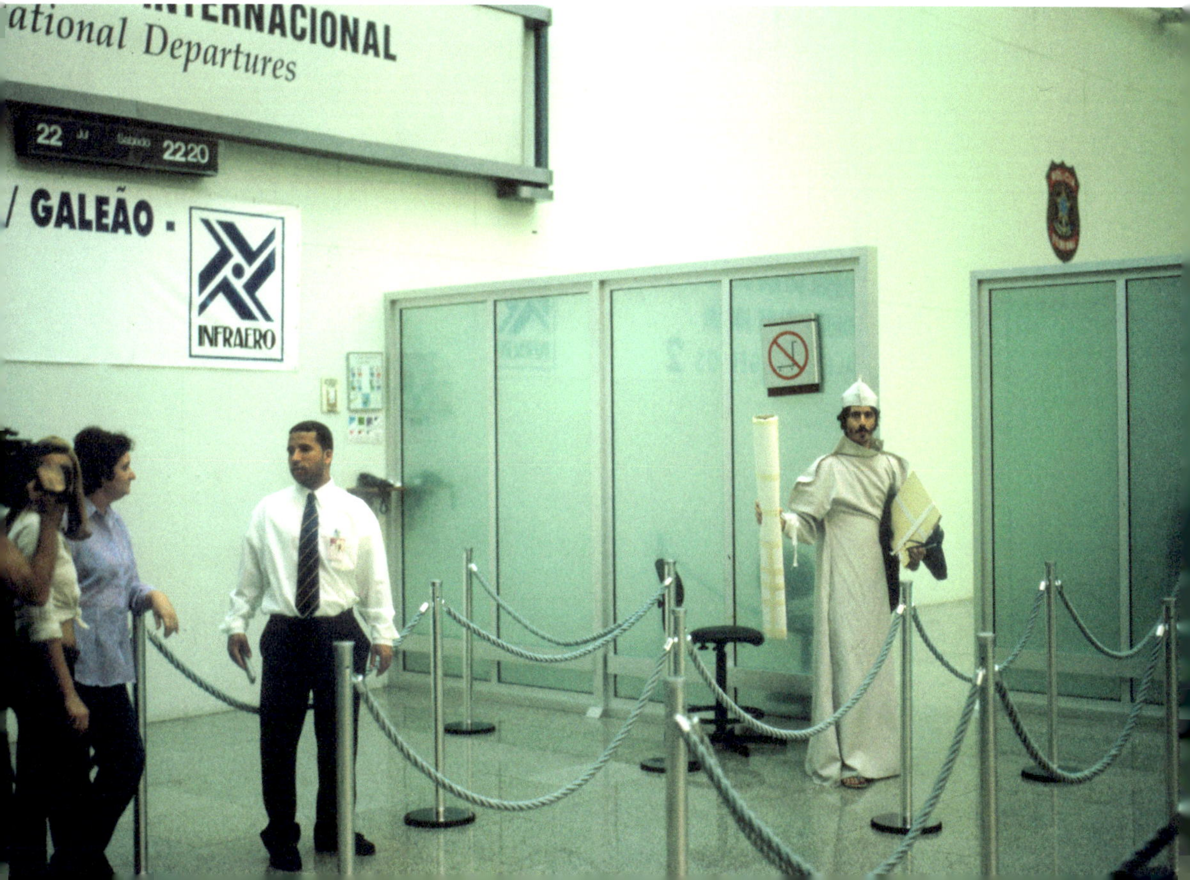

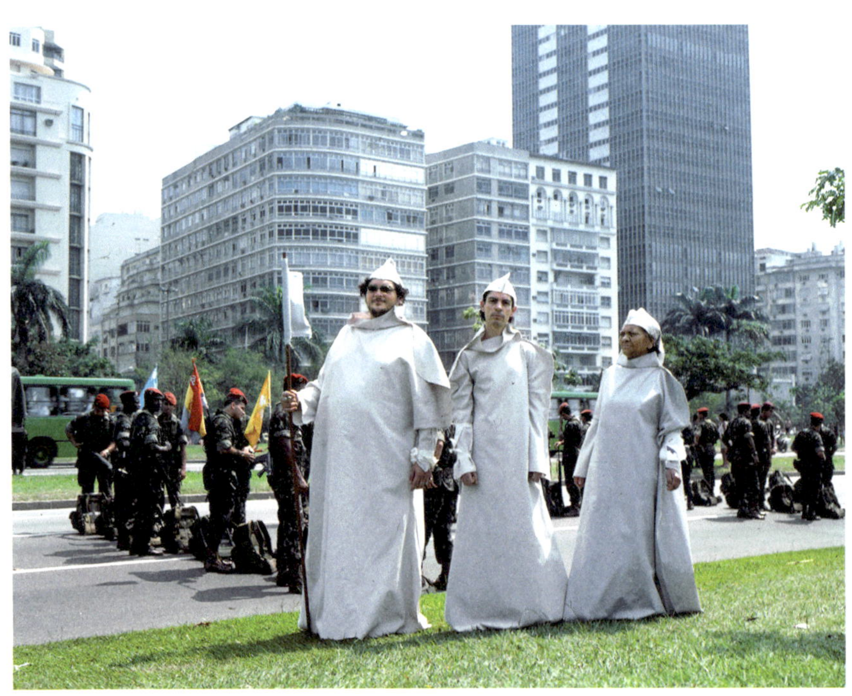

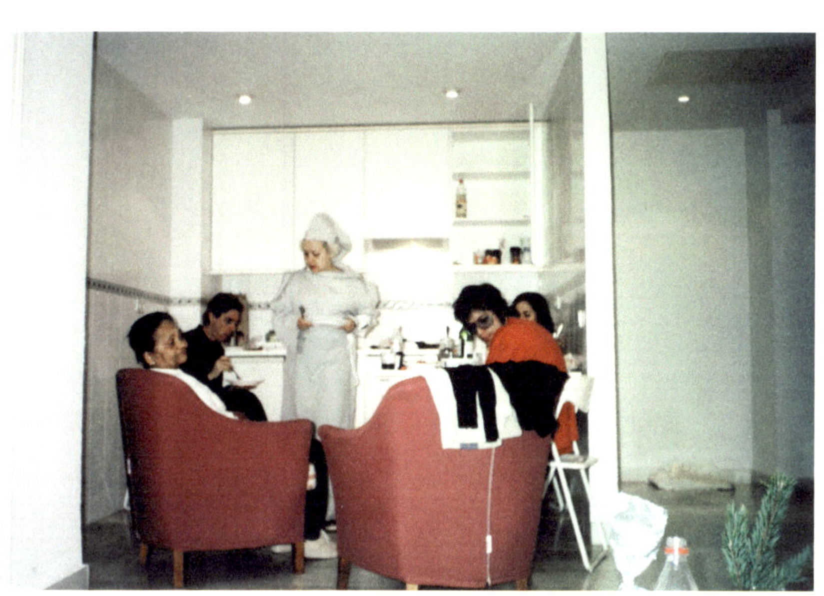

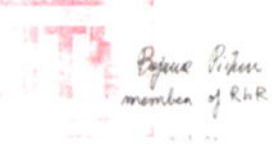
UGOVOR UGOVOR UGOVOR UGOVOR UGOVOR
UGOVOR O AUTORSKOM DJELU

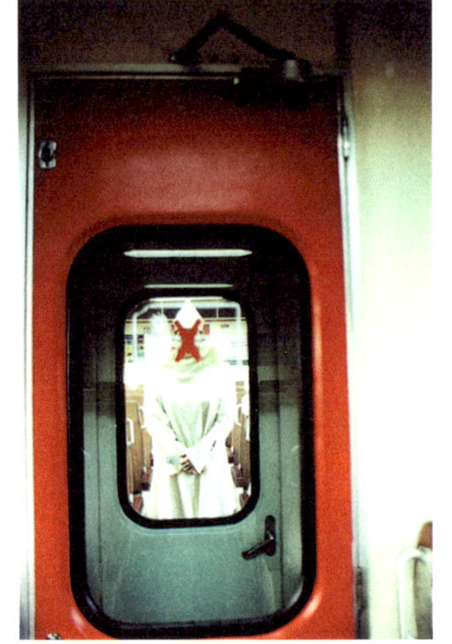

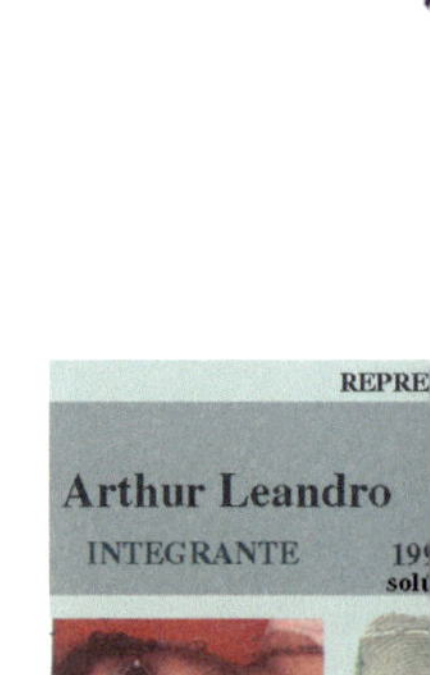
REPRE
Arthur Leandro
INTEGRANTE   19
solt

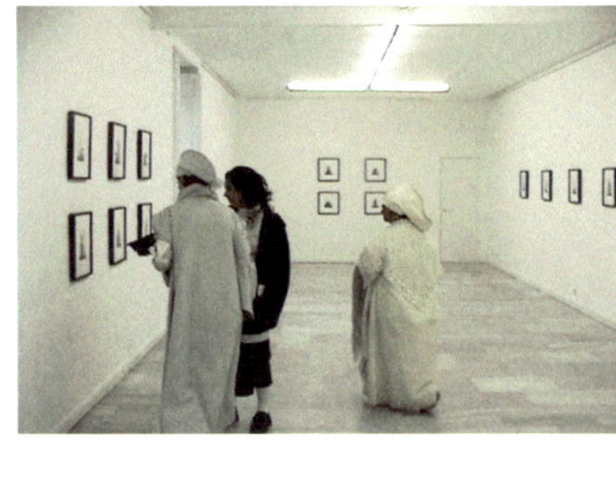

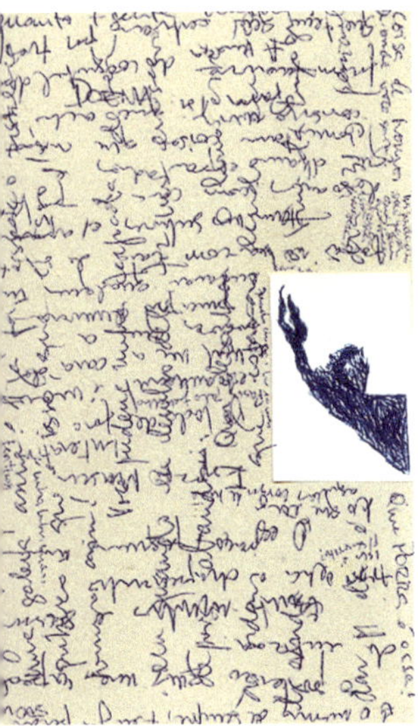

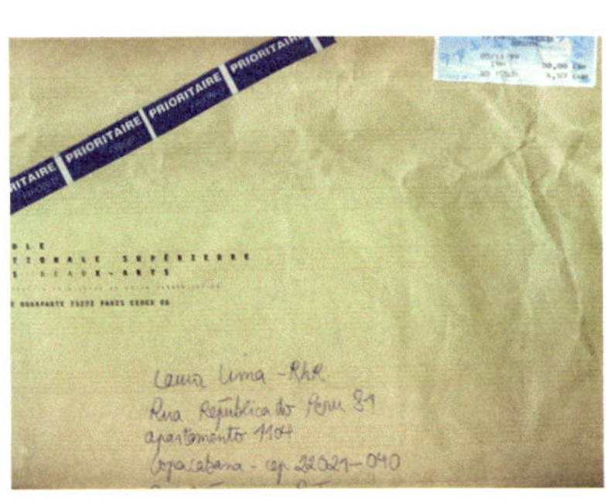
PRIORITAIRE   PRIORITAIRE
PRIORITAIRE

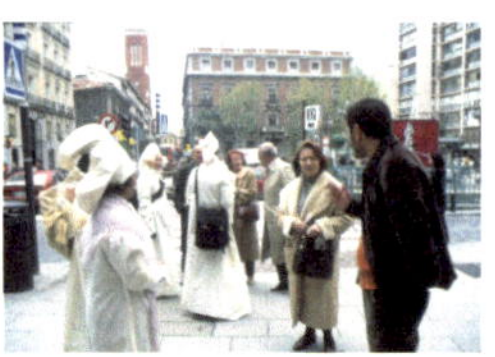

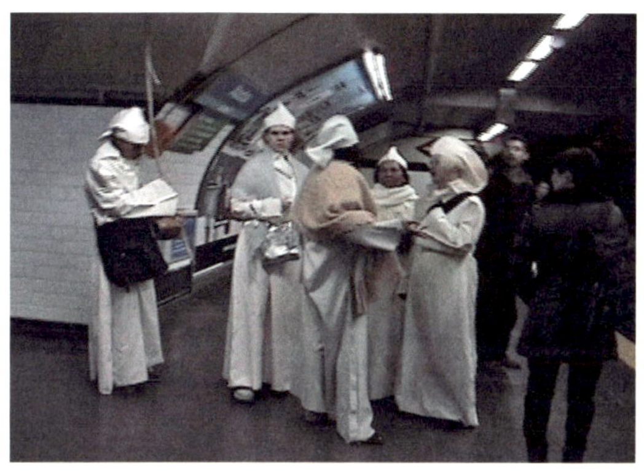
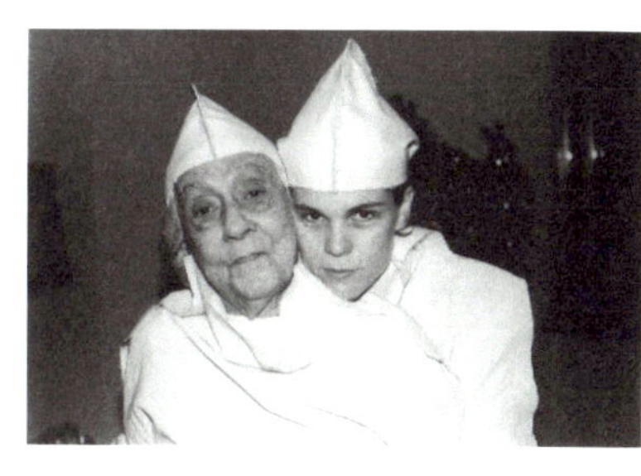
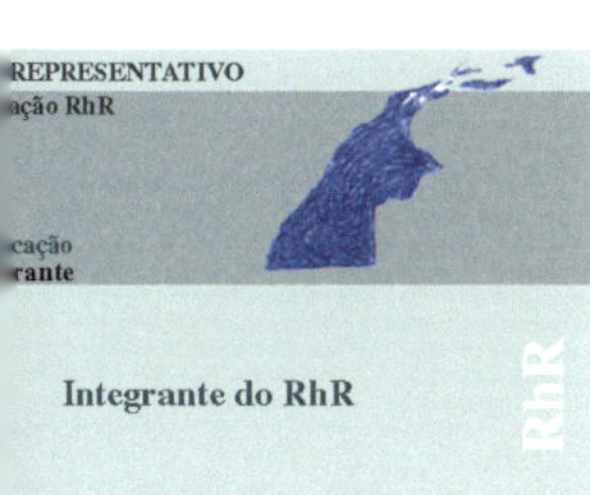
REPRESENTATIVO
ção RhR
cação
rante
Integrante do RhR
RhR
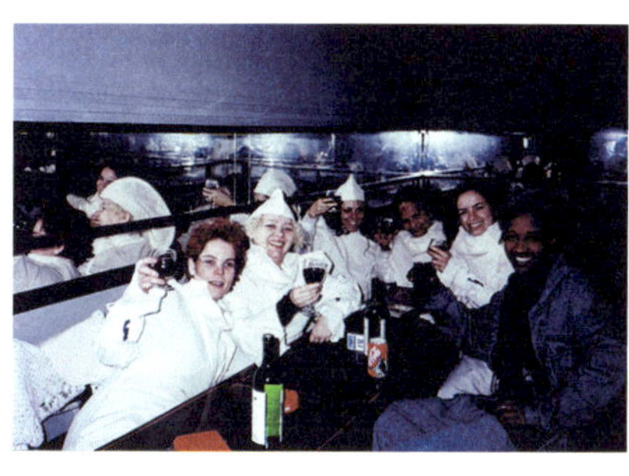
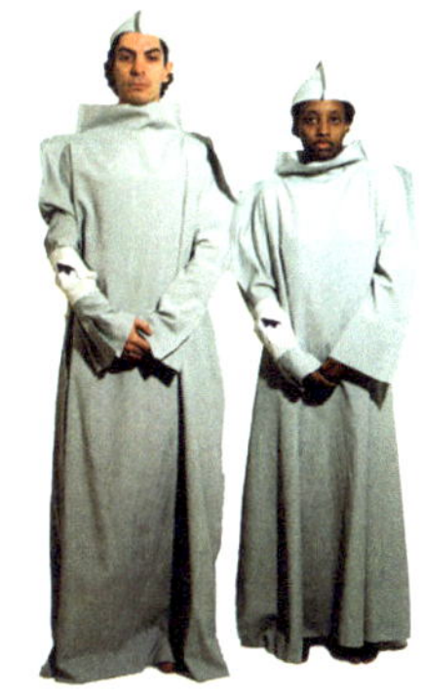
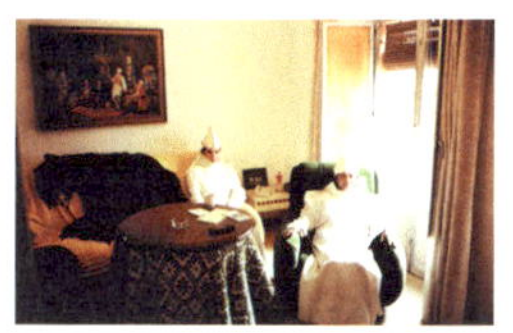
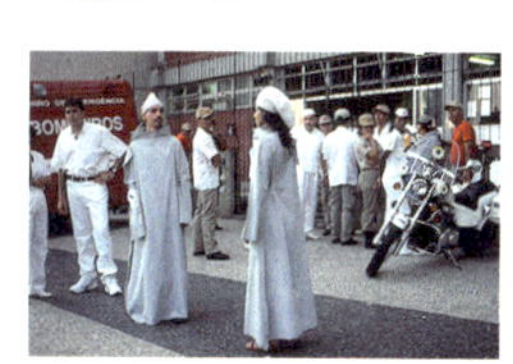
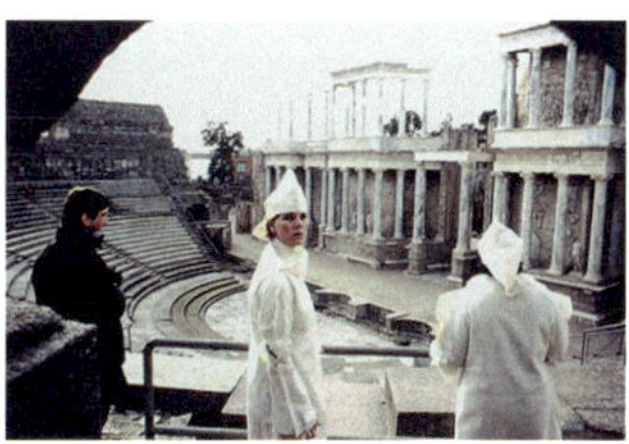
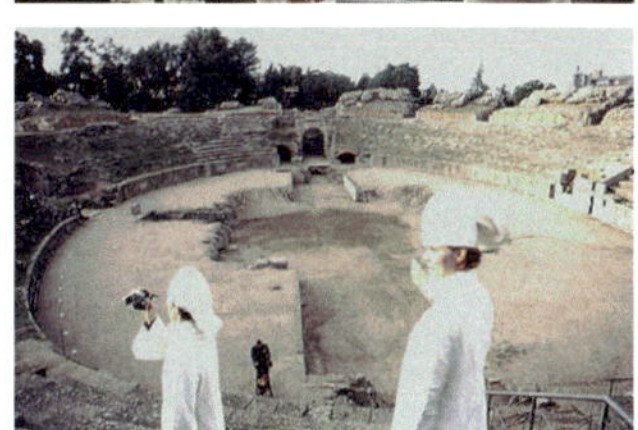
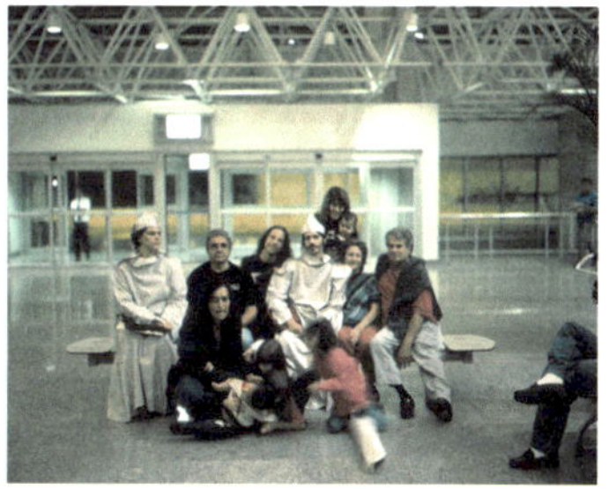
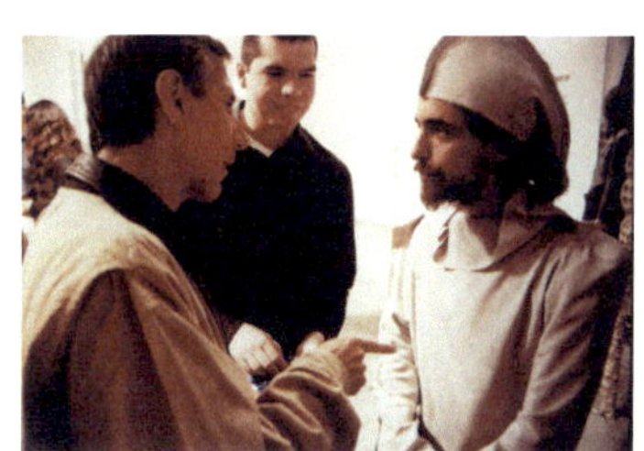
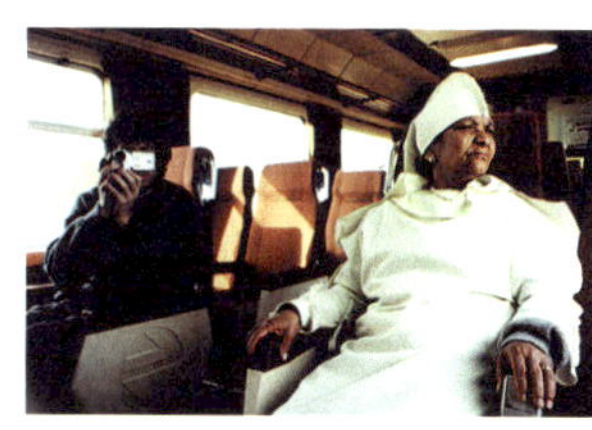

Man = Flesh / Woman = Flesh

Homem = carne / Mulher = carne

Cow / Vaca, 1994
Cow, water, food, and landscape. Dimensions variable
Courtesy of the artist, Photography: Laura Lima

A cow from the mountains was brought to an urban beach.
She remained in the landscape for one entire day.

Fighting / Marra, 1996 / 2001 / 2006 / 2010
People, fabric. Dimensions variable
Collection of Instituto Inhotim, Photography: Olle Kirchmeier, Views: Bonniers Konsthall

Two men, naked from the neck down, are attached together by means of
a two-sided hood cloaking their heads. They wrestle and fight against each other
until they are tired. No one wins this fight.

Candy / Bala, 1996 / 2000
People, metal, sweets, chair. Dimensions variable
Collection Modern Art Museum of São Paulo, Photography: Vivia 21

A man has his mouth held open by an apparatus. A candy has been put on
his tongue. He stays like this until the candy disappears.

Hips / Quadris, 1996 / 2000
People, fabric. Dimensions variable
Collection Modern Art Museum of São Paulo
Photography: Laura Lima, Views: 24th São Paulo Biennale

Two men are connected at the hips. They walk around everywhere
in a peculiar manner, with feet and hands on the floor.

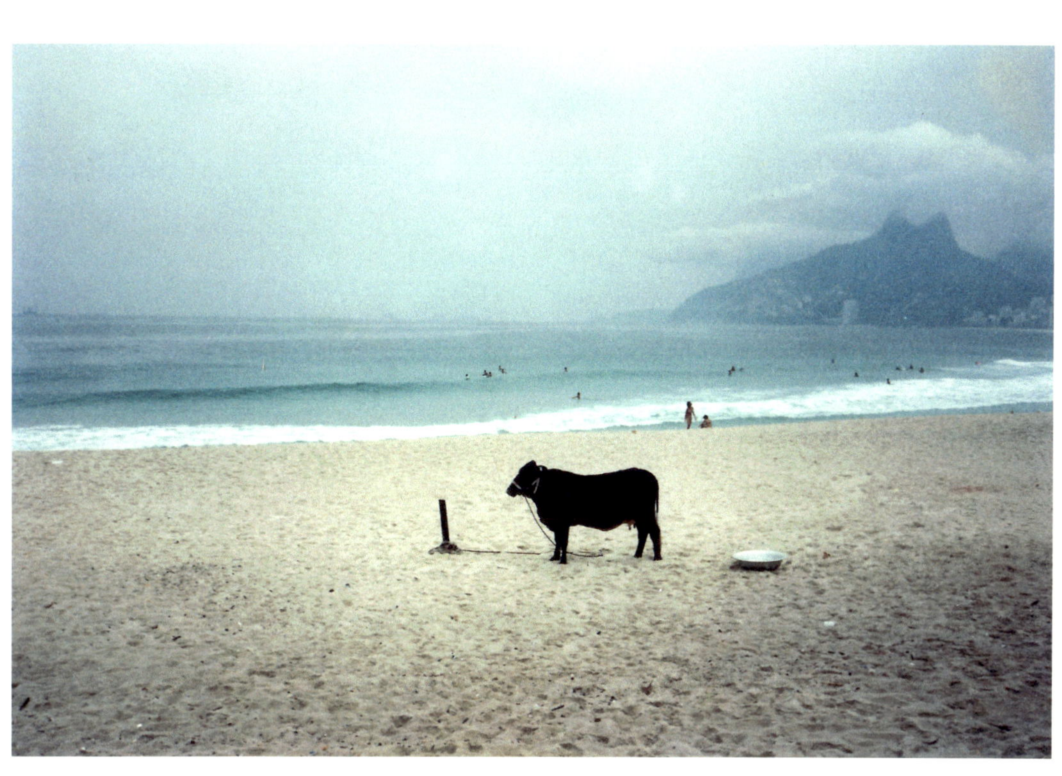

Hair + Hammock / Pelos + Rede, 1996 / 2009 / 2010
People, hair, special glue, fabric, metal, ropes
Dimensions variable (hammock 2200 cm long)
Courtesy of the artist, Photography: Sérgio Araújo
Views: Casa França-Brasil, Rio de Janeiro

A couple reclines together on a twenty-five-meter-long hammock that crosses the entire
space of the exhibition. It seems their only task is to lie back in a relaxed sort of
"dolce far niente." The eyebrows of the man and the pubic hair of the woman have been
lengthened by hair extensions so long that they touch the floor.

Doped / Dopada, 1997 / 2006
People, fabric, threads, special nails, sedatives. Dimensions variable
Collection of Instituto Inhotim, Photography: Eduardo Eckenfels
Views: Instituto Inhotim

A woman, dressed in a white gown and connected to the wall by a long tube of crochet,
is sleeping under the effect of sleeping pills. She remains there until she wakes up.

Flat / Baixo, 1997 / 2010
People, fabric, lamp, wood. Dimensions variable
Courtesy of the artist, Photography: Sérgio Araújo
Views: Casa França-Brasil, Rio de Janeiro

A ceiling was constructed forty centimeters from the floor. A man or a woman with
a peculiar body shape (known as "with a disability") lies on the floor in this compressed
space. The viewer has to bend their body to see the image.

Architecture Puller / Puxador Arquitetura, 1998
People, architecture, straps. Dimensions variable
Courtesy of the artist

The Landscape Puller / O Puxador Paisagem, 1999 / 2013
Dimensions variable
Courtesy of the artist, Photography: Oliver Santana. Views: MUAC, Mexico City

The Columns Puller / O Puxador Colunas, 2002 / 2011
People, straps, columns, architecture. Dimensions variable
Collection Pampulha Museum, Photography: Eduardo Eckenfels
Views: Museu da Pampulha, Belo Horizonte

A naked man is pulling the columns of a building, or the landscape that is outside
the place he is in, or the architecture he is attached to. In all three versions of this piece,
the man uses an apparatus constructed and connected to the object he is pulling.

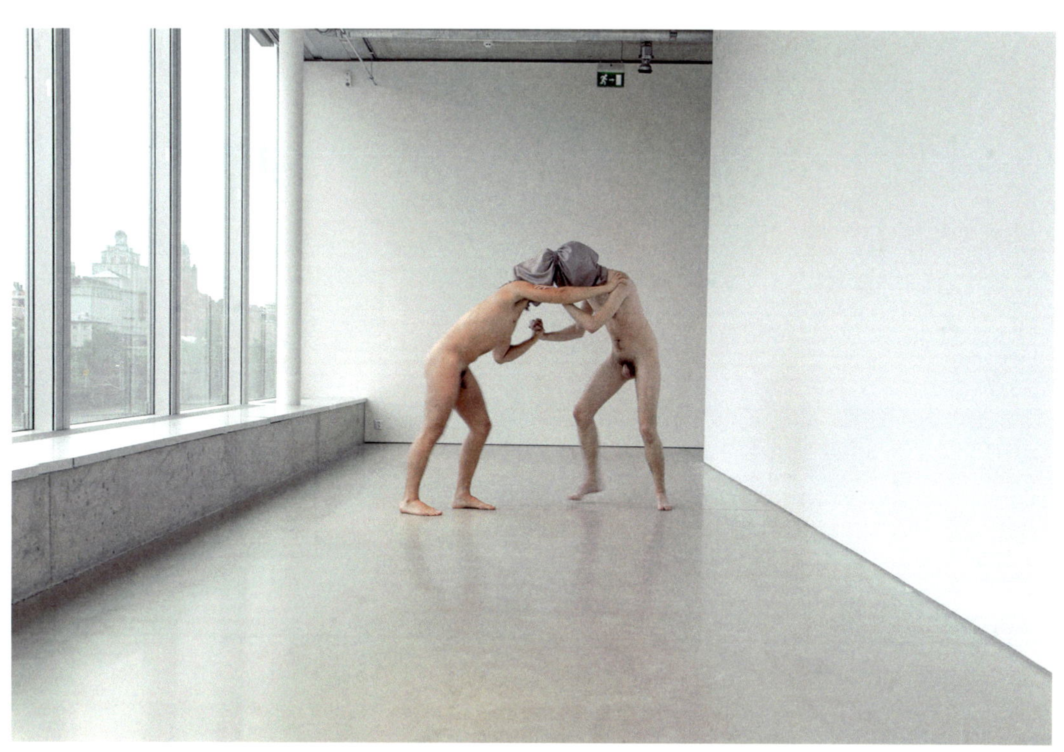

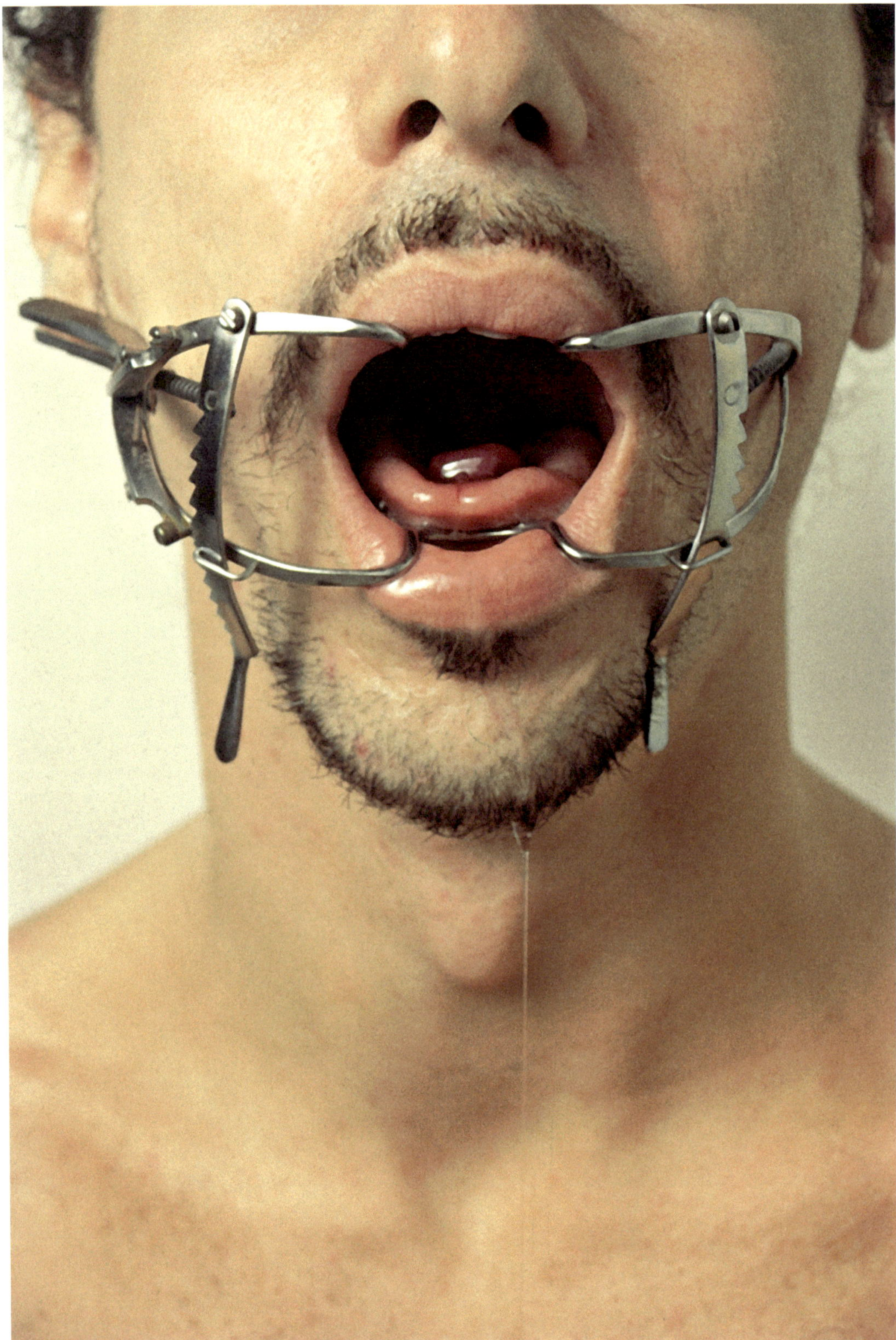

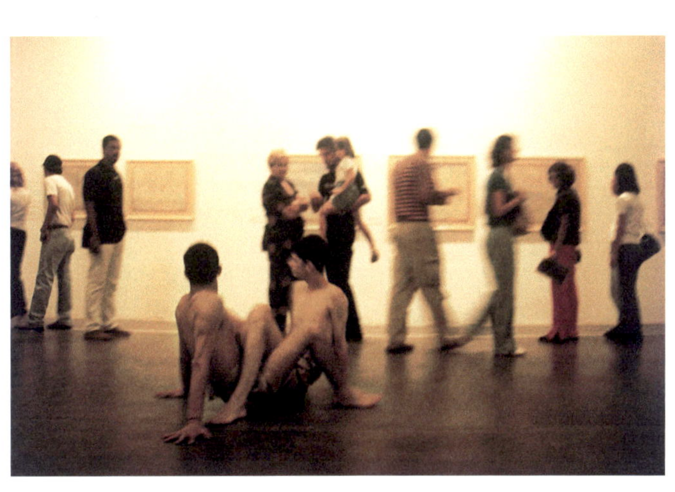

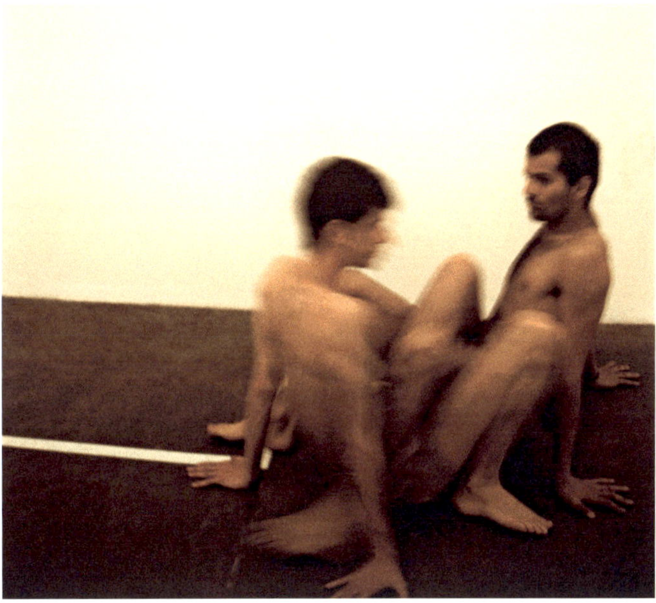

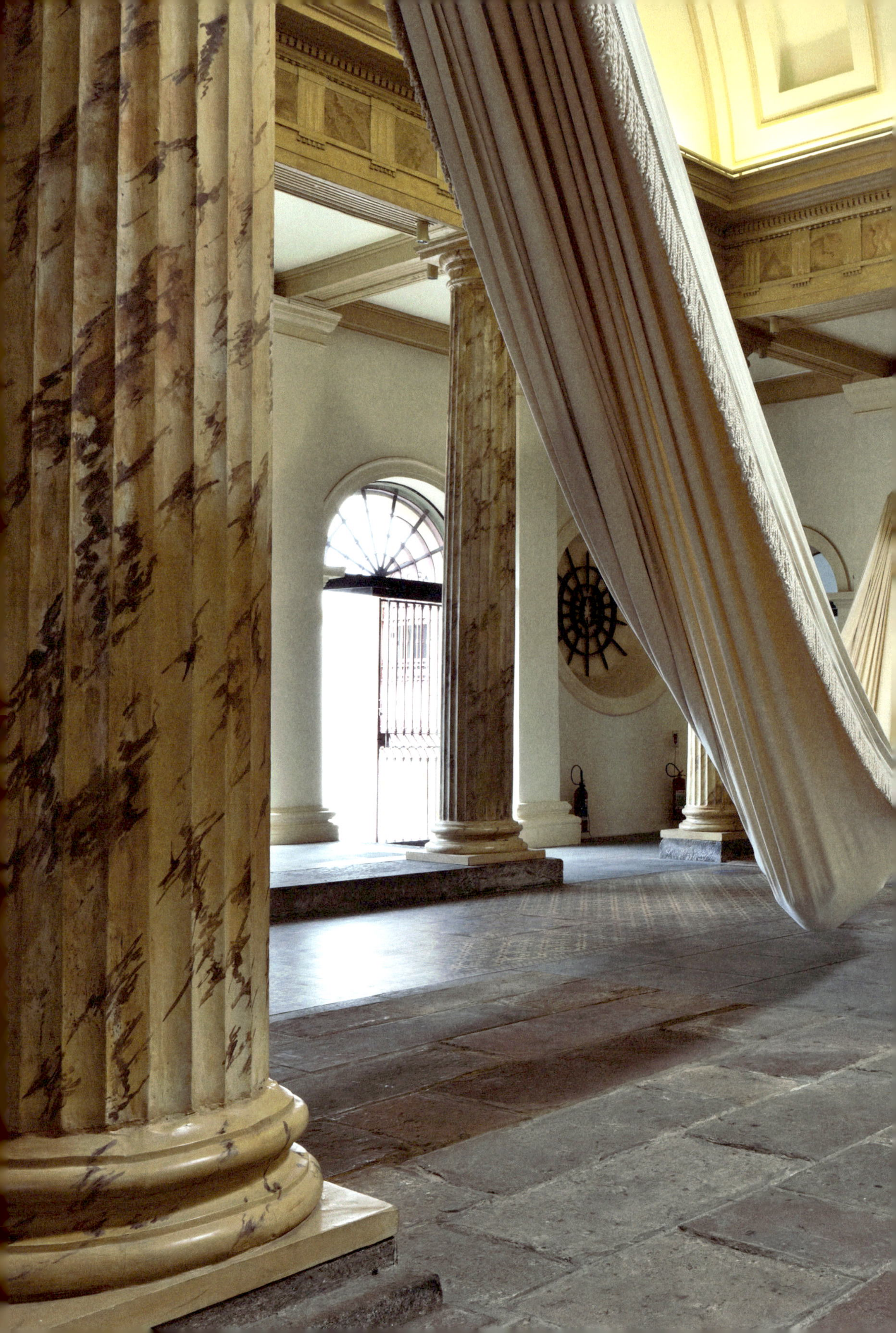

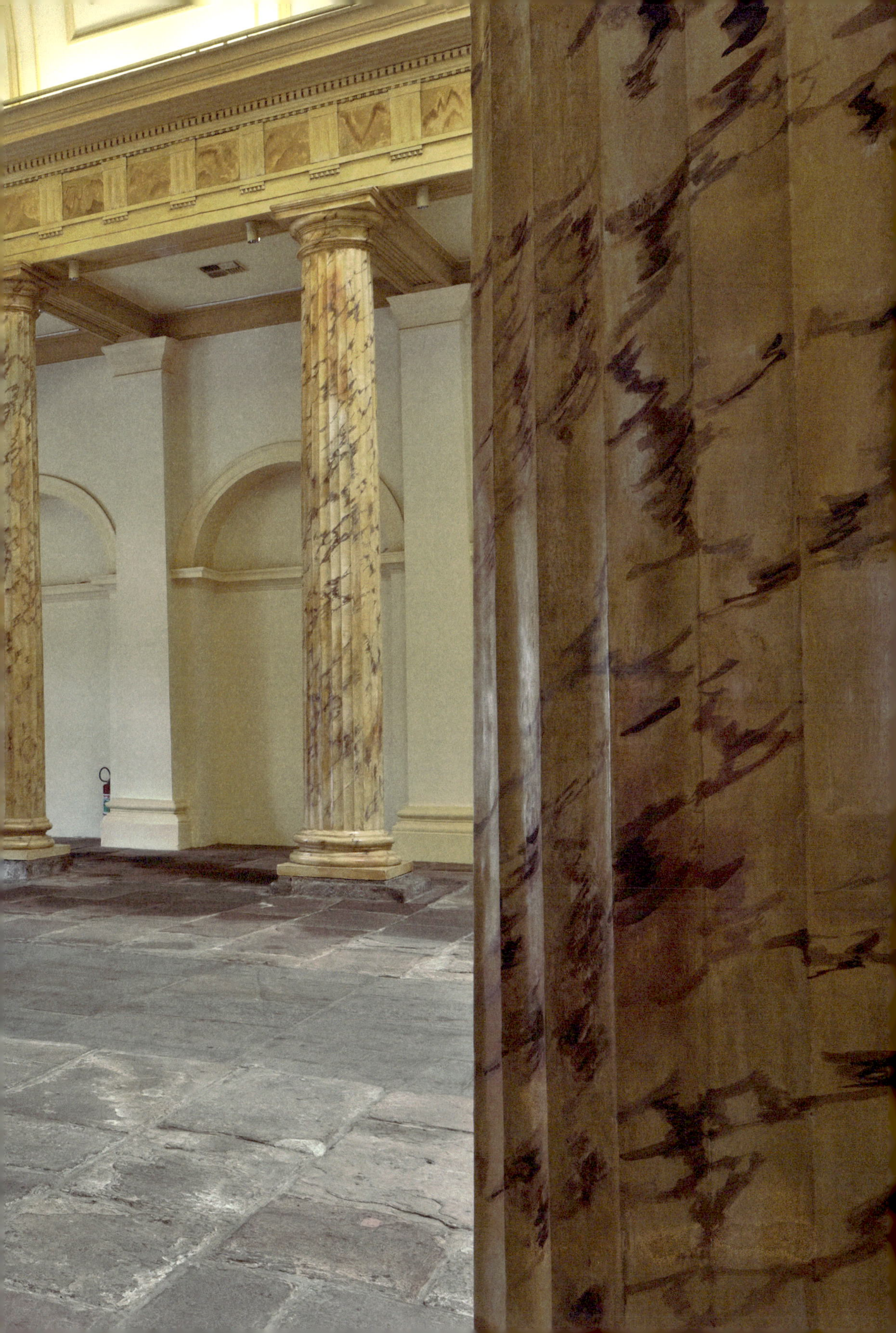

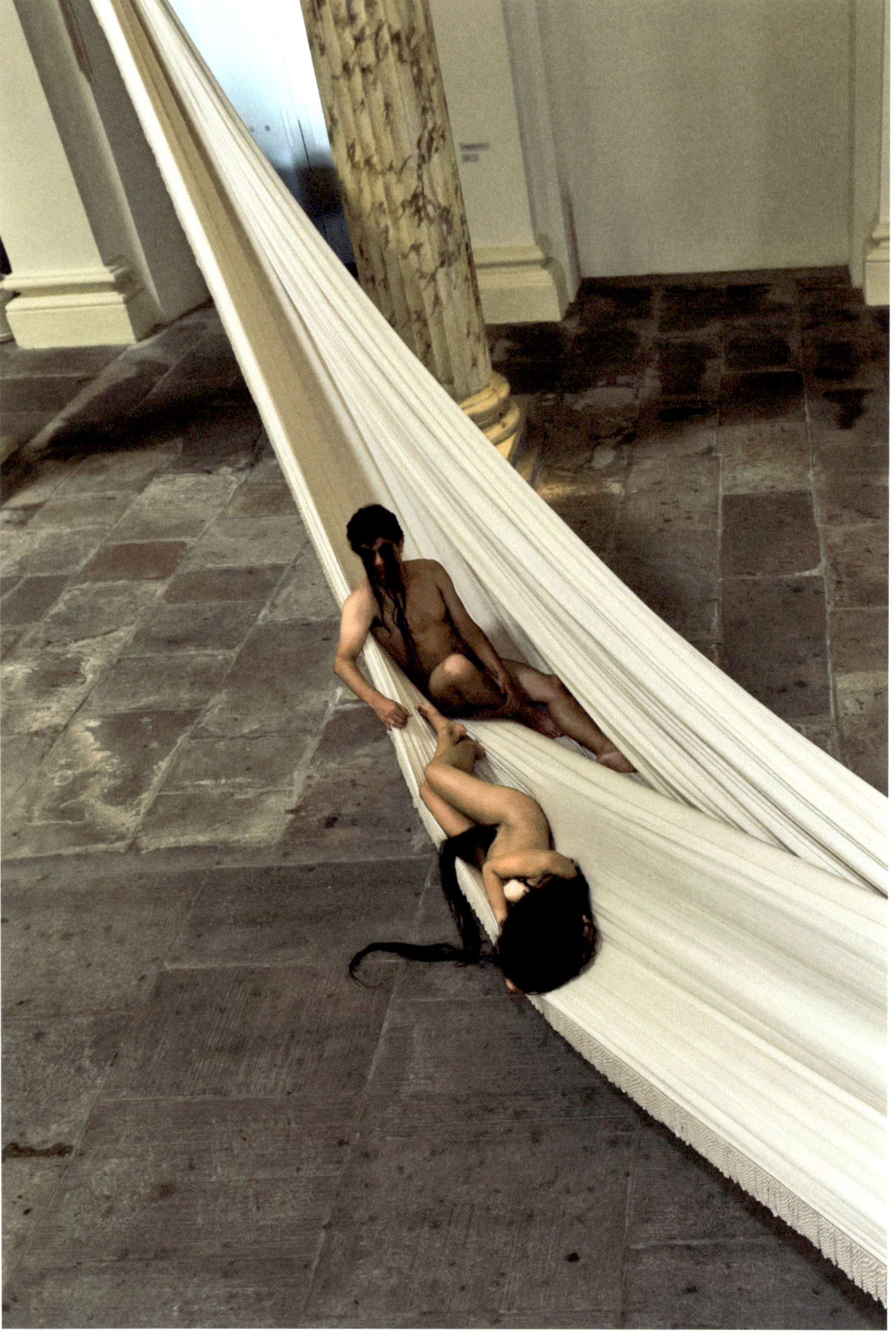

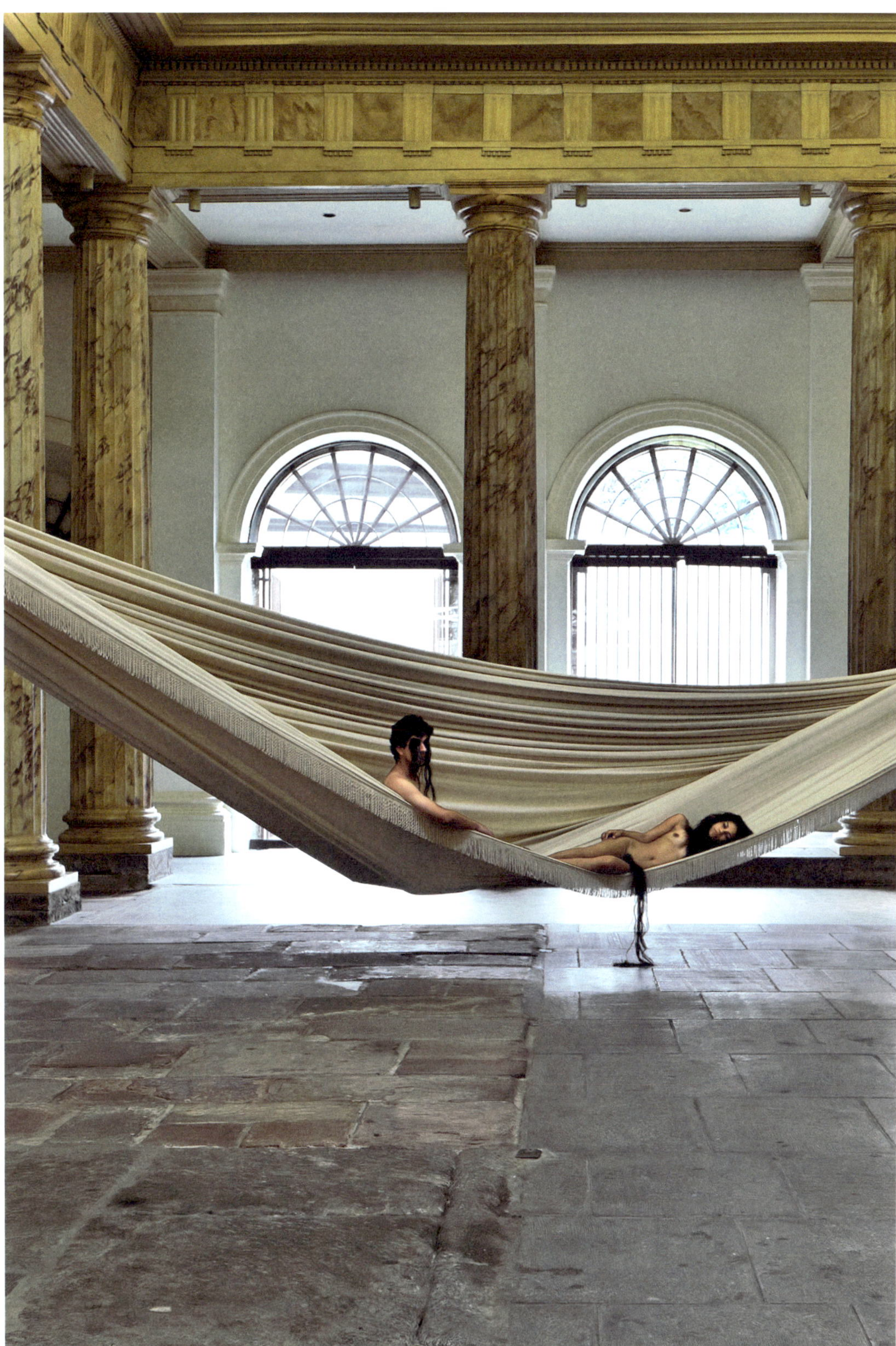

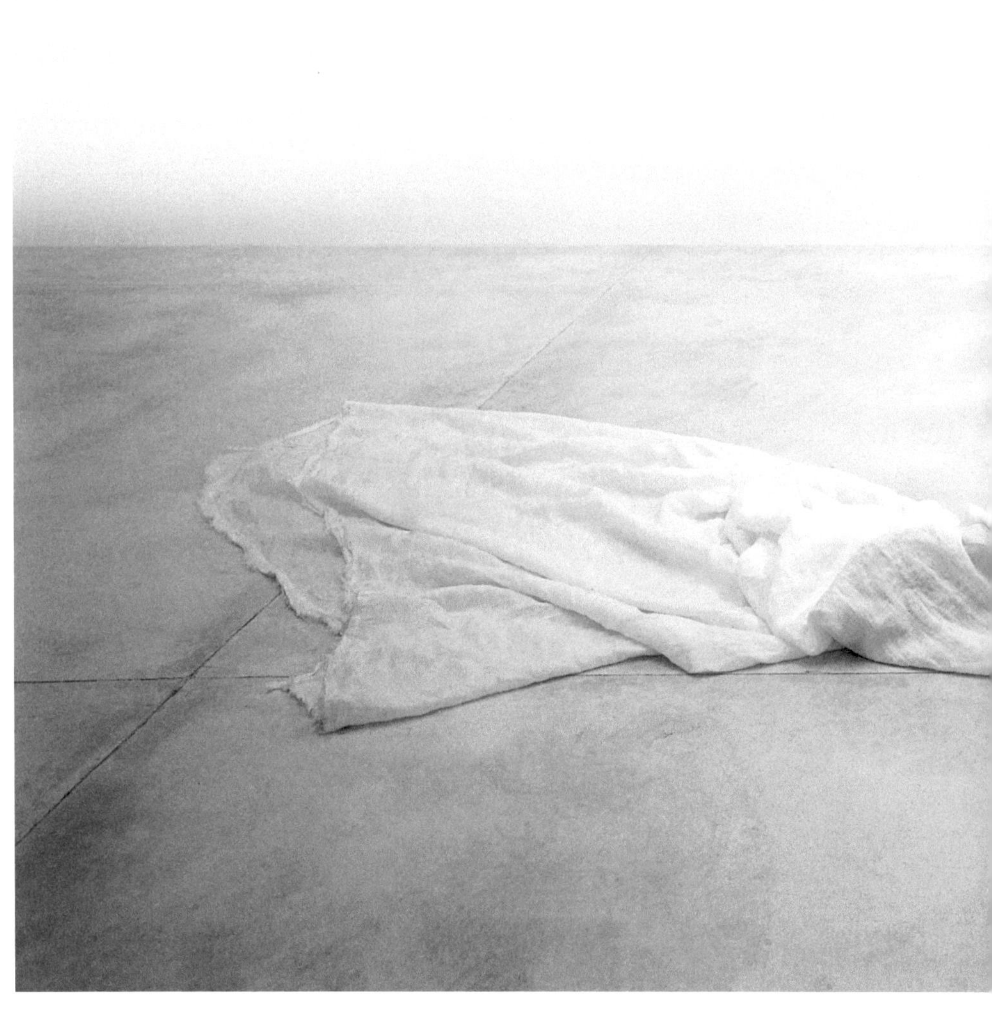

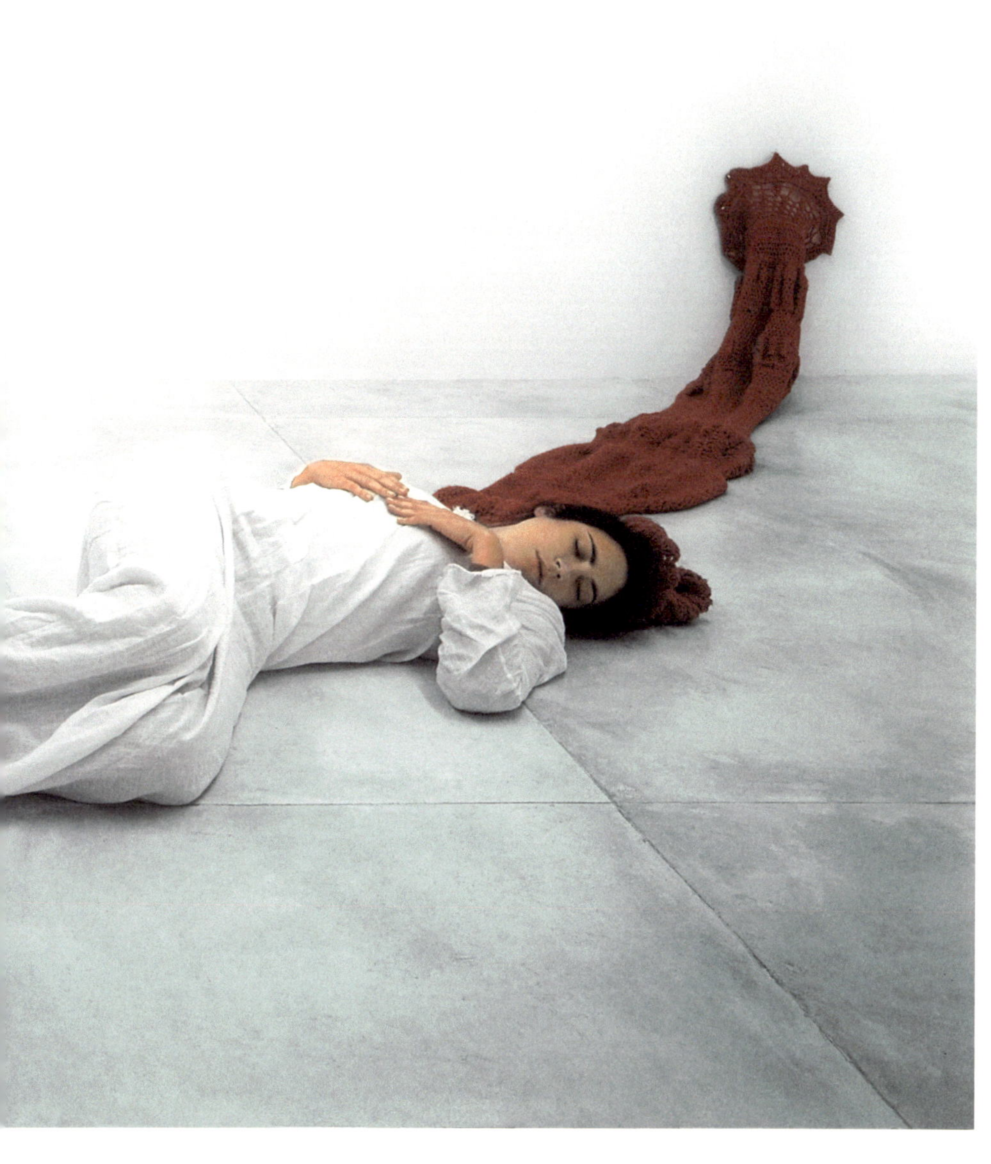

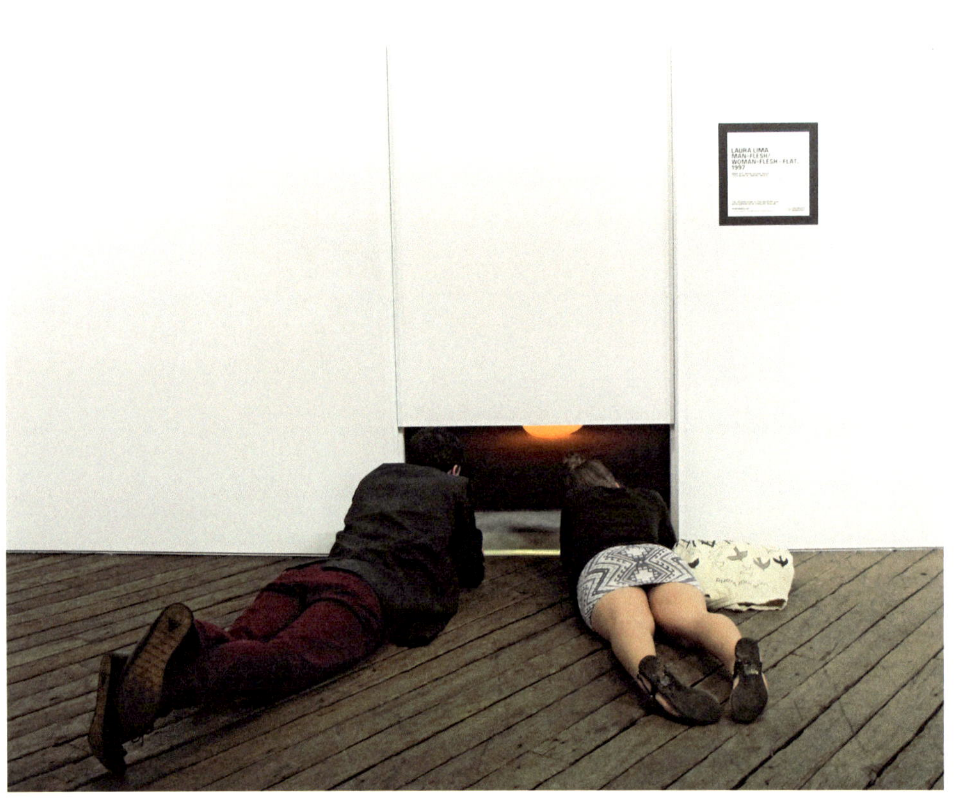

LAURA LIMA
MAN-FLESH/
WOMAN-FLESH - FLAT.
1997

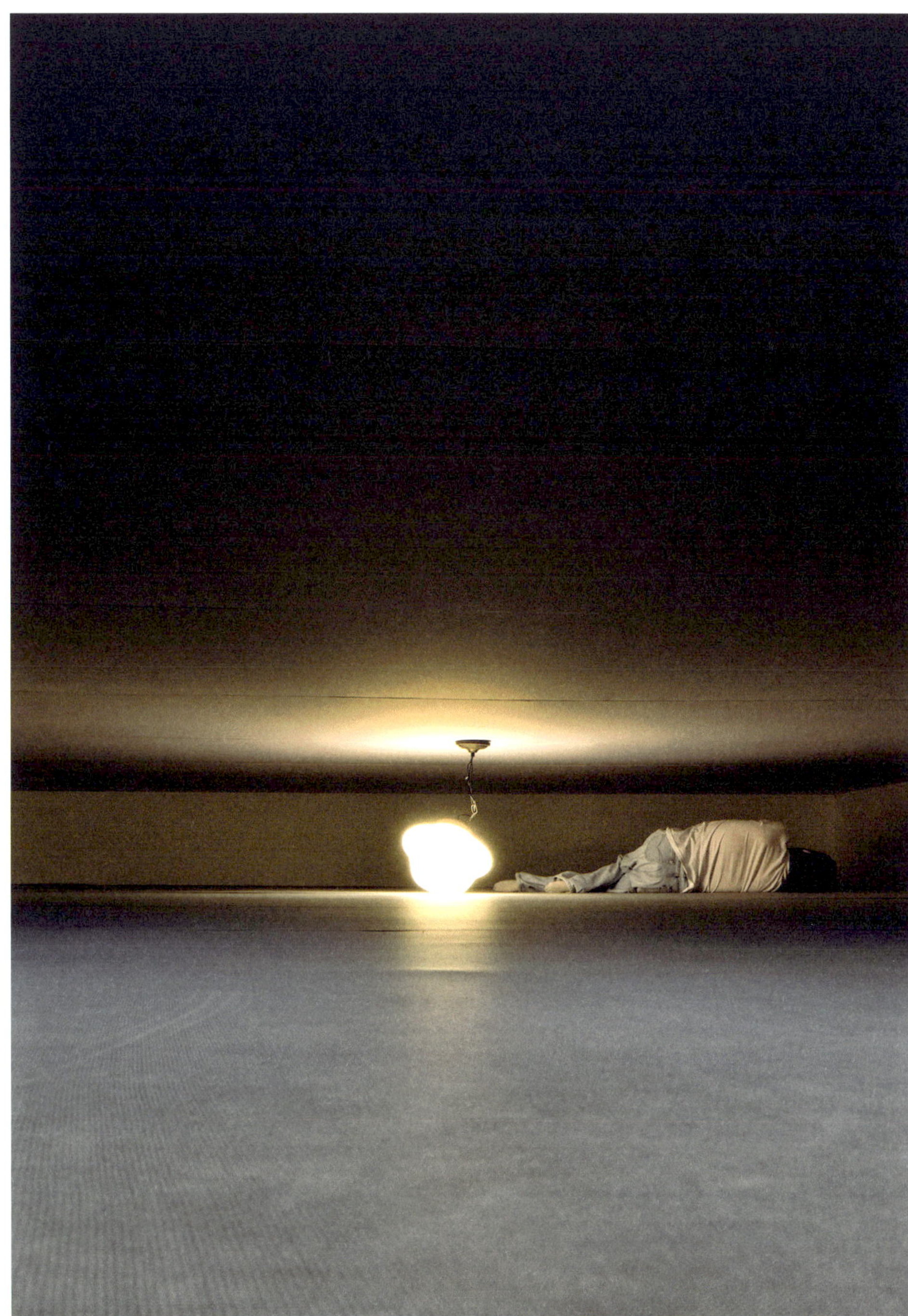

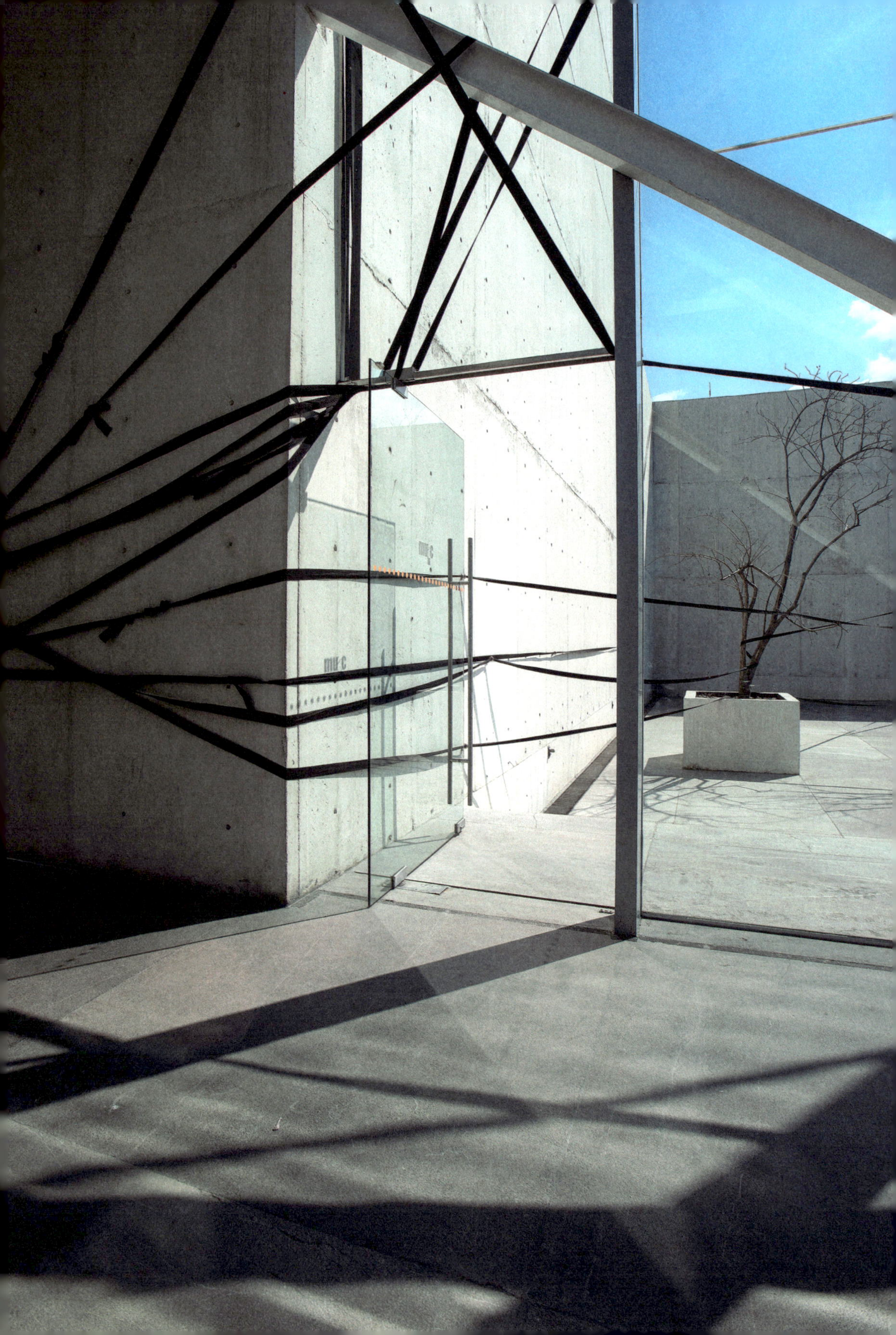

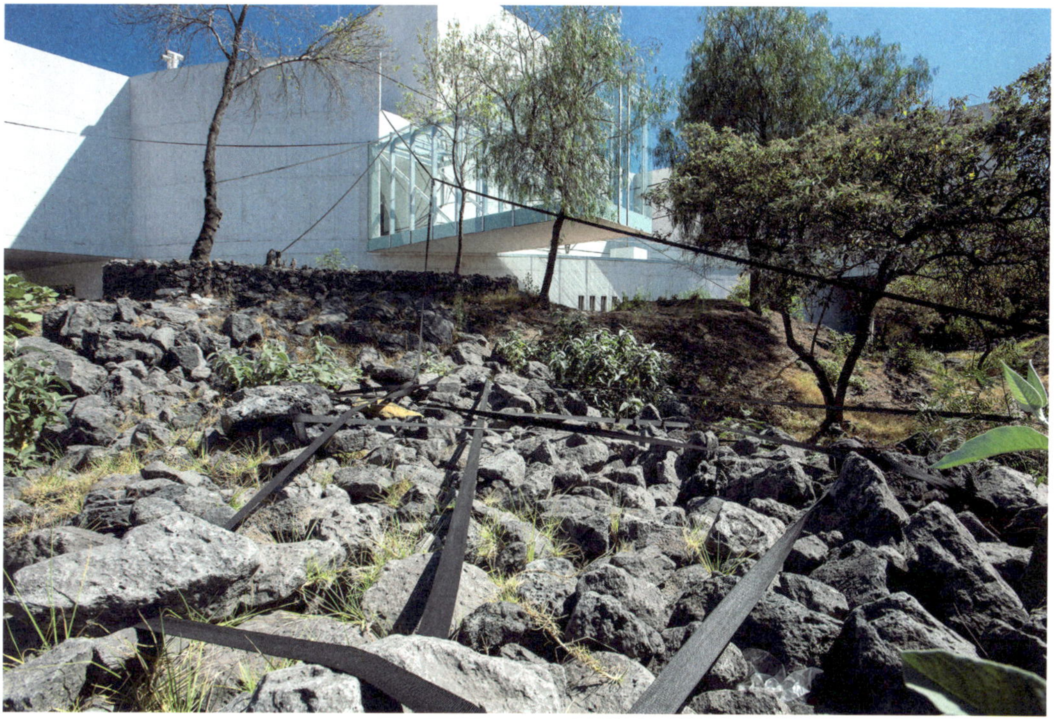

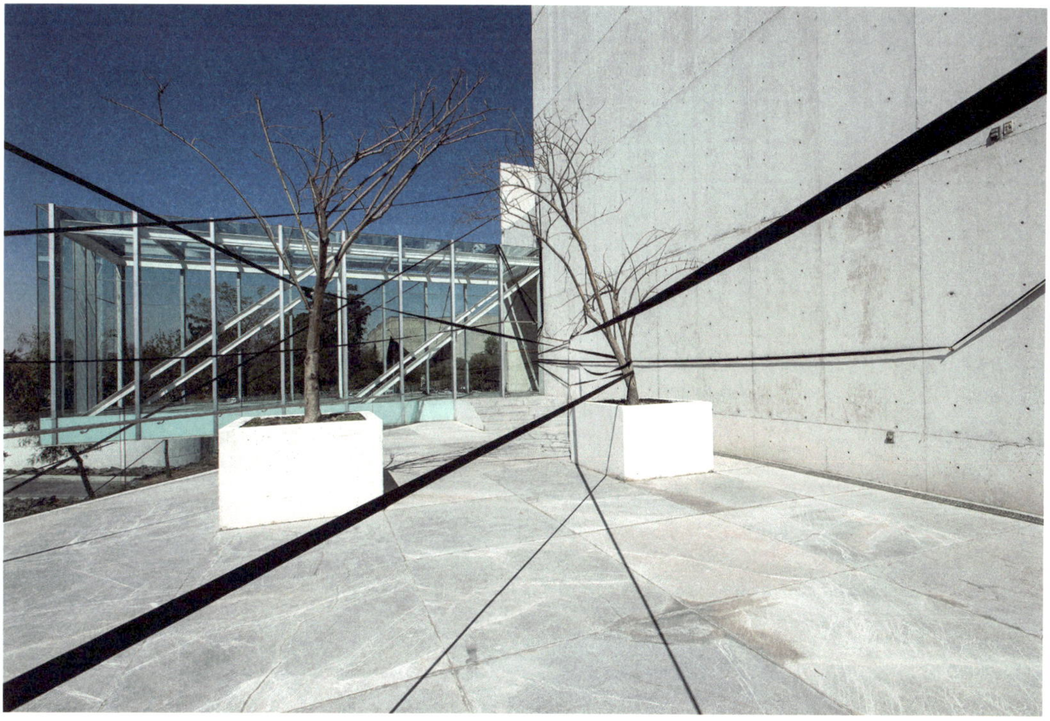

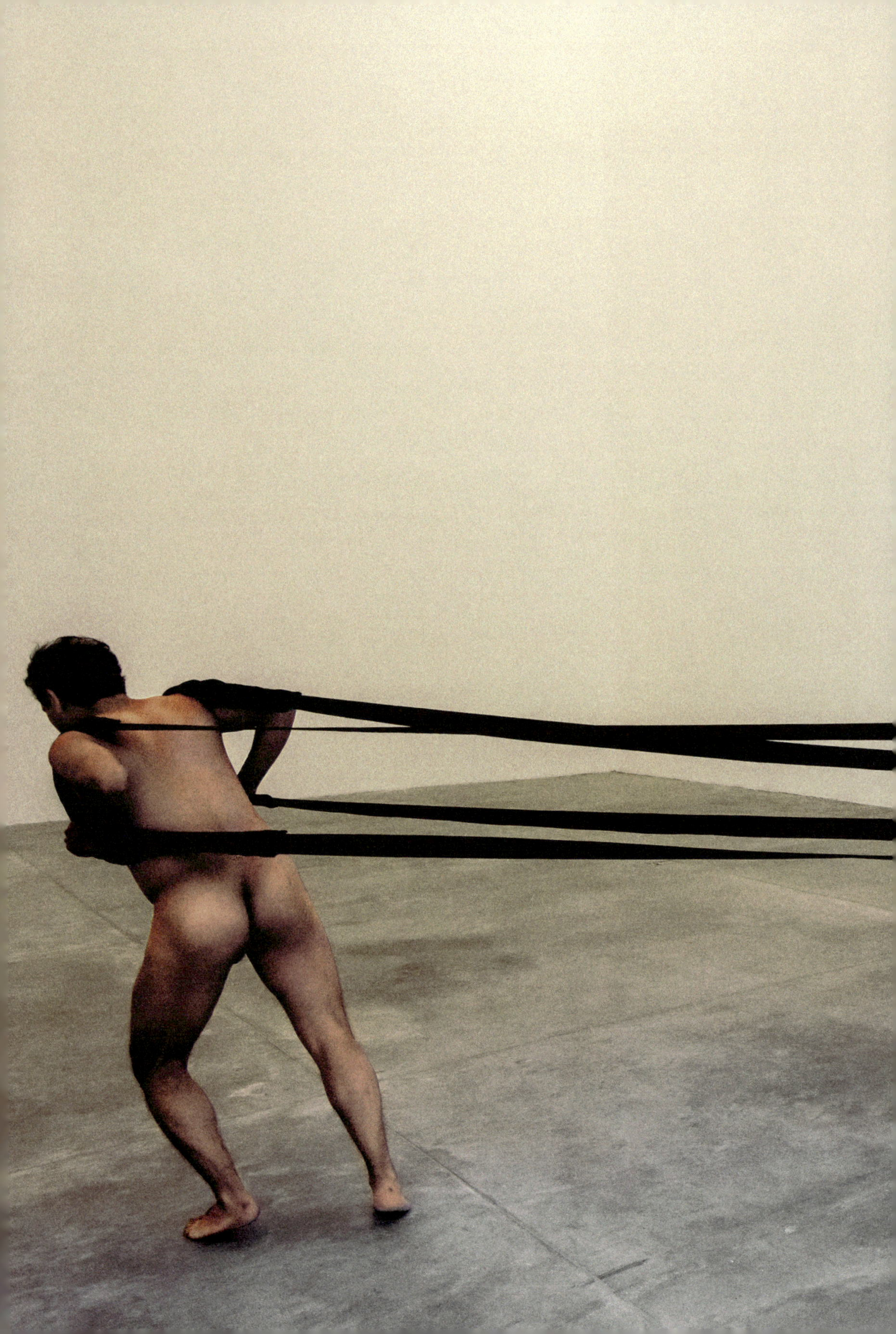

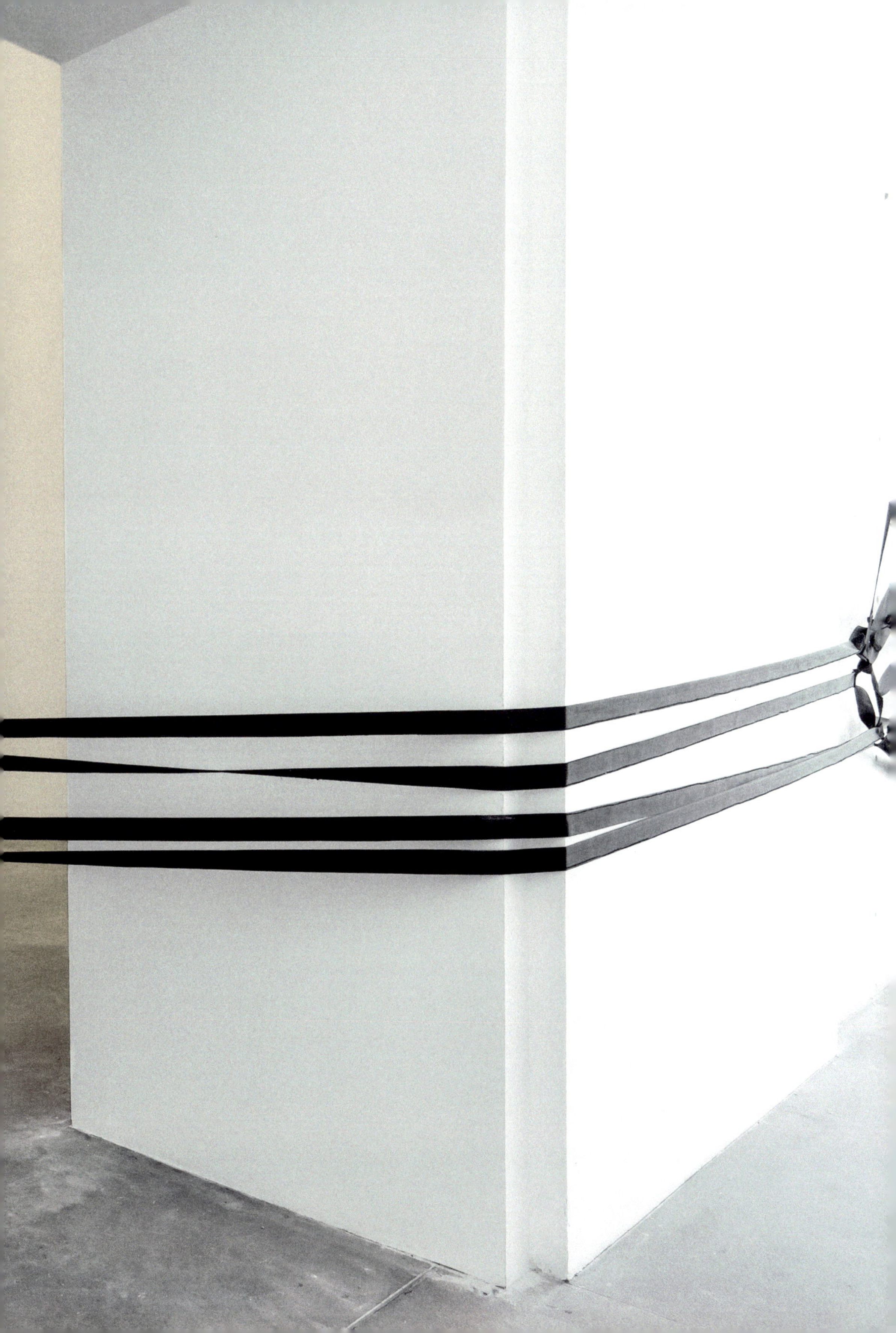

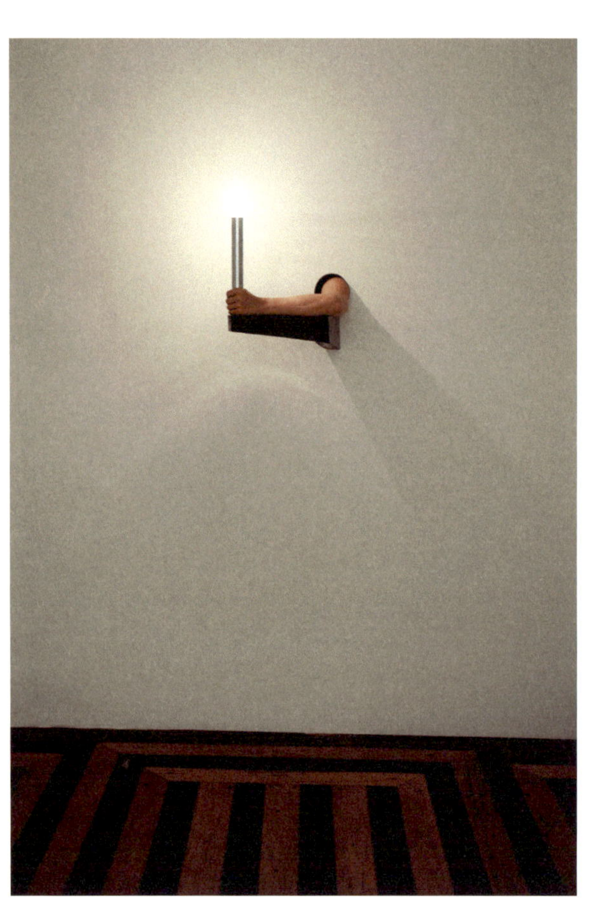

Cloud

Nuvem

Human hands and ears protrude from the gallery walls holding lamps, photographs, and
drawings and rolling cigars to offer to the public. In this intoxicating atmosphere,
the public is invited on a kind of nonsense tour. The artist organized two groups for the
exhibition so that participants would trade places each day over the entire month,
thereby maintaining a constant presence of body parts and their poetic substance in the
gallery space. To enhance the strange atmosphere, the architecture of the gallery
was modified and fake walls were constructed, so the public could not see the participants
holding the pieces. In addition, the artist created fake imagery on photographs of art
nouveau ambiences, confounding the viewer as to what was real and what was not.
A fumoir inside of the gallery gave visitors the opportunity to smoke with modified cigars
and pipes; the smell of mint, smoke, and chocolate was everywhere.

Cloud / Nuvem, 2009
Arms and ears of people, glass, black and white photographs, wood, light, mint,
chocolate, paper, metals, cigars and cigarettes, fire, smoke, pipes, sand
Dimensions variable

Courtesy of the artist, Photography: Laura Lima, Ana Torres
Views: Laura Alvim Gallery, Rio de Janeiro

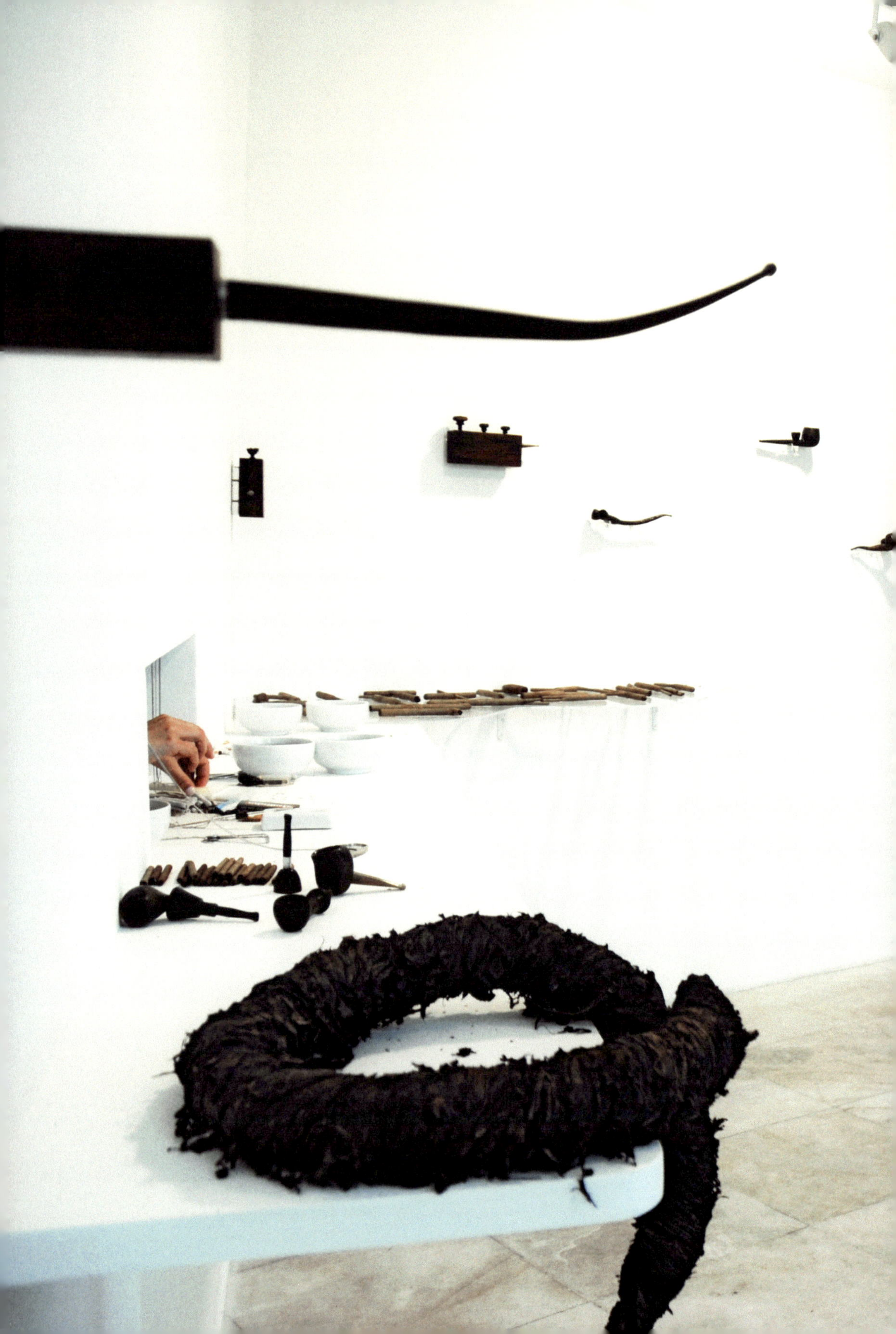

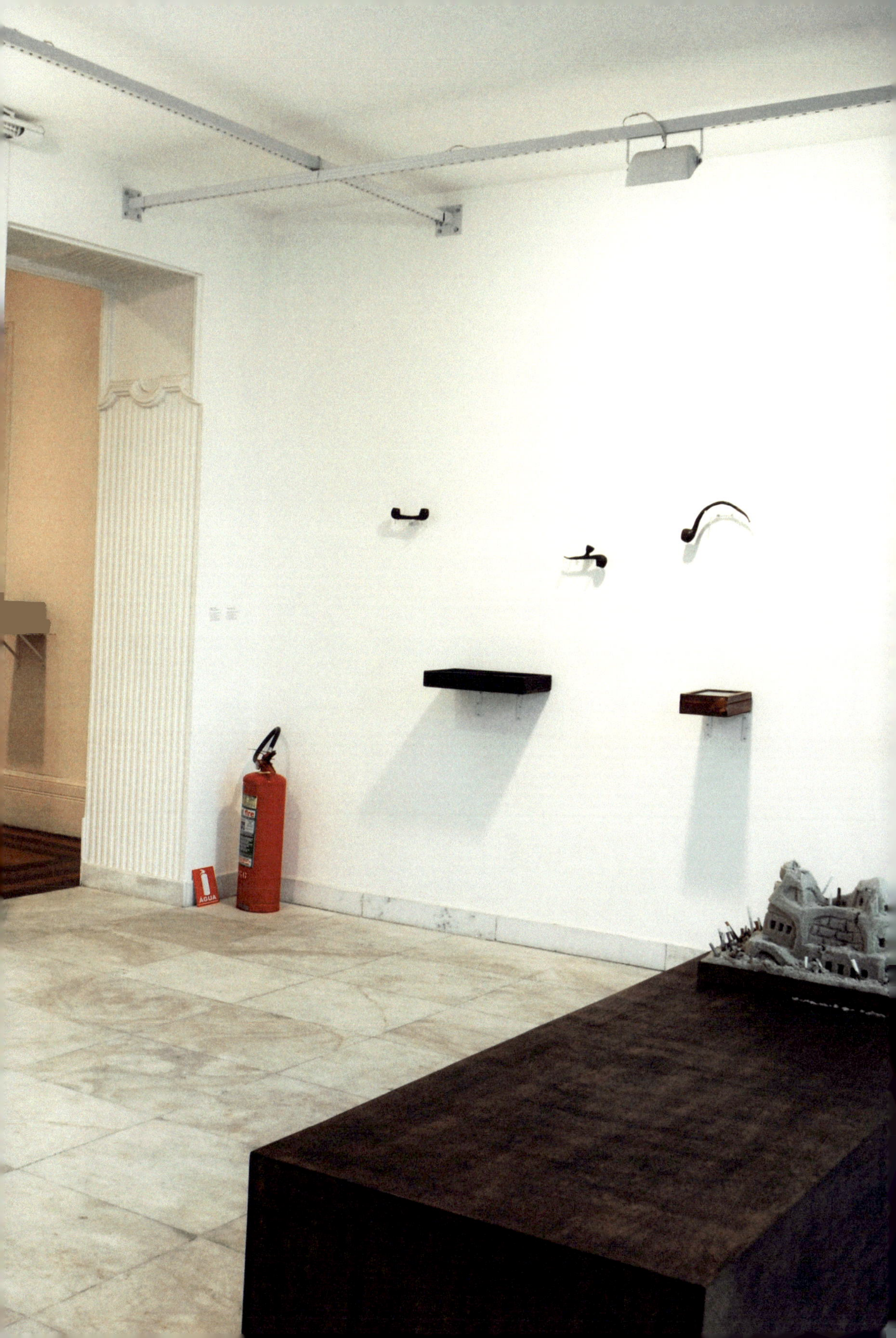

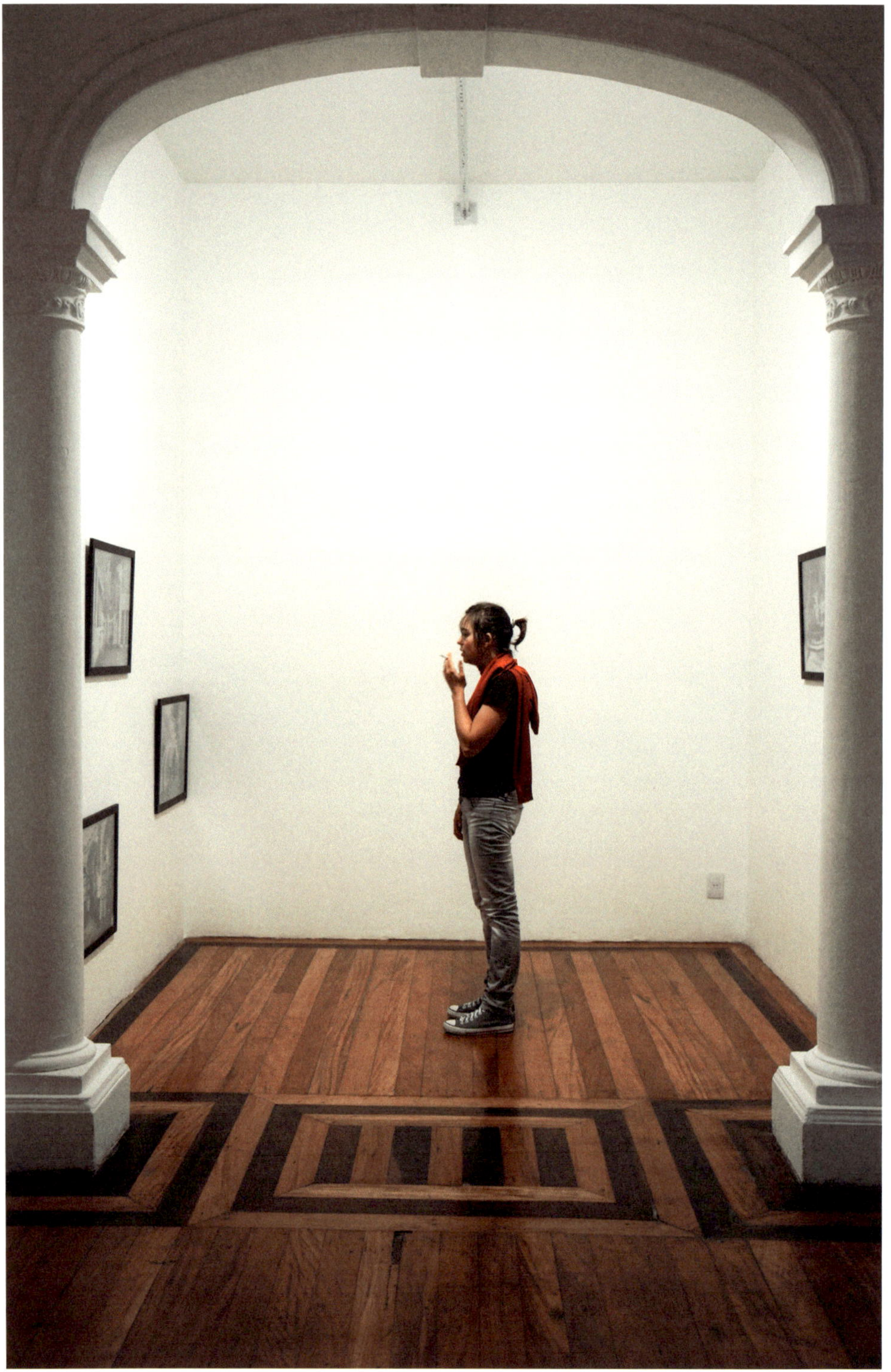

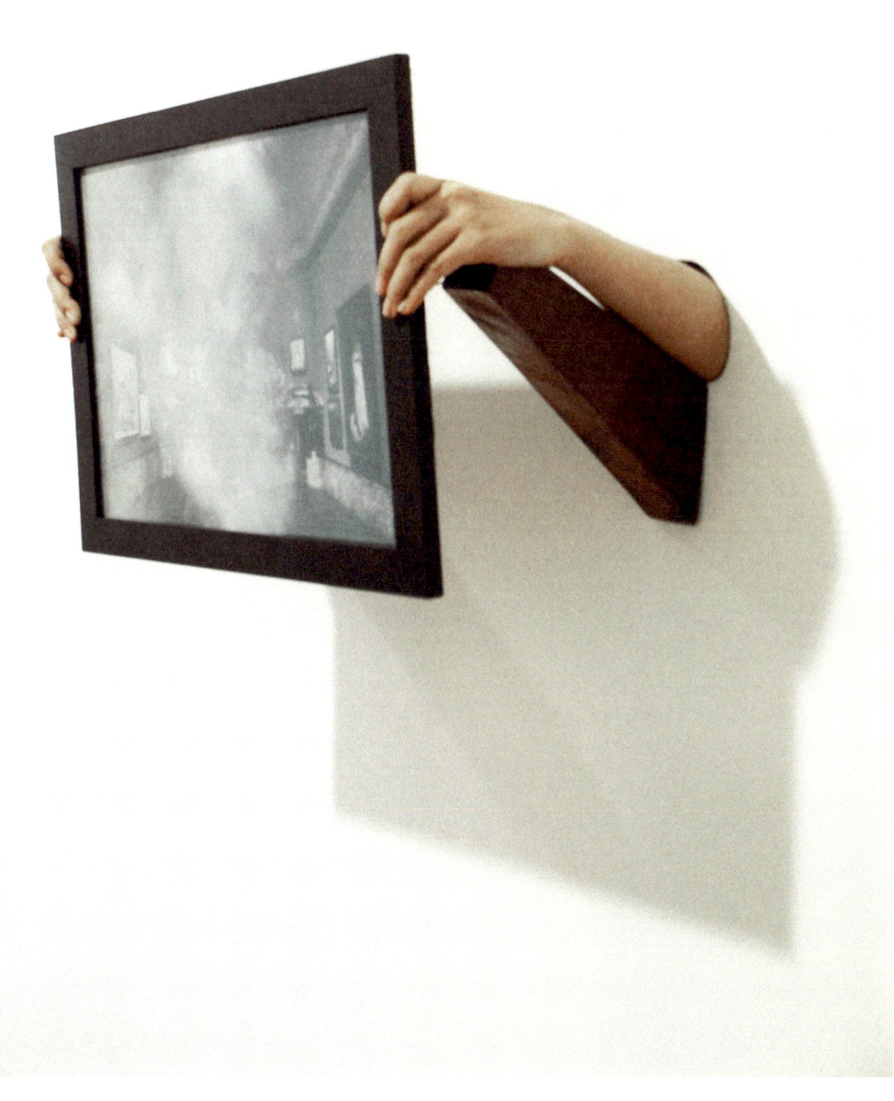

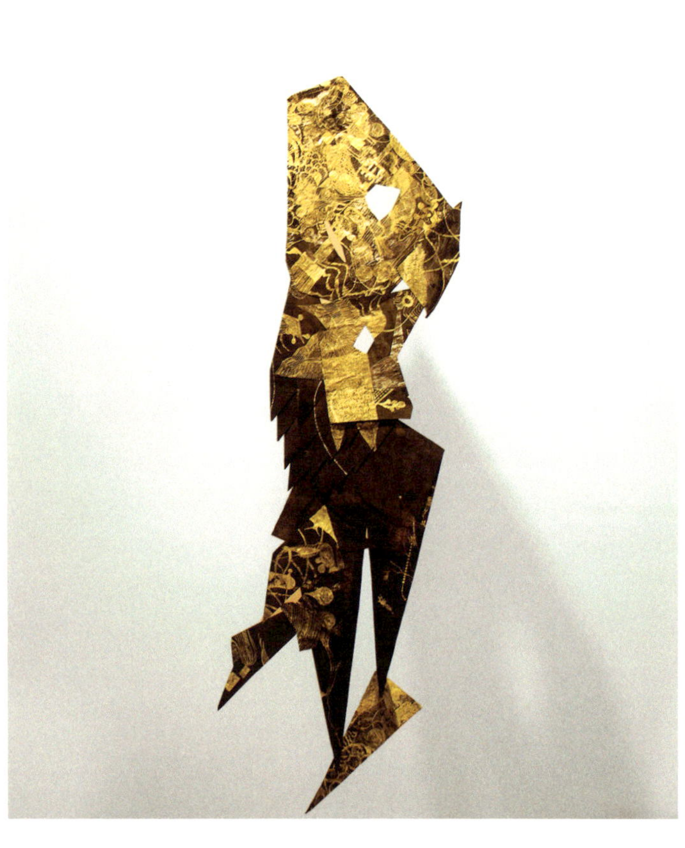

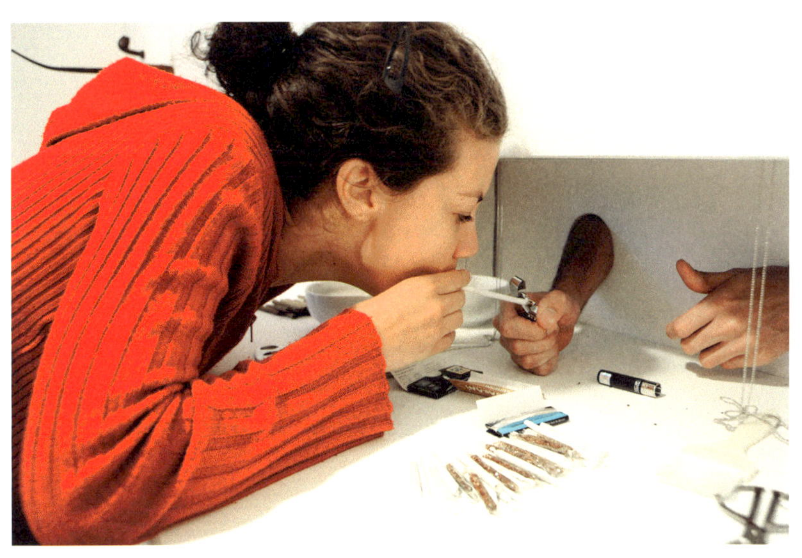

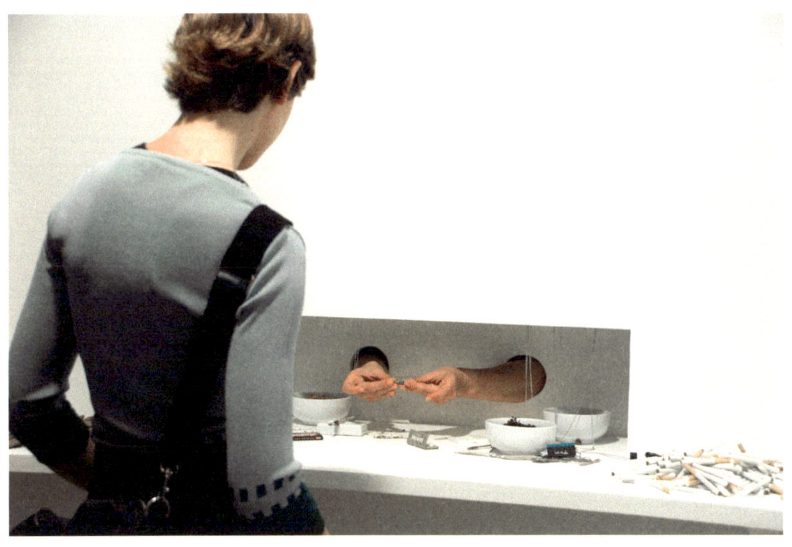

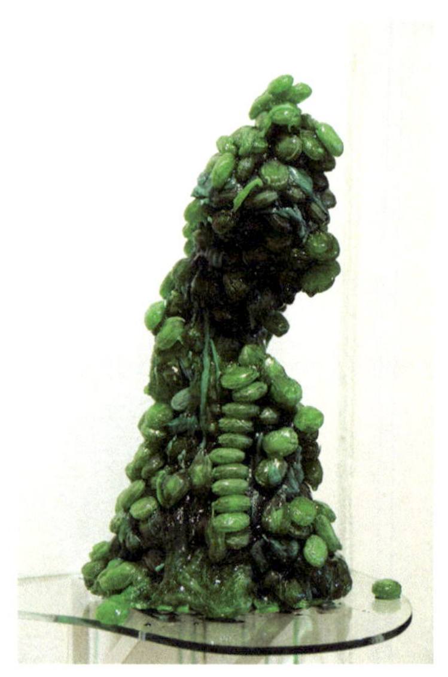

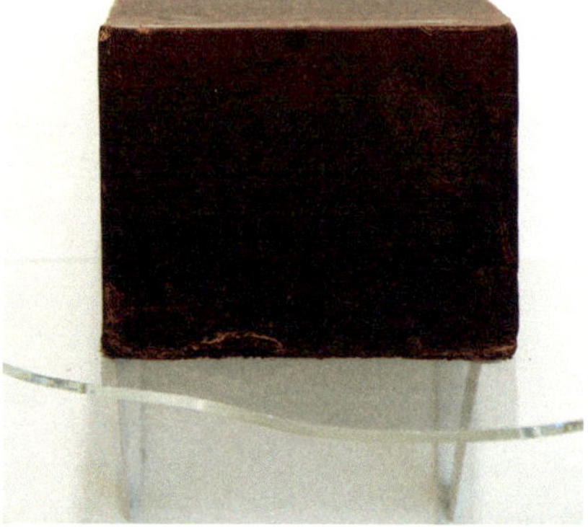

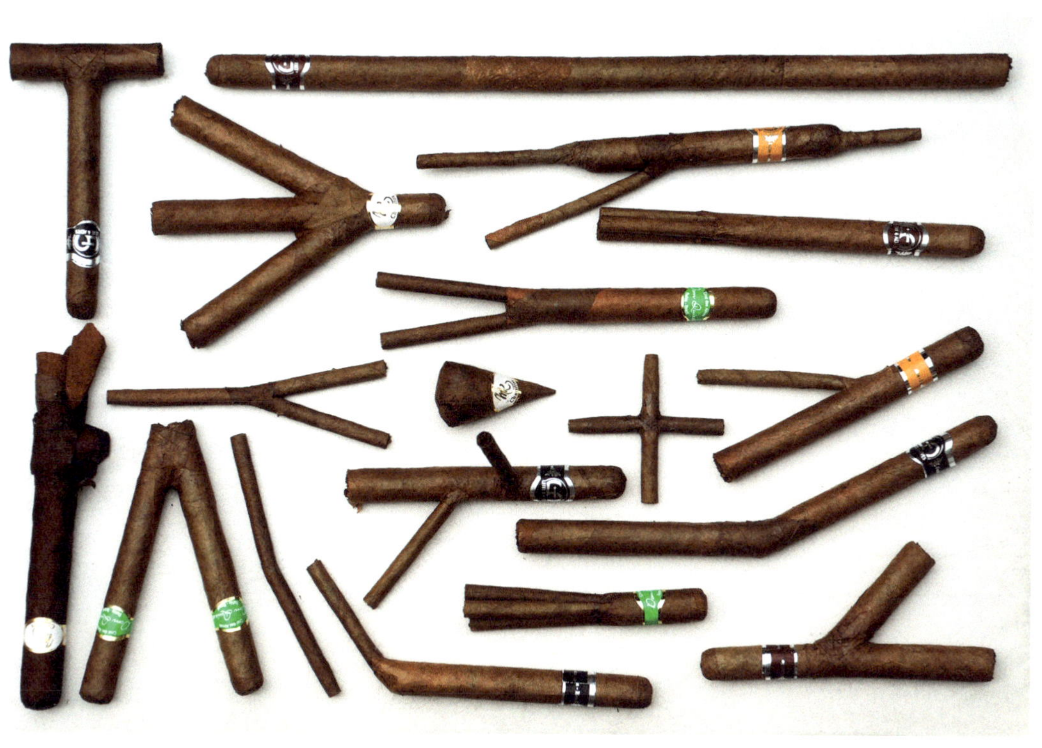

Choice

Escolha

Three opera curtains of different colors invite the visitor to a completely darkened room,
where he or she loses all sense of space. Inside the room, there is a secret:
something may happen. For the installation of this piece, only the staff of the museum
hosting the exhibition knows what is inside the room. The artist keeps the
secret forever. The institution shall not divulge the atmosphere and the secret of the piece.

Choice/Escolha, 2010
Fabric, dark space, cold temperature, secret element
Dimensions variable

Courtesy of the artist, Photography: Sérgio Araújo

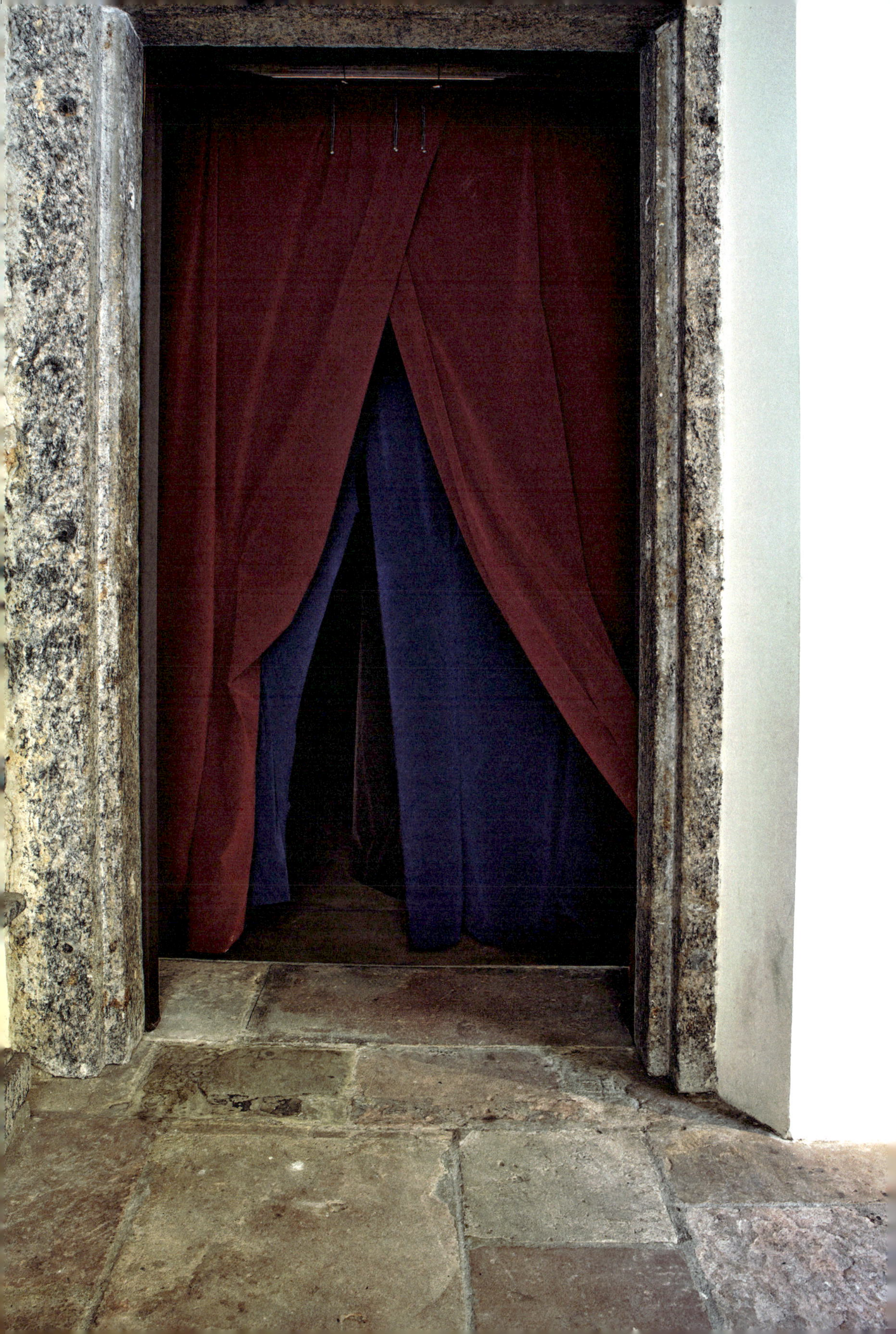

Wheelchairs

Classical modernist chair designs, such as those by Charles Rennie Mackintosh, Marcel Breuer, Ludwig Mies van der Rohe, Eero Saarinen, or Ray and Charles Eames, are transformed into wheelchairs through the addition of wheels.

Wheelchairs, 2011 / 2012
Wood, metal, rubber, straw, leather
Dimensions variable

Courtesy of the artist, Photography: Rafael Adorjan

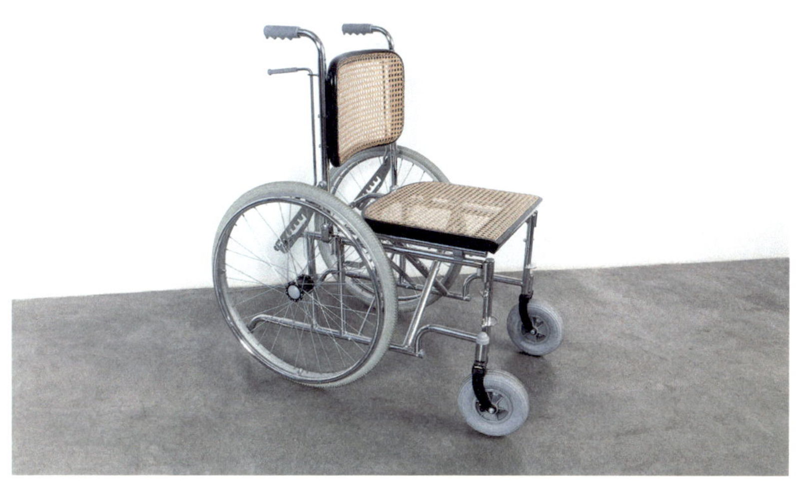

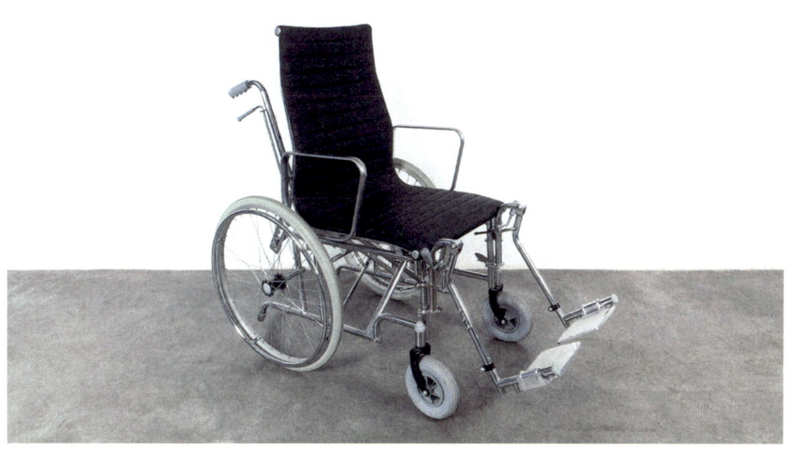

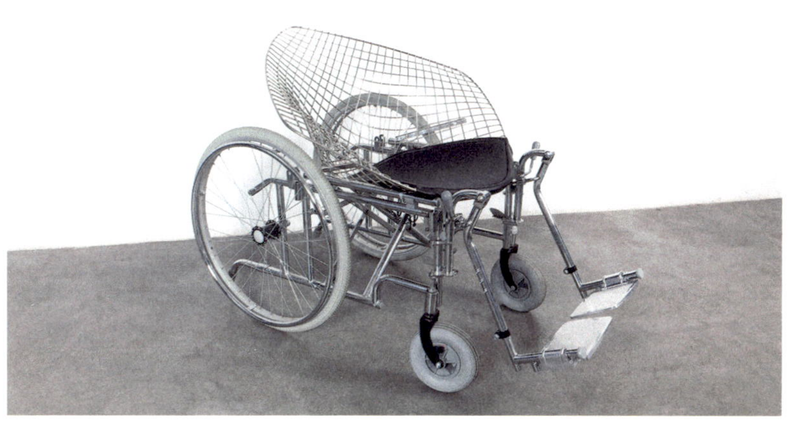

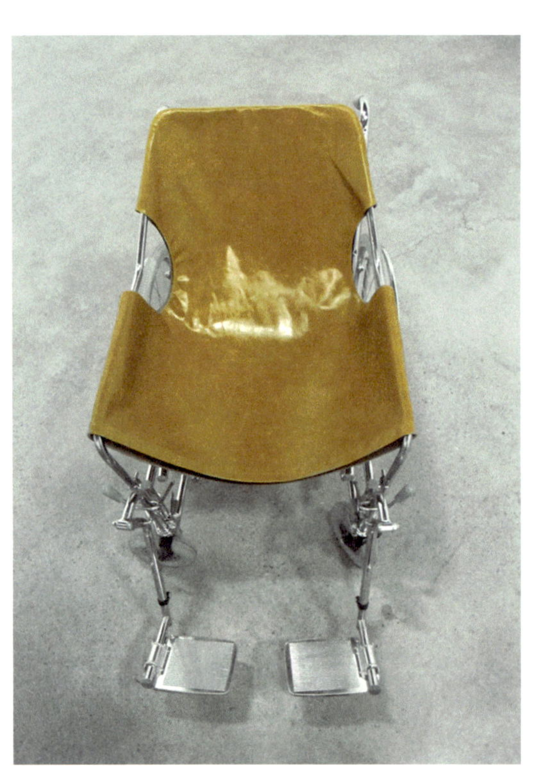

Sara Arrhenius

Cinema Shadow

149

Sometimes, the experience of handling an artwork and installing it in an exhibition has its own particular story to tell and encapsulates some of the work's significance and specific character. When we showed Laura Lima's *Marra (Fighting)* at Bonniers Konsthall as part of the exhibition *The Spiral and the Square* curated by Daniela Castro and Jochen Volz in 2010, it was not the first time that I had seen Lima's works. A few months previously, in an exhibition at Casa França-Brasil in Rio de Janeiro, I had wandered around in her peculiar world inhabited by magicians, dreamy men and women in hammocks, and enigmatic objects. But carrying out the preparations for exhibiting her work added a further dimension. It goes without saying that organizing exhibitions of contemporary art frequently throws up tasks that are far from the conventional museum routines, whether in depositing works, transportation, or installation. But with Lima's art, for those of us who were working at Bonniers Konsthall, the preparation process became something more than an everyday matter: a meaning-filled ritual that prepared us for the showing of the art piece, but which also became a part of our experience of the work. *Fighting* consists of two naked men clad only in two hoods connected at the top, which simultaneously hide their heads and join them together. Bound together and deprived of sight, the two men wrestle their way through the exhibition space throughout the exhibition's opening hours. Our task was to find people to take part in the work—an assignment that involved an unusual series of meetings, conversations, and negotiations, and which became for us a process of increasing involvement, as we, together with the artist, tried to anticipate, imagine, and pass on a kind of game plan for what was to happen, a kind of mental script to share between us.

The material that we had to deal with, and which is Lima's *prima materia,* was the body. It recurs in nearly all of her works. She stages, investigates, and exhibits the body's presence, its capacities or incapacities. She uses the body's physical form, letting its volume, warmth, and smell take place in the exhibition space. She tests out its strength and its movements, and the way that it can be controlled, restricted, and intensified. The participants we were looking for were not actors who would learn a role that was to be repeated. What Lima needed was participants who would encounter their opponent and the situation for the first time. This directness and what happens in the untried encounter between the two men are an important part of the work's mode of expression. In the encounter, the men develop a method that allows them to move together without falling over and, at the same time, to fight against each other. In this collision, a syntax unique to the moment will be created.

The structuring of the body's movements, as well as the space that Laura Lima creates around the body using objects and staging, are important generators of meaning in her work, which comes across particularly clearly in *Fighting*'s pared-down aesthetic. It is not just flesh that stands before us, but a body that has been shaped by our culture and by our symbol system. The special design of the hoods that bind the two men together, evoking associations in the viewer; the naked body in the museum space; the simple changing room implying a time both before and after the performance; the men's movements and the place of the viewer as stipulated by Laura Lima: taken altogether, this creates a matrix of cultural significances that mean that the work is filled with meaning and is readable by the viewer. A matrix created and guided by the artist's instructions forms the skeleton that to a certain extent defines the work and the situation that is the work's inherent potential. Within this framework there is a kind of script, a set of instructions that also makes it possible to reconstruct the work. The objects and the instructions create a situation that accommodates both limitations and possibilities. This is a language within which the bodies move, and which makes them readable for the viewer, but, like every language, it has room for a rich register of ambivalence, nuances, and possibilities for interpretation, which emerge every time two men encounter each other. By using this method, Lima's work takes on a powerful dynamic. It has an inherent possibility for change, and it is actually only first created at the point of intersection between her instructions and the participants' interpretation of them.

The fact that the body is Lima's primary material inevitably sets its stamp on the experience of her works, and gives them both a powerful tangibility and volatility. Since she uses the body as a sculpture in the art space, rather than as an actor in a performance, her works resound with the sculptural problems that have been worked on throughout art history. The giving of a form, or a Gestalt, to the body's weight, strength, and movement is then transposed into its opposite. Here, the translation from the soft, living body to solid, dead matter becomes a translation from the reference to art history's perpetual sculptured bodies to living, mortal flesh. At the same time, the expanded field of art and dematerialized art objects of the late 1960s, with the development of environments and performance as a more porous and elastic definition of the field of sculpture, have obvious resonances with Lima's work—as do that era's interchanging and experiencing of the psychology of perception and cognition and its development toward group-dynamic methods in psychoanalysis. Here it seems unavoidable to mention Lygia Clark's late work during her time in exile in Paris, where she developed a method for teaching in which she and her students created works for expanded and sensory experiences, subforms that came close to being therapeutic sessions. In Lima's use of the living body, as often in her work, there is also a nod toward older, more demotic image forms. There are associations here with the *tableaux vivantes* so popular in the nineteenth century. This form is primarily found among amateurs as a favorite mode of social intercourse in the bourgeois salon, but also in the popular vaudeville theater, cabaret, funfairs, and pornography. Through its mixture of image and theater, high and low culture, professionals and amateurs, it has links with Lima's interest in hybrid art, in what arises in the encounter between various artforms, cultural norms, and image cultures.

The performative character of Lima's works means that time takes on a decisive significance in them. Time is one of her great themes and is central to her work. In *Fighting*, the flow of time is made manifest through the work's lack of either a beginning or end. When it was shown at Bonniers Konsthall, it began when the exhibition opened and ended when the space closed for the day. This is one indicator of the way that *Fighting* relies less on the tradition of theater than on that of sculpture. The work is there for the entire exhibition period.

The possibility of viewing the work for different lengths of time and on different occasions makes it possible for the viewer to experience how it changes over time. Having a work go on uninterrupted stifles expectations of a clear beginning and end. But it equally challenges the notion that the artwork will be the same regardless of when we choose to view it. The passage of time becomes tangible and an experience in itself. But the passage of time also sees the emergence of the differences, shifts of meaning, and changes that require time and patience from the viewer in order to be noticed.

In *Fighting*, Lima does not let the viewer take part in any way other than specifically as a spectator. There is a distance here between the person who sees and the person who is being viewed. This is an important aspect of the work. Instead of trying to dissolve the distance between work and viewer, she emphasizes that, in this situation, we are specifically voyeurs, creating images of bodies by seeing.

The tension between script and performance, instructions and executed work, and the distance between viewer and viewed are the key themes in Laura Lima's work. In her *Cinema Shadow* from 2012, these themes are also put to the test and artistically taken to an extreme. To date, this monumental filmic work has been produced twice in different versions, once in London and once in Rio de Janeiro. In the course of the work, a body of films is created from scripts written by the artist, the idea being that the piece can be developed, reconstructed, and preserved by using an archive of the films and their scripts.

If *Fighting* is a work that I have seen and spent a lot of time with over an extended period, then *Cinema Shadow* is a work that I still only know from a distance, through conversations with Laura Lima, reading her script and notes, and looking at documentation. The work's underlying conditions, intentions, and possibilities are accessible and illuminated. But what really happens when the cues in the script, the underlying conditions that the artist has laid down, and the atmosphere that the pictures allow us to intimate, are still hidden in shadow? Distance is also a crucial concept in *Cinema Shadow,* something that makes it stand out against Lima's earlier works with their accentuation of corporeal presence in space. *Cinema Shadow,* by contrast, is based on the distance of the viewer from the live performance that is at the heart of the work: seated in a cinema, the viewer sees the projection of a live recording in real time of a scene that is being played out in a building somewhere else. Every day is a take that lasts different lengths of time in the different versions of the work. *Cinema Shadow Unspecified* was shot in an apartment in London and was shown simultaneously for three days at Short Wave Cinema. The first day's take was three hours long, the following one four, and the last day a whole eight hours. The second version of the work, *Cinema Shadow Segundo,* has a total of one hundred hours of film, in which more than fifty people took part. This was made and shown over thirty-three days, with a three-hour take made each day in a new room in the building where the film was recorded. The participants play their roles according to a script written by Lima, amid scenery built by the artist for each day's take, as laid down in the script. Every day is a new take on a new stage. The only "editing" done on the film is this daily change of scene. The actors are a mixture of amateurs and professionals. In some cases the actors write their own lines of dialogue, in other cases they do not act but are themselves. In this way, various levels of fiction and reality are seamlessly interleaved. At one showing, Lima also displayed the script to the public by placing it on the door of the cinema. Lima instructed the actors during the filming and made changes to the script. She also moved back and forth between the recording location and the cinema. The work was thus totally open and dynamic during the showing, and as a viewer one found oneself inside the creation process. While the work was being shown, the viewers came and went, sitting and watching for various lengths of time. As with many of her works, *Cinema Shadow* can be described as an atmospheric and associative flow of time, rather than as a coherent text that is dramatized. People, objects, colors, places, and words act as catalysts for chains of situations and relationships. The work's title, like Lima's earlier work, evokes associations with archaic images that are precursors to film and photography. Here, she reminds us of the shadow play that was a popular pastime before photography and the diorama. What she is interested in is the distance between the object or the person behind the screen and the likeness on the screen, but also in the way that the images in a shadow play are created continually and simultaneously with the movement of the actors behind the screen. Just like the images on the projection screen, by which the viewer is captivated at the cinema, there is a magical aura around the shadow-play images. It is as though we are transported back to the time before the birth of film, when the moving image that appeared on the screen was still an unfathomable miracle—wizardry with light—which today has become an everyday banality.

By creating associations with visual technologies from earlier eras, Lima conjures up a primordial scene of seeing, a kind of model for the economy of desire that directs our seeing. As Laura Mulvey taught us, this could actually not be any clearer than it is in the classical cinema situation, where, alone and unseen in the velvet-black darkness, we are able to watch and enjoy what happens on the gleaming screen in front of us. But Lima creates an insecurity in this situation by not granting us the safety of a clear narrative or a dramatic climax. Here, instead, we are placed in front of a series of events that resemble life itself, a continuum that goes on without beginning or end—a stream which shifts between the direct and the literary, dream and waking, symbol and reality.

Web cameras and various forms of surveillance equipment, smartphones, computer programs that report exactly where we are and what we are doing—these are all rooted in our fascination with seeing an event just as it happens, even though we are somewhere else. To do this, we agree to live under an extreme degree of recording and surveillance. If we do not see, we do not exist. And, in many ways, we imagine that life cannot be lived without being watched. Today's cult of docu-soaps and reality shows merely serves to highlight this contemporary mode of subjectivity. Nothing hides in shadow any longer. However, *Cinema Shadow* is absolutely not a reality show about making a film. It suggests to us something entirely different: an artwork that before our very eyes transports us back to the early magic of film and the image, that makes us experience the physicality and materiality of film paired with its capacity to dematerialize the body and have it be an illusion on a screen shining before us in the darkness. *Cinema Shadow* is an artwork that comes into existence in the moment and that is projected in front of us. *Cinema Shadow* is beyond the image culture of our time's insistence on the real. Instead, *Cinema Shadow* generates poetry's dreams and fiction's possibility of otherness. Nevertheless, it is impossible to think about *Cinema Shadow* outside the paradigm for seeing that we have created with today's technology. The favorite genre of our time, the docu-soap or reality show—TV programs that purport to register reality by following close on its heels or by having the camera running in locked rooms—promise closeness to unfiltered reality. Yet the reality that is put forward is always strikingly conservative and seems mostly to confirm the feeling that nothing can be changed. The world is as it is. As an artwork, *Cinema Shadow* exists on the reverse side of that visual paradigm, both as a symptom and as a catalyst for a critical understanding of our time's relationship with the image and with the camera. But perhaps most important of all, it is a radical proposal that, with its poetic dynamic and unpredictability, tells us that everything could be different. The world and the image are not fixed to appear in a given way.

Different ages make their own images, thereby expressing the longings and visual utopias of the time. The early documentary also had ambitions to depict the world as it actually was. Its various schools of thought held different notions of the camera's role, and I think it is interesting to set these in relief against Lima's *Cinema Shadow*. The early American documentary chose the "fly on the wall" metaphor for the eye of the camera. Invisible, neutral, and recording. What the camera registered was reality. A totally different notion of the age and the camera's truth is found in the documentary that was developed in the so-called *cinema verité* school with, among others,

Jean Rouch's anthropological films. Here the camera becomes an active catalyst for creating a situation that could not exist without it—a situation that can trigger and reveal another reality and truth that the participants themselves were not aware of. In this tradition, the camera's presence becomes a precondition for being able to portray a reality that could not be achieved without the camera. It is not an invisible witness, but a visible co-participant.

This awareness of the functions of the recording apparatus and of how the camera, the director, the viewer, the actor, together with the script, the scenery, and the object, are inscribed into a structure that creates its own energy, self-generating desire, and its own truth, is also found in *Cinema Shadow*. It cannot be seen in its parts, as a film, a script, or a performance. It is not a film, a script, or a performance; rather, what Lima has created is an entire structure for seeing—a structure that determines the relationship between the written script and its staging, between the viewer and the performance. But at the same time, realizing this structure will in itself involve interpretation and change: the actual version exists in the moment that it happens. Its truth and its poetic power lie in the entirety, and how and when we choose to use the situation decides what the work will be and what experience we will have. This applies, regardless of whether we are the viewer who chooses to stay in the gloom of the cinema for hours or just for a moment, regardless of whether we are the actors who, starting from Laura Lima's script, develop possible lines of dialogue or actions, or whether we are curators who, in the future, starting from the archived material, will again stage *Cinema Shadow* somewhere. In a way, Laura Lima's work is never what we see in front of us, but always the entirety of the situation, the script, the place, the actors, the scenography, and now also the archive, which becomes a potential source of an endless number of realized or unrealized situations and images.

Cinema Shadow

A film is filmed and projected at the same time following instructions on a script.
The instructions are open to adaptations, depending on time and space and
when and where the film is built, including objects, sequences, ideas, and technology.
No prerecorded images are used. *Cinema Shadow* is filmed and projected at the
same time through the technique of streaming/broadcasting. Two places are necessary:
a cinema and the film set. Filming and projection are simultaneous but they
happen in two completely different places. The public only has access to the place where
the film is projected but not to the film set, thus deepening the mystery and
highlighting the atmosphere implicit in cinema projection—the space of illusion. Although
filmed live, with all the paraphernalia used to make a film, and projected in real
time, the film's images are fictional constructs. *Cinema Shadow* adheres to several basic
questions that define it, while retaining its ability to deal with the unexpected.
The films may last the duration of an exhibition, one or two months. They also can be
shorter—timing is in relation to the situation and the script. Each "fiction" on
Cinema Shadow has its own instructions, like a "play." A film can be made many times, it is
only necessary to access the script. *Cinema Shadow Archives* can be shown at a
movie theater. The public, just as in the streaming version, may return to watch the film.

Cinema Shadow, 2011 / 2012
People, movie score, HD film or live stream, movie theater, cameras,
different objects and materials, special locations
Dimensions variable

Cinema Shadow film archive:
Unspecified, 2012, duration 15 hours. P. 159–61. Filmed in a studio in London and
project simultaneously at the Shortwave cinema, in Bermondsey Square, London.
Commissioned by the State of Rio de Janeiro and produced by People's Palace Projects and
Andrew Mitchelson. Featuring Stella Rabello, Robson Rozza, cone and more. Camera Anna
Azevedo and Camera special guest Vivienne Dick. Created and directed by Laura Lima.

Segundo, 2012, duration 100 hours. P. 162–168. Filmed and projected live at the cinema
of Fundação Eva Klabin and Caixa Cultural in Rio de Janeiro. Commissioned by Eva Klabin
Foundation and produced by Susy Muniz. Featuring Zaba Azevedo, Ronald Duarte
and others. Created and directed by Laura Lima. Co-directed with Emanuel Aragão, music
of Domenico Lancellotti, clothes Bruna Lobo, light design Andrea Capella, camera
Tay Nascimento. *Segundo* was created at the house of Eva Klabin for the Projeto Respiração
curated by Marcio Doctors.

Courtesy of the artist

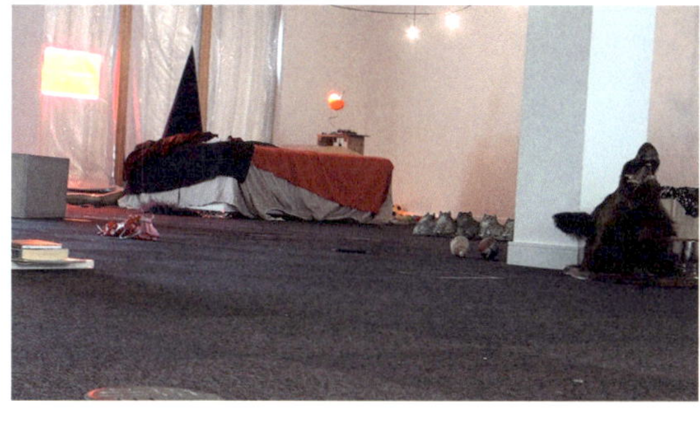
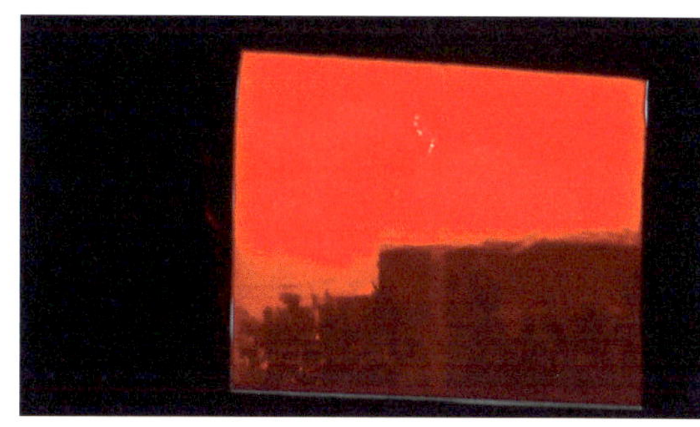

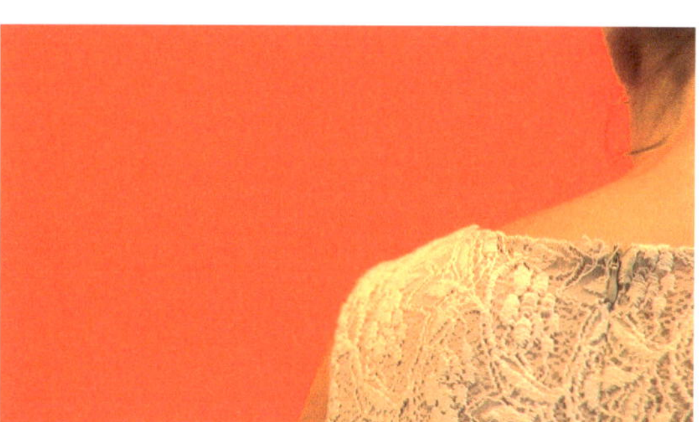
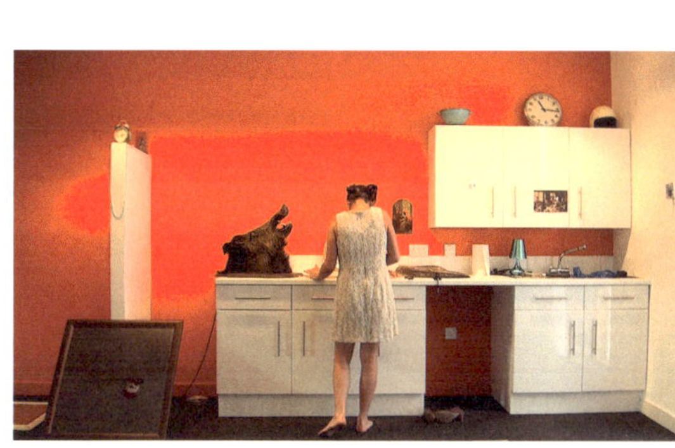
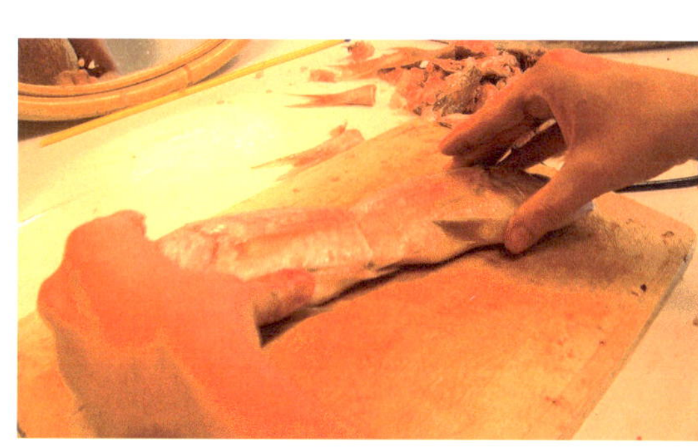
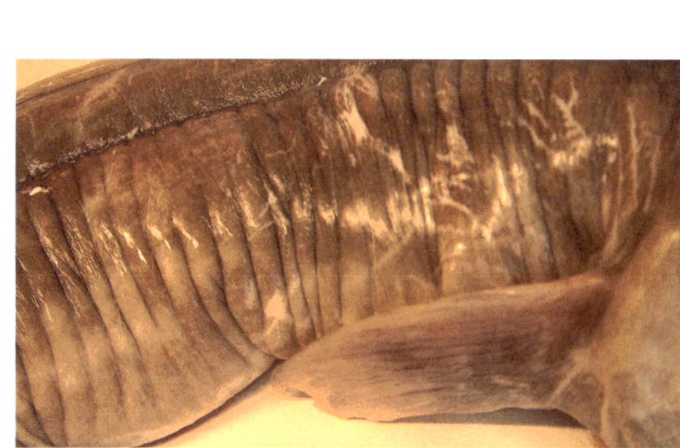
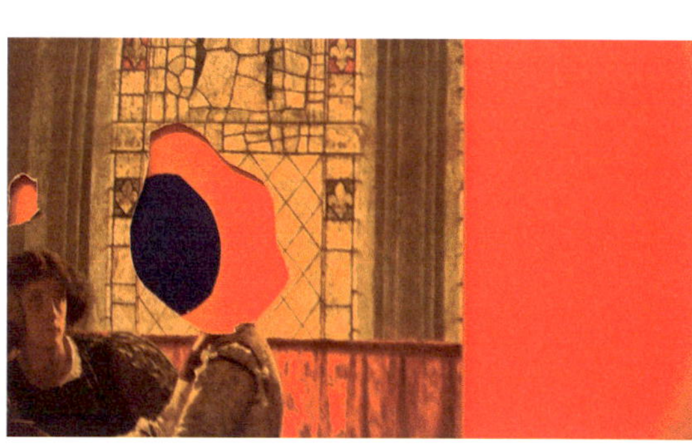

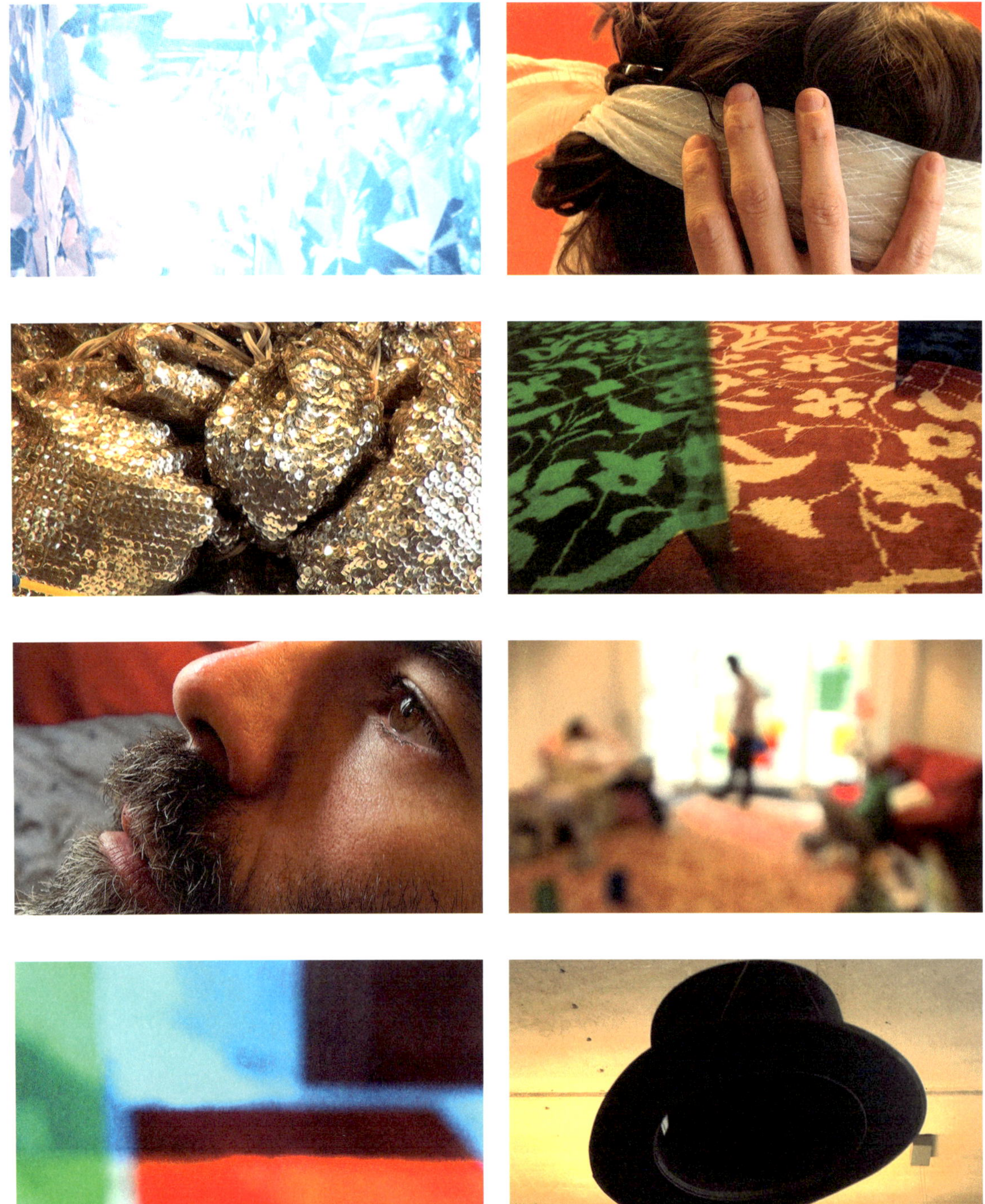

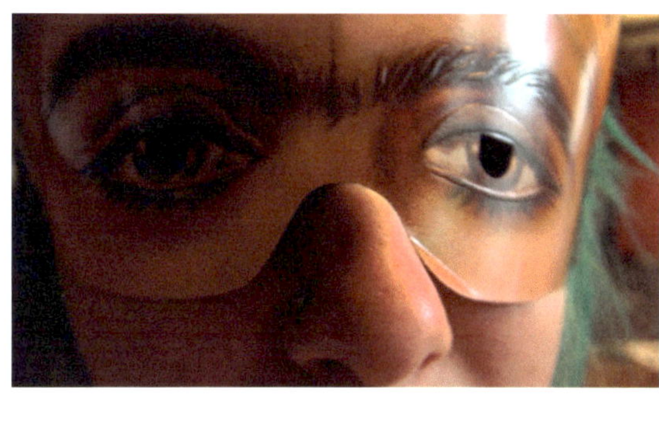
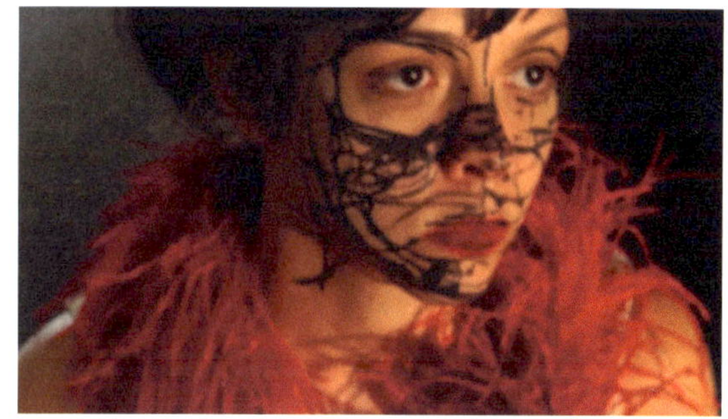
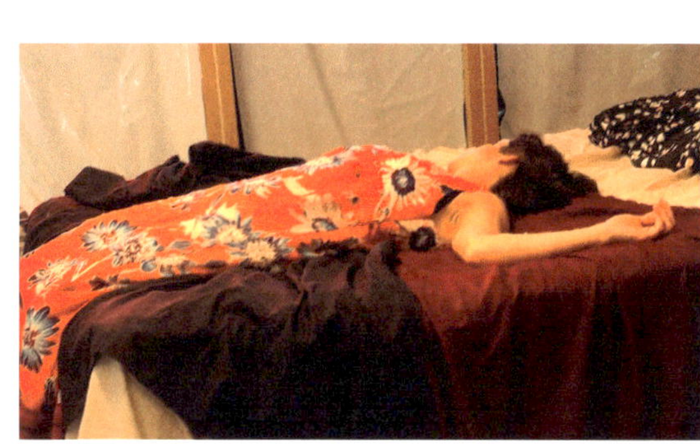
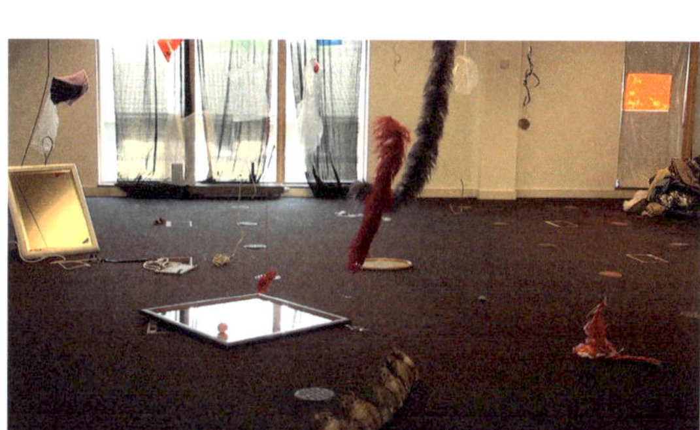
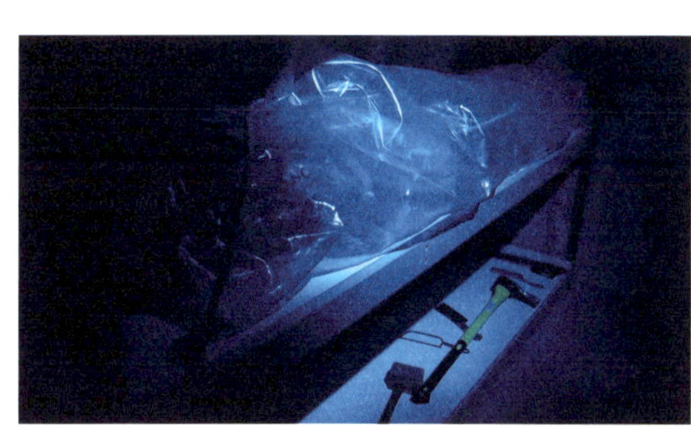
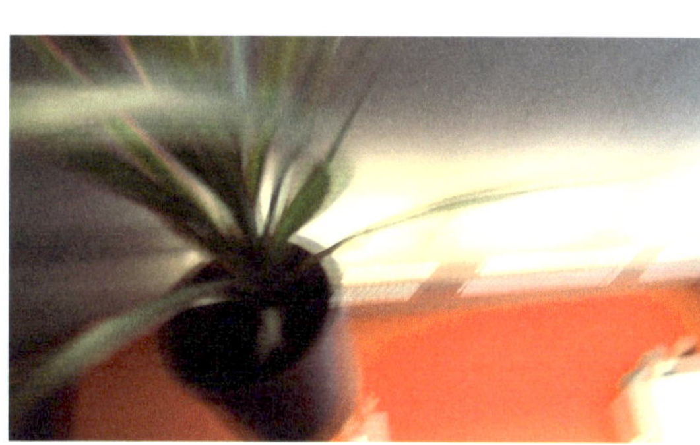
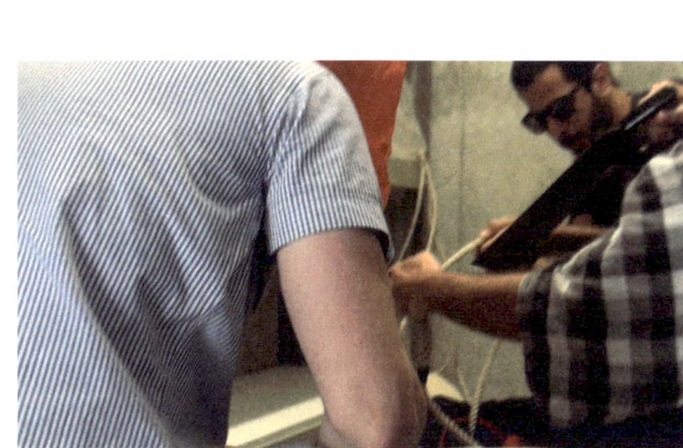
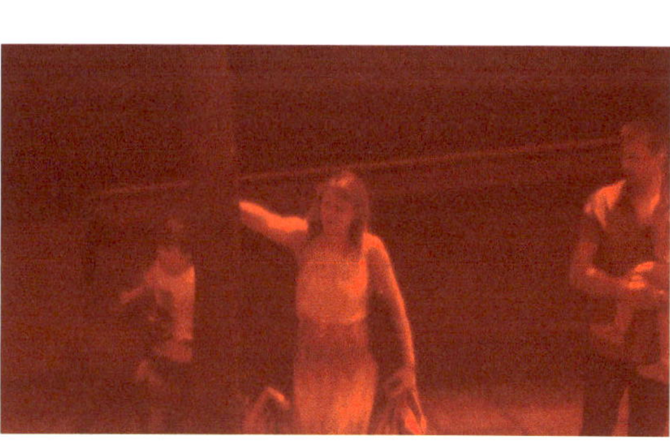

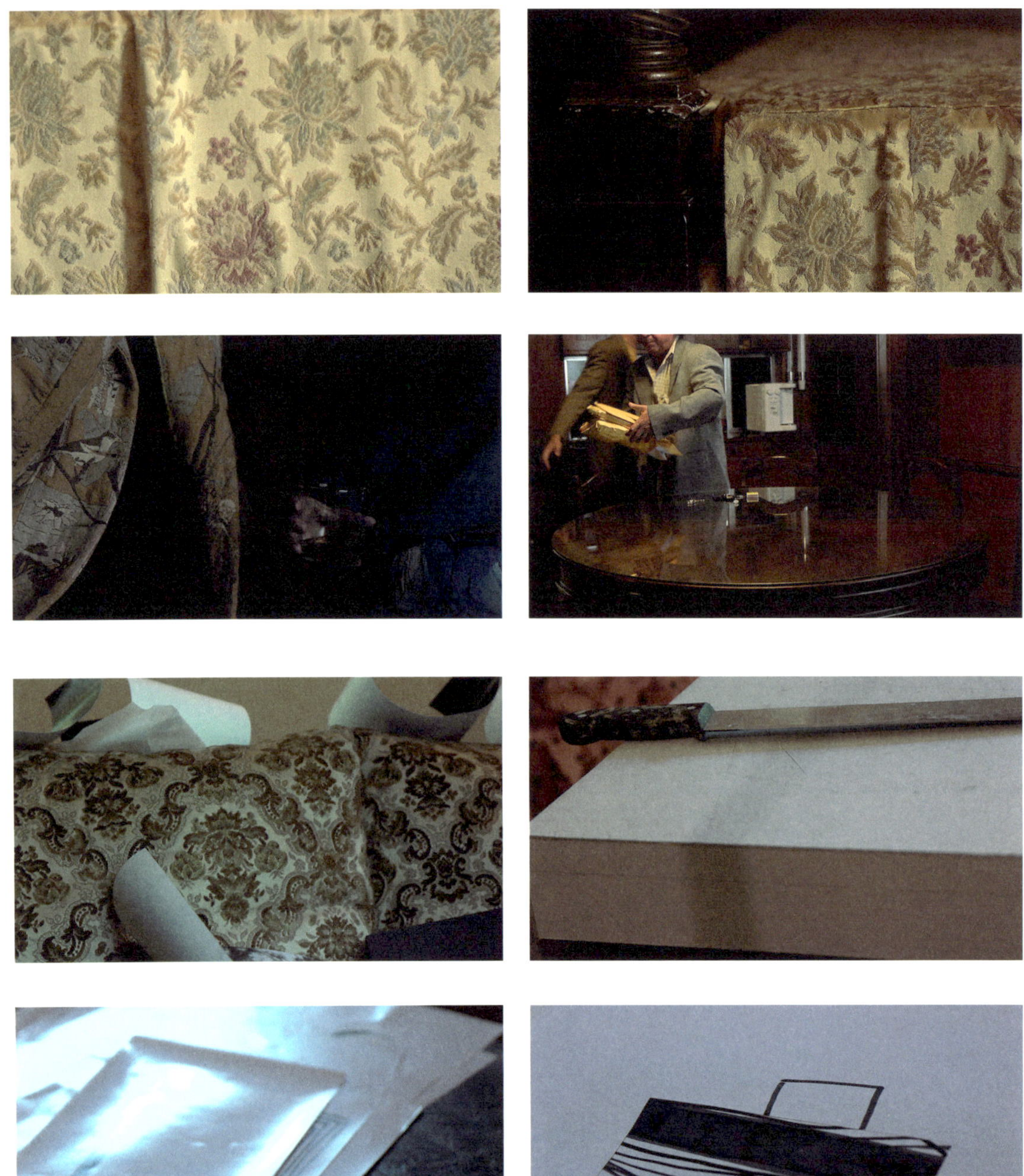

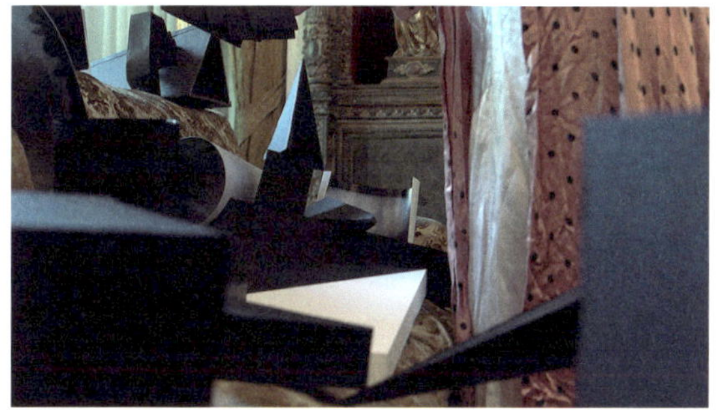
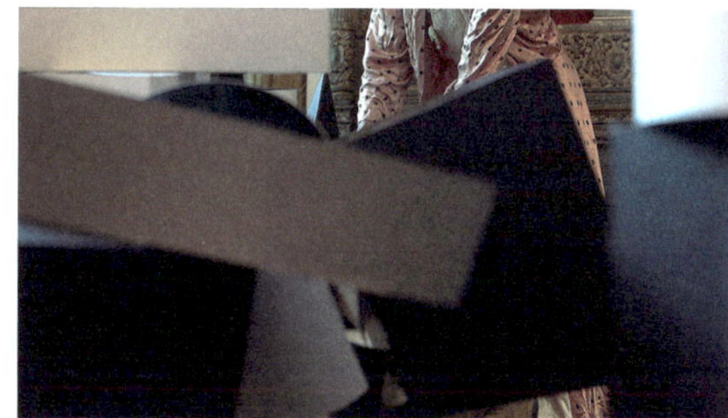
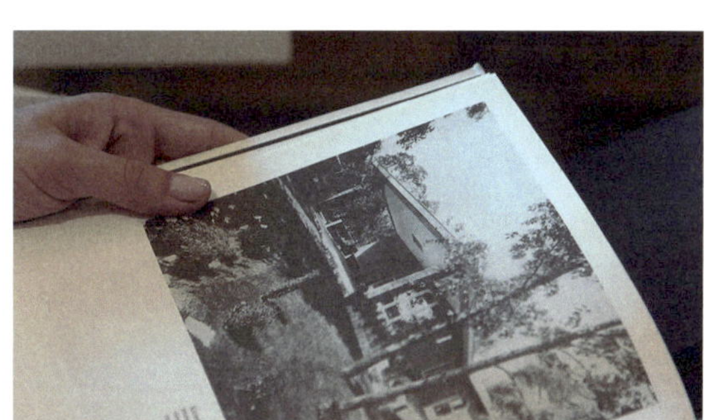
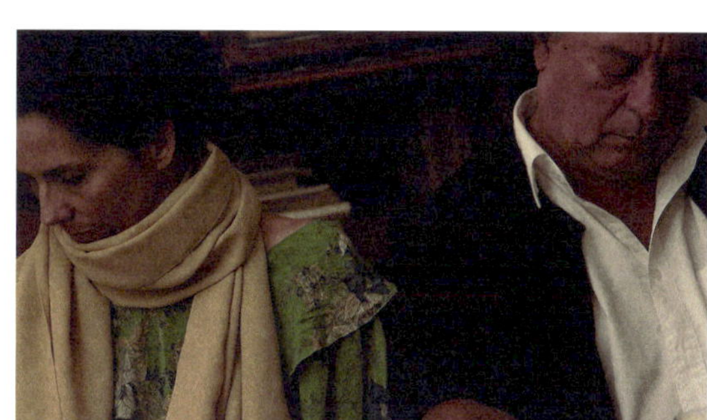
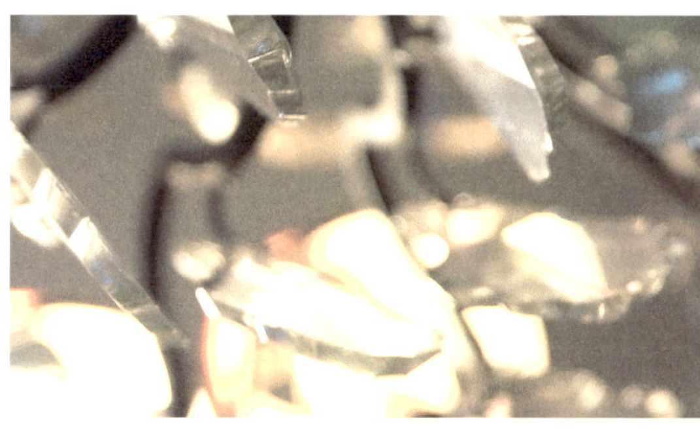

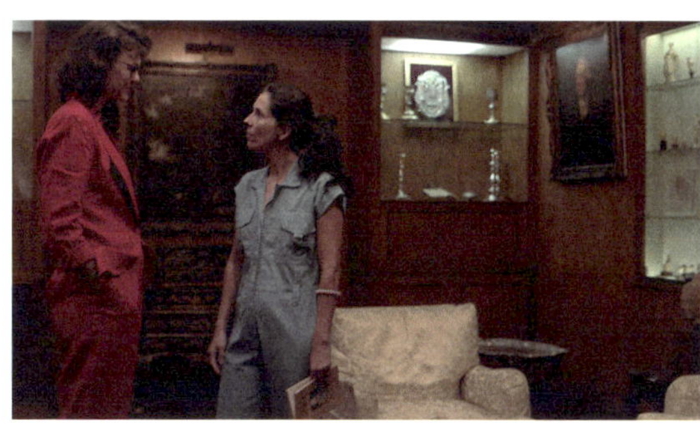
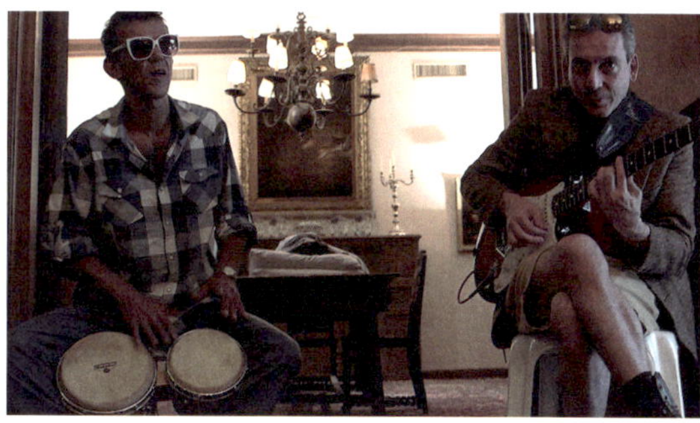

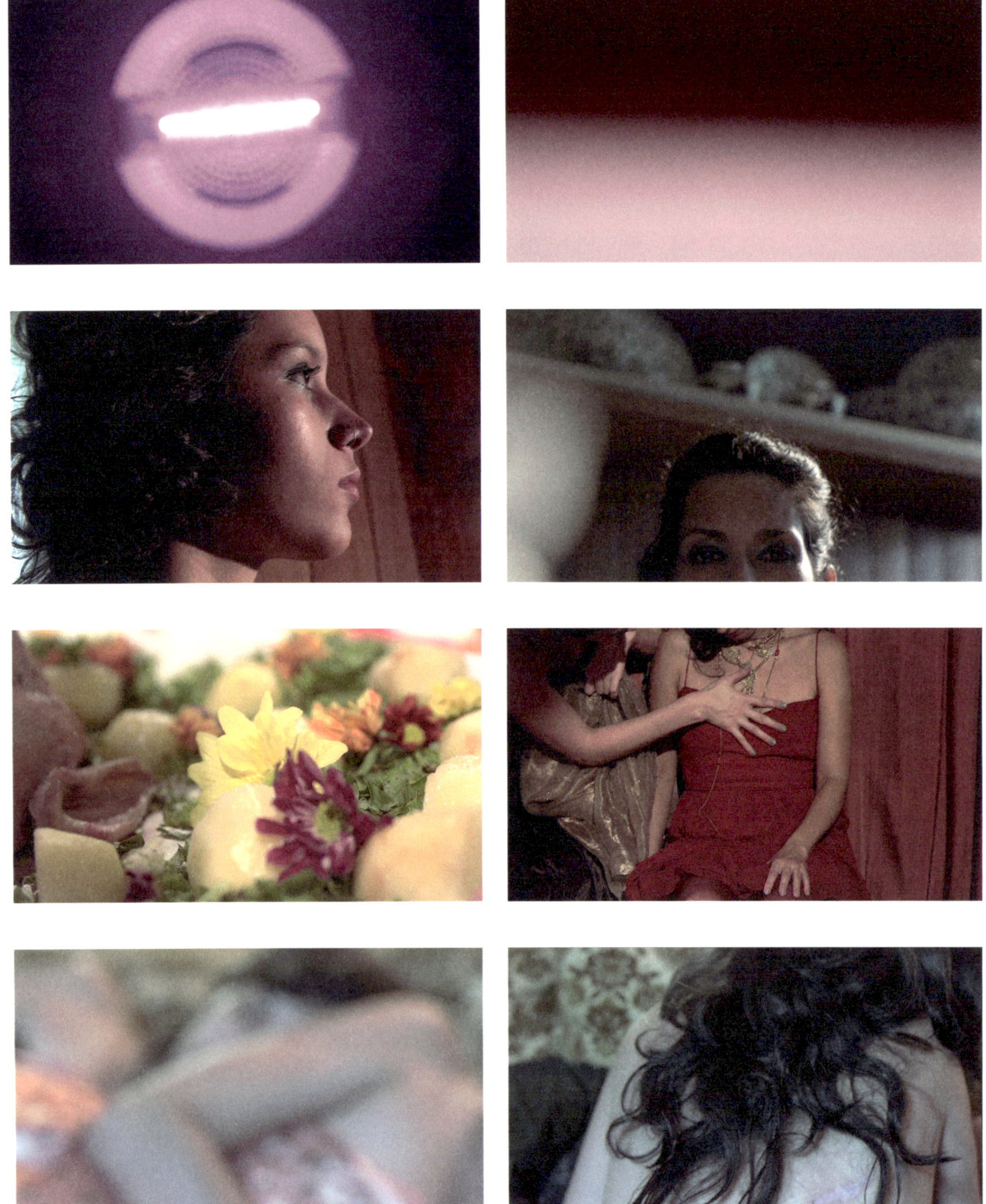

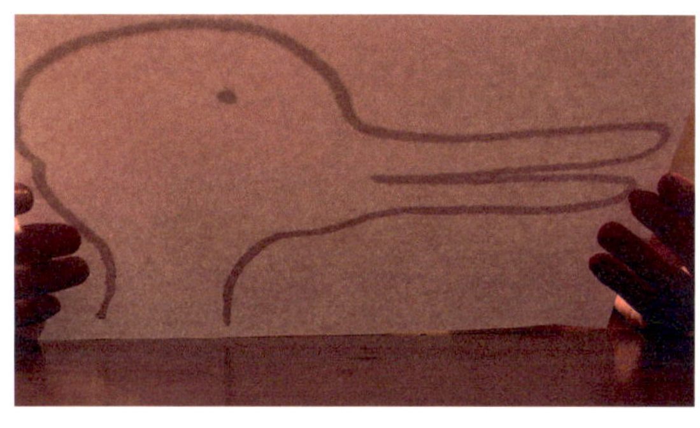
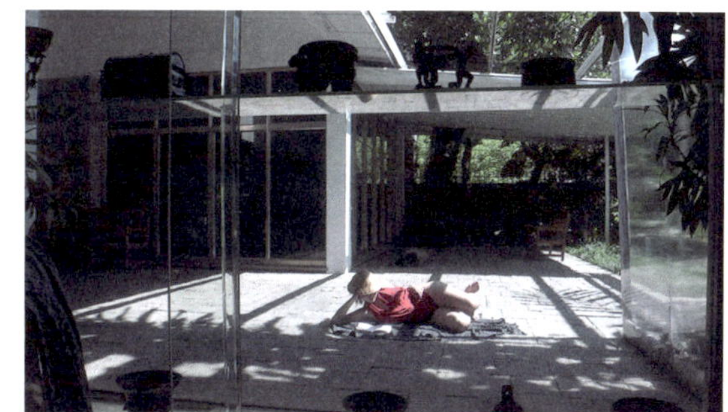
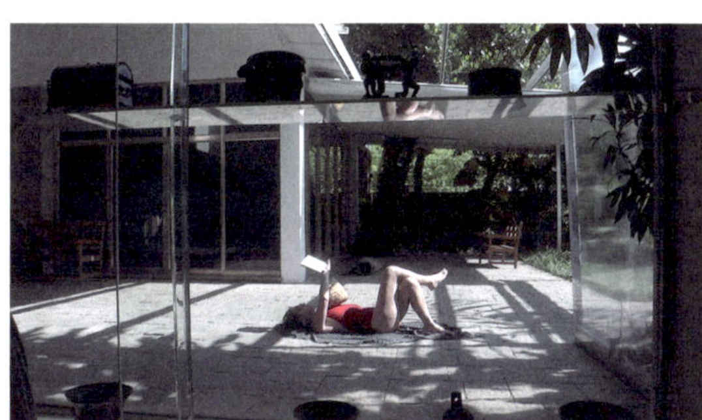
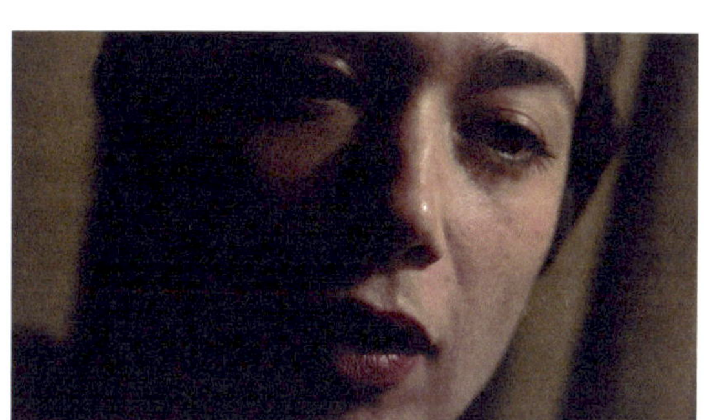
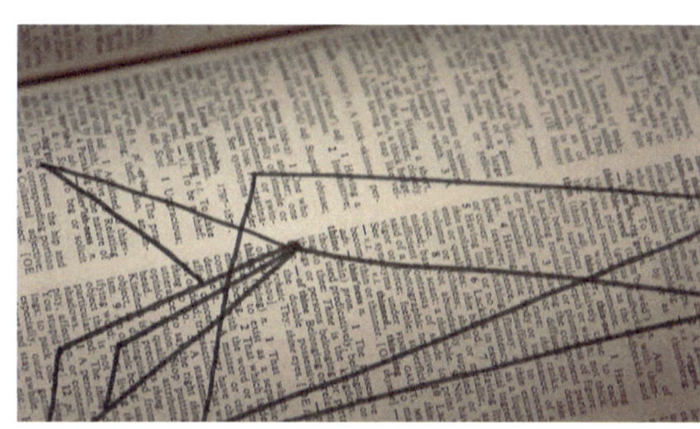
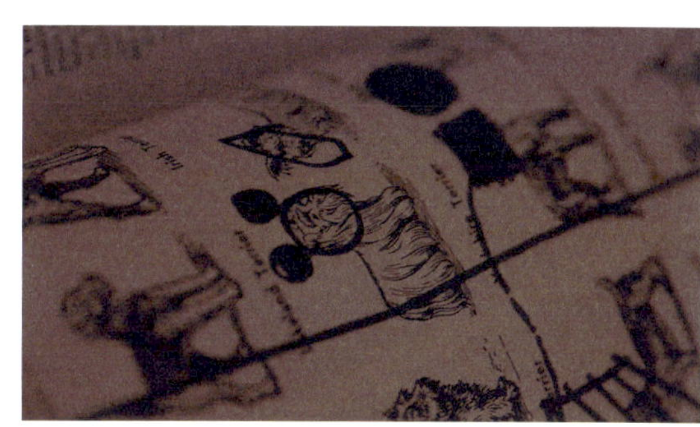
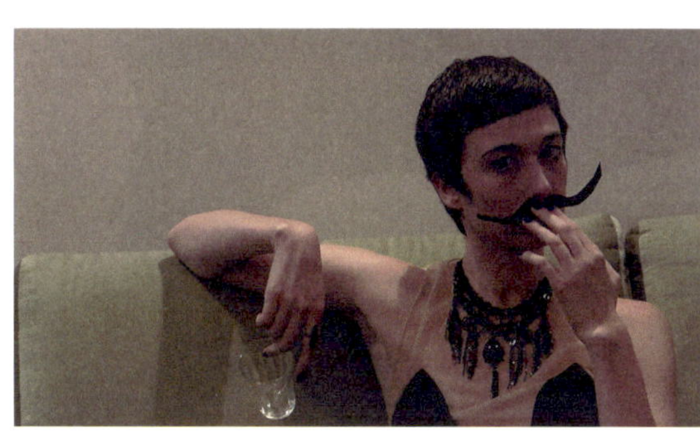
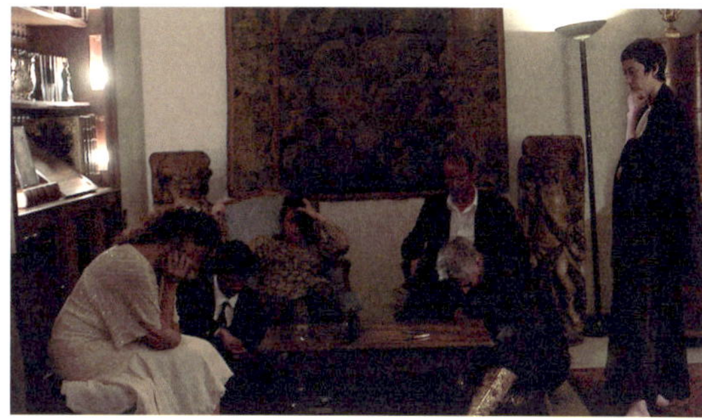

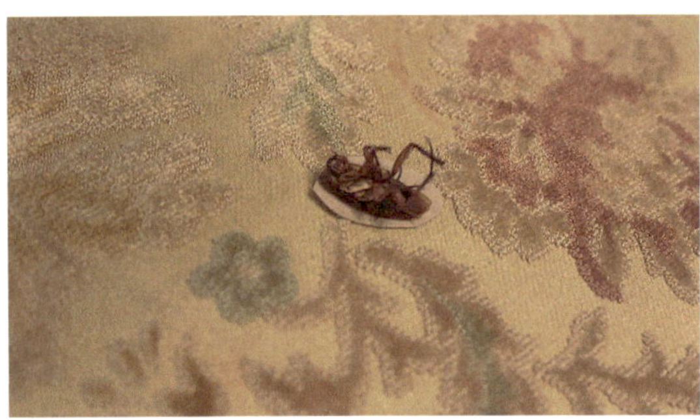
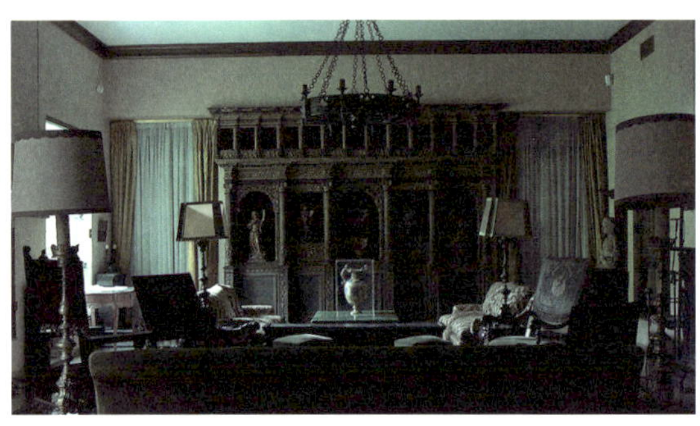
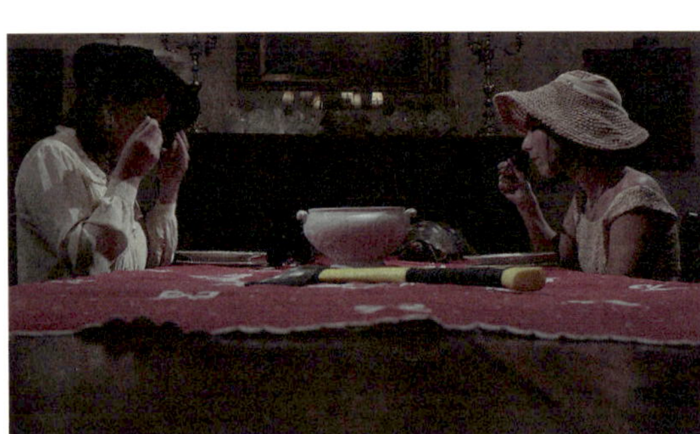
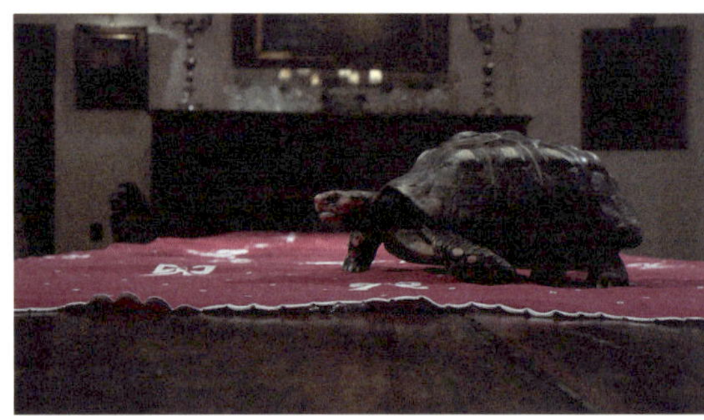
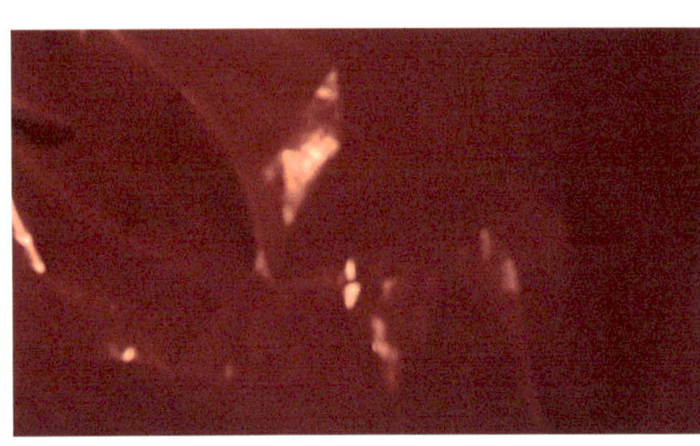
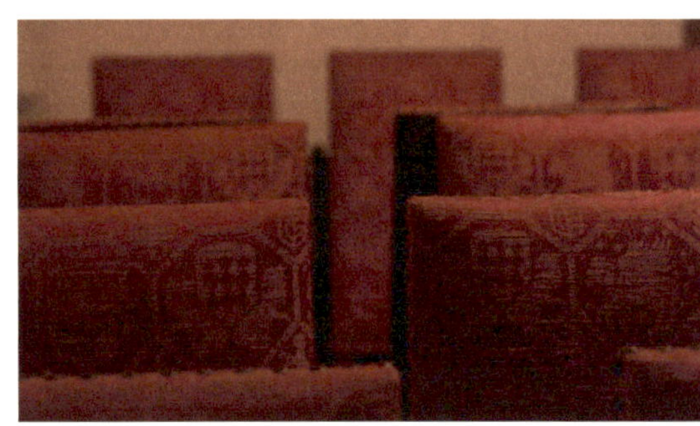
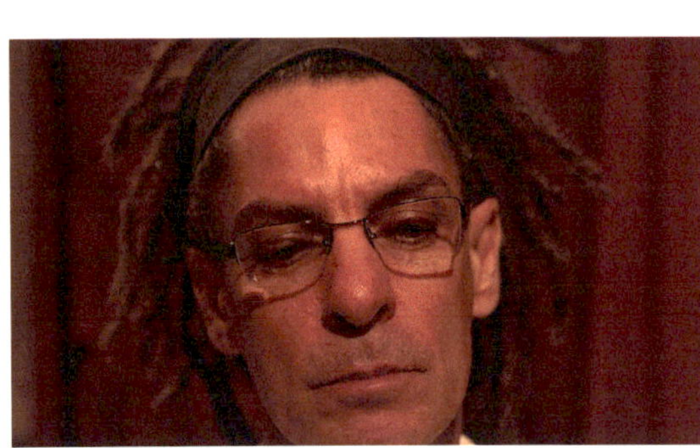
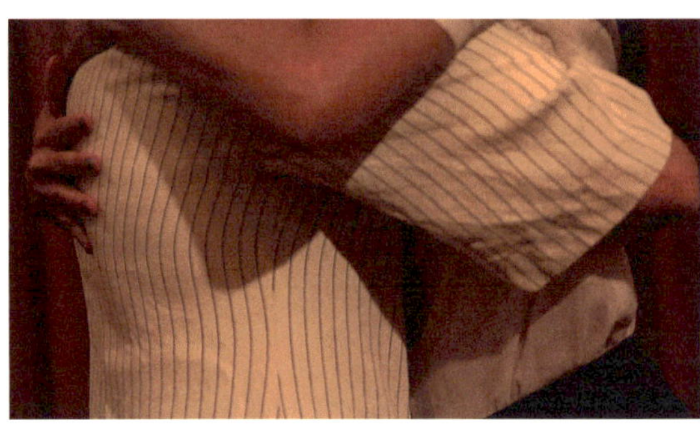

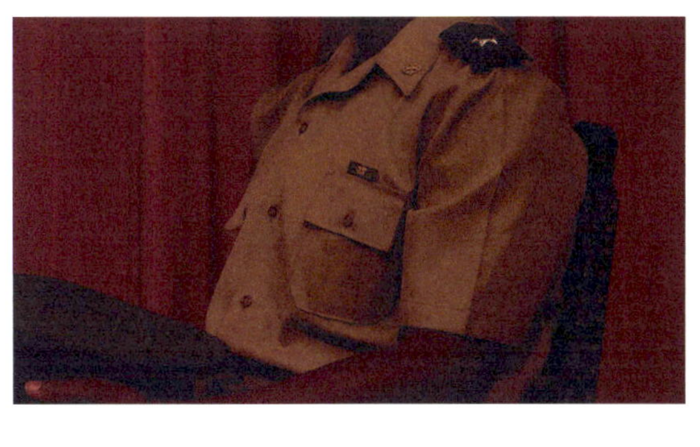
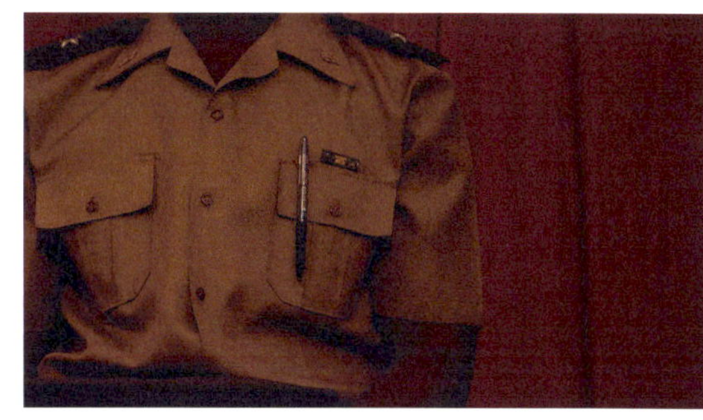
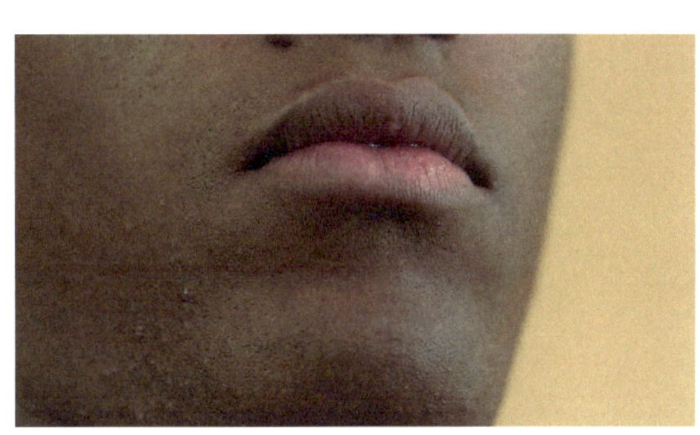
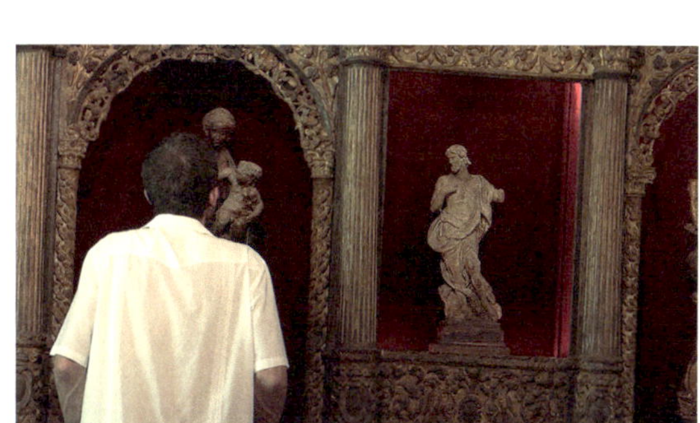
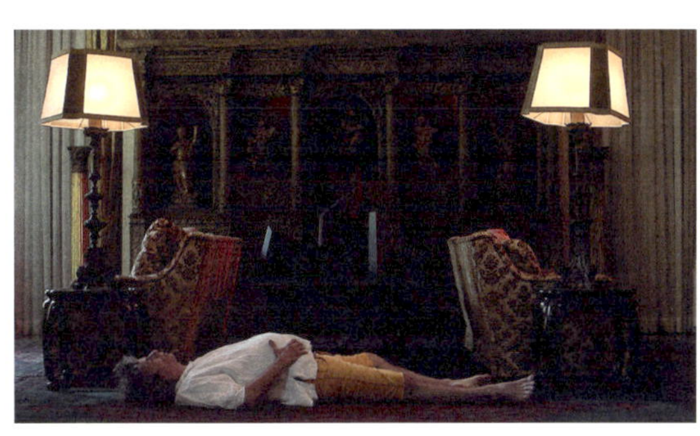
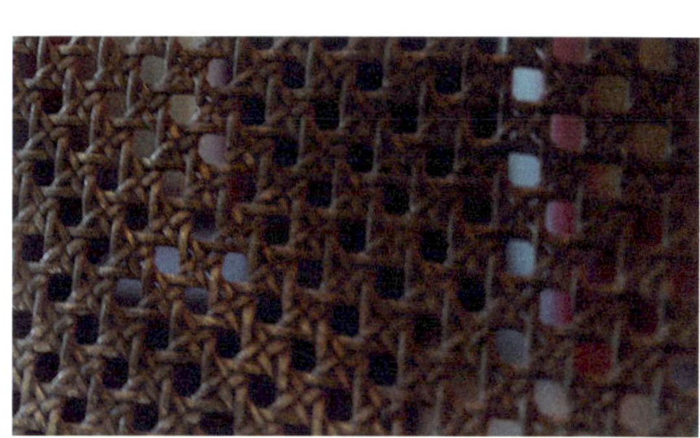
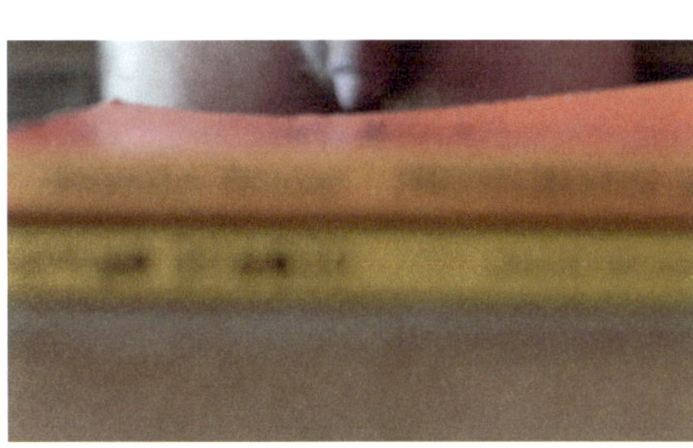
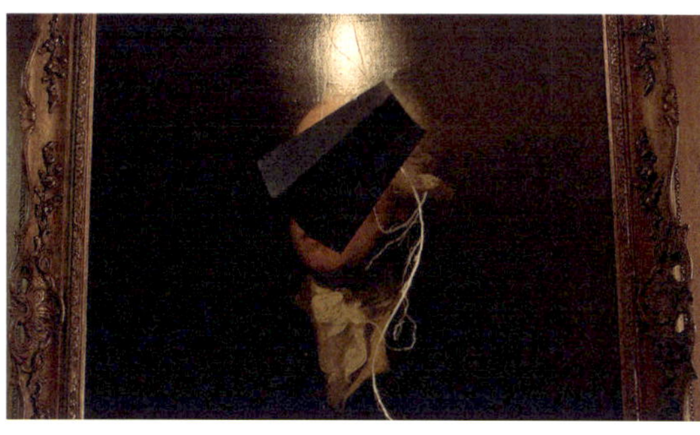

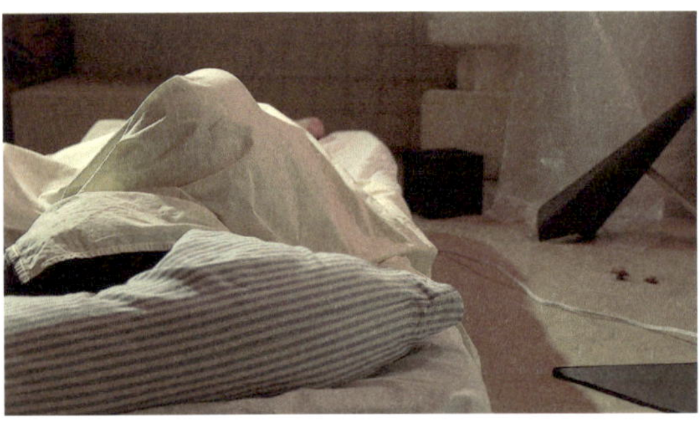
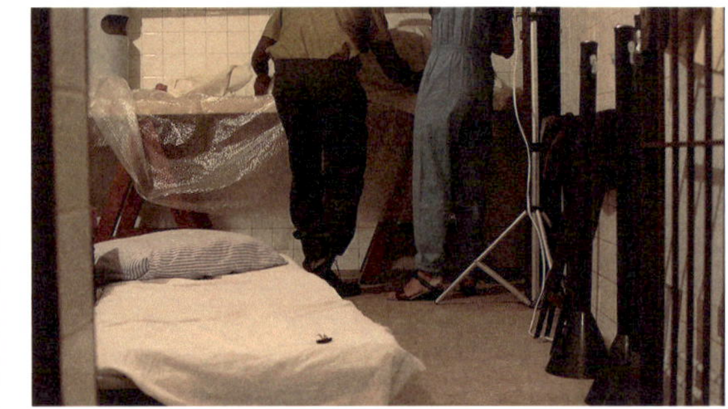
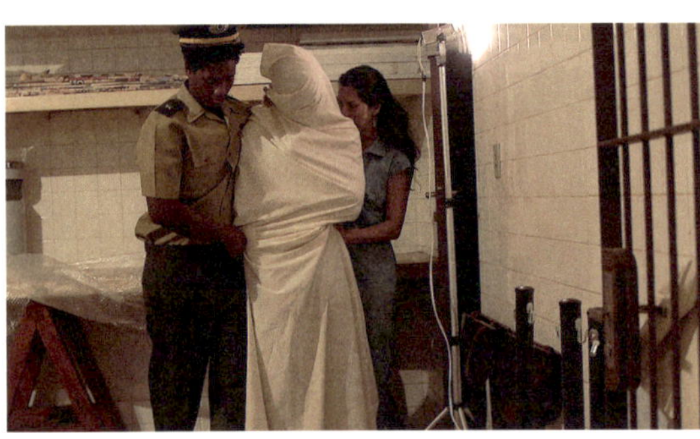
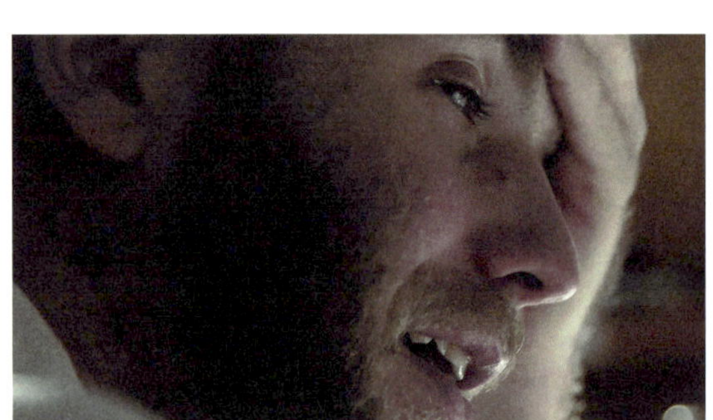
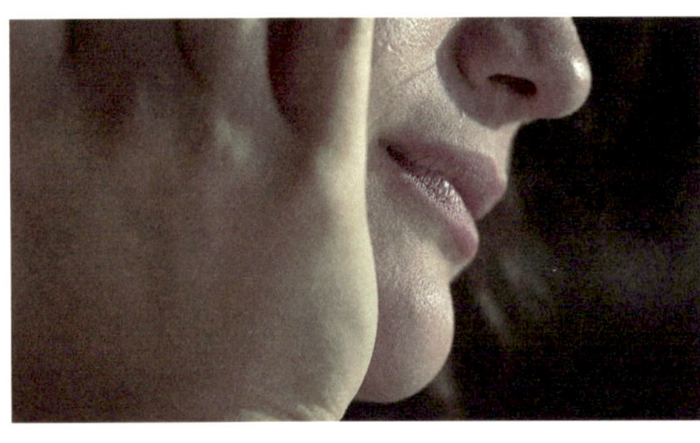
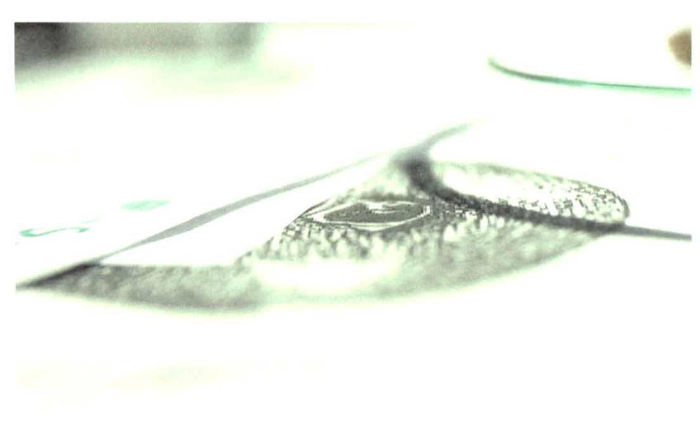
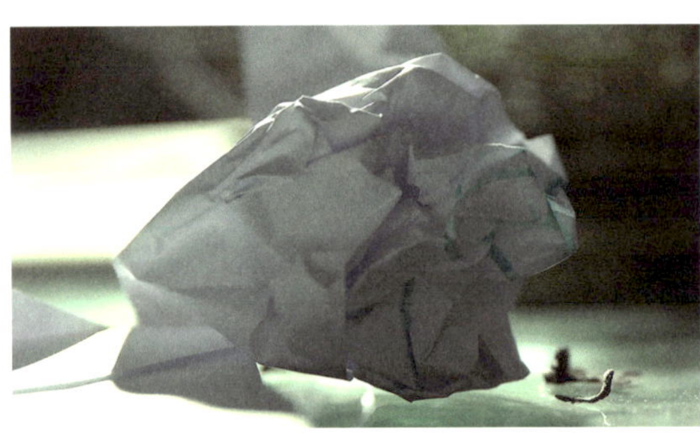
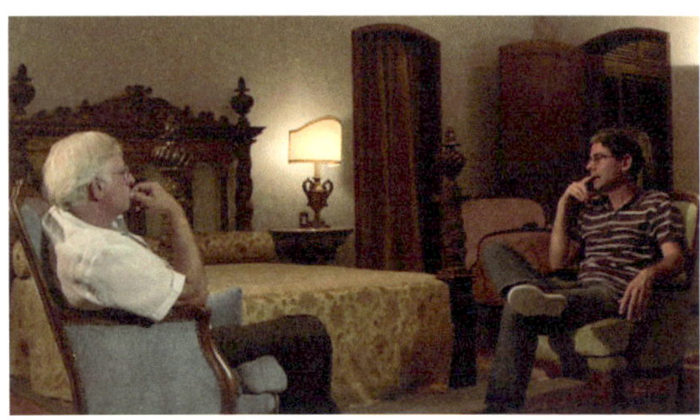

Interview with Laura Lima

by Ronald Duarte, Inês de Araújo,
Felipe Scovino, Daniel Toledo,
Simone Michelin, and Analu Cunha

169

Inês de Araújo—You studied philosophy and went directly into something that is not exactly performance. How did you start your artistic career? You followed a unique path and developed a work that does not fit well into any category.

Laura Lima—I can answer by going deep into the past, to where I lived in the countryside of the state of Minas Gerais, in a town without many cultural inputs and with a very strong Catholic influence. In my home, however, we talked about Marxism, about Lula and having a worker in power, about Cuba, about the possibility and freedom to be atheists. Those subjects were taboo, because those were the 1970s and 1980s, childhood and adolescence, decades of great political changes in Brazil due to the dictatorship and post-dictatorship periods. I was born into this kind of ideological "foreignness." A sort of ostracism and incommunicability. When I moved to Rio, I gradually adapted, but never completely lost that feeling. When I was still very young, something dramatically changed my life: my younger brother, who was very close to me, had a psychotic break. That was when I began to see things in a completely different way. Everything begins with madness, I mean, precisely in the construction of language, in the structure of reason and construction of meaning.

Simone Michelin—In your early work, when you were still a philosophy student, you already created a theoretical apparatus, certain concepts, as in the case of *RhR*.

IA—We started to talk about *RhR* due to one of your constructions, the philosophy of ornamentation, and the issue of clothes and the body.

I could start there in order to talk about this trajectory, however, it is too early to go into that, because there is a whole previous construction. *RhR* began in 1999, I am still talking about the time I started to study at Parque Lage (Free School of Visual Arts in Rio de Janeiro) in 1991, and my philosophy studies, constructing from 1994 what would be the foundation of my whole artistic thinking. At that time, I chose not to study fine arts for a political reason: studying philosophy seemed to be the most interesting way to approach art. Without technical knowledge, I worked more densely on the general conceptual apparatus of the work. One has to think the web, based on its own triggering events. In 1994, as a participant in a group exhibition, I brought a cow from a mountain to the urban beach of Ipanema, in Rio de Janeiro. The cow was there for a whole day and at the end of the day, it was taken back to its place of origin. That work—the displacement and the cow's image—marked the beginning of my ideas for *Homem=carne/Mulher= carne (Man=flesh/Woman=flesh)*. From then on, I started to work with living things, and it was important to consider that *HcMc* started with an animal.

I started to build a system of notes, a hybrid using drawings and words, since they were not independent drawings that said something *per se,* nor were they texts containing the description of an idea. The ideas were organized in those notes; I created my own library of references and transformations, and the use of philosophy was important in this process. Then I started to create a construction system and a glossary intrinsic to the process. Explaining more objectively, *HcMc,* was the point of convergence of several ideas to be constructed with the presence of living beings, especially humans. In *HcMc,* there is no hierarchy between humans, animals, or objects; between animate and inanimate, which means to say that the individual in the work is not the one who "experiences," who constructs subjectivity. The tasks given to people shape the image, or the animals in the contexts to which they are linked.

The images of *HcMc,* constructed with living beings, should be present the whole time in the exhibition, from the first to the last day. We needed an arsenal of people for the work/image to be present.

This system of equivalences with living beings and the permanence of the work on all days of the exhibition were very unusual at the time, in Brazil and abroad. I had a lot of difficulty with the realization of these ideas, since the institutions were used to those structures only in the case of inanimate objects. In Brazil, there were only a few galleries, mostly in São Paulo, that could support exhibitions as complex as the ones I proposed; museums or institutions were rare.

SM—What is the glossary you mentioned? And why did it appear? What is its function, what does it say? Are you renaming things?

The glossary is not for display. It appeared in order to create notions within the work and rearrange words, creating meanings belonging to specific contexts. They work intrinsically to develop thoughts about how the work

operates, or to think paradoxes or noises in the meaning the work generates due to its nature, like, for example: recognizing that the person who participates in *HcMc* in equivalence to the apparatuses has their own inherent characteristics, and that is why they are called "person=flesh" (another word in this glossary). It is understood that the work will be inexorably influenced by each living being doing it.

After *HcMc,* I created works with different philosophical constructions, where I no longer give tasks to people= flesh. By completely changing the philosophies of construction of the works, I began to realize that they are different instances, which restructure the work's poetics as a whole, offering new points of view. These instances are not isolated, they have a lot in common with each other. Sometimes a term appears flirting with several instances, as is the case of my ornamental philosophy. I have already added two words to this glossary: "Instances" and "Ornamental Philosophy," and so we go on unveiling it.

IA—Do you display the glossary alongside the works when you exhibit them?

No. The glossary appears with the creation of the work. It could serve as a critical and theoretical apparatus for the one who writes, or when I talk about my own poetics, as in this interview, for example.

IA—How do you choose the people? How do you hire them?

RD—Is it true that *HcMc* had this peculiarity of not allowing actors to participate?

That is not true. I think it is easier to work with non-actors, because there are no previous layers of knowledge, the person performs the task without having to access elaborate codes. Non-actors are at a different level of domestication. It is easy for the construction of the work, but not always easy to find them. However, even with actors, many tasks are so specific and demand so much concentration that the work itself neutralizes those layers of knowledge. On the other hand, this rule is not that cruel. The image of the work and the process to construct it is such that, frequently, participants initiated in this way appear, and they can be amazing. Anyway, actors or non-actors, working with people means to flirt with the unfathomable. Updating the images with people is a permanent struggle. It is fascinating; on the other hand, that part of the work leaves, goes home, takes a bus—the risk I run thinking that the image may not be there the next day is huge.

I could add that the institution is also a body, like I am a body that is outside my works; the institution is a structure that functions to gather other bodies. Depending on the demand, the institutions must devise a complex plan to deal with the works, which require people as participants. When this happens, I think of Kafka. Actually, I always think of Kafka. (Laughs.)

The enigma of that is that actually this whole structure does not talk only about the body, but about time. The discussion around the body is a historic discussion anchored in many artistic movements and therefore easily activated by critics who talk about my work. I always saw the work with its image permanently in a museum, gallery, institution, wherever it is displayed. But, before that, working with the living requires that time is primarily considered. No body is related to the work if we do not consider that its time is limited. The body is in the sense of humanity. The body is in the sense of a living being and the fragility of its existence. The question of carnality, reification of the human, is a political exercise and an exercise in the construction of meaning and poetic symbols.

No, I do not distance myself, I am part of this flesh. Carnality here is used as a poetic possibility for constructing— I needed that as an artist. There, in the beginning, asking myself what I would work with in the future, in my cauldron I sought to bring together matter and the web-of-life experience and something unfathomable. In the first years in my studio I worked with things that rotted and images that disappeared, I threw candy into creeks to be eaten. I usually made things that disappeared, then I started to work with people and animals.

The tasks necessary for the realization of *Man=flesh/Woman=flesh* are an integral part of the work—museums or collectors buy the work and agree to a lot of rules that should be followed because otherwise the work will not be the real work. I offer a detailed *modus operandi,* and it cannot be modified in the least.

SM—Is it a kind of contract that the institution has to sign with you as an artist?

It is a set of instructions I establish, like a contract. The institution is responsible for the work and its conceptual integrity, because one needs to respond with quality and assume one's own role.

Felipe Scovino—I think your work establishes a dialogue with many other artists, but perhaps most of all with these three artists, each one in their specificity, Lygia Clark, Hélio Oiticica, and Flávio de Carvalho. The reason for that is the fact that all four of you think the body in a manner that is not within the physical realm. Lygia, for example, in the disappearance of the body with her sensory objects, Flávio de Carvalho thinking the body as an ironic and sarcastic act. Flávio brings up the social way in which the body can be used, and Hélio thinks the body more like a suspended place in the social realm. Why did I mention those three? I want you to talk a little about the expression you used, carnality, or the way you think and use the body. Those artists, too, failed to qualify what those actions were for them. You were talking about this situation of yours in relation to the museum and, for example, with Flávio de Carvalho, the works *Traje de Verão* (Summer Outfit) and *Experiência no. 2* (Experiment No. 2), do not really exist: there are only accounts, and they happen orally, the work is not sold, it exists photographically because someone photographed it, otherwise it would have disappeared. Those are situations that were somehow kidnapped by art history and the artist often has no power over his or her own production. How does that shift happen, the reverberation of the work?

I agree with some of those things, indeed. My glossary serves me, yet I do not find the word to respond to the use of the word "performance," a category into which people normally want to include works with people. I create a system, but I know that it is rigorous without being rigorous, because I accept unfathomable things, constitutive and constructive paradoxes. I remember that when I received a phone call in 2000 saying that my work was going to be acquired by a museum, I did not at the time have something that responded to an art object in a strict sense; instead, I create a structure for the *modus operandi* of each one of the works acquired. The method for the creation of instructions for artworks has antecedents since the twentieth century with many artists. That was not the difference—it was the whole historic conjuncture that started to be linked with it. Before that, the market wanted me to consider the work's documentation as a work in itself, but I refused to accept that as an ontology of my work. The museum's board was already experiencing the way I dealt with the market. At that time, they made a fuss in the newspapers: "Brazilian museum buys performances for the first time"—my own works. On the other hand, it was interesting to see the institution's attempt to deal with itself, abandoning its inertia and updating itself; however, the glossary was still the same, the same set of tools, and the works repelled this denomination.

IA—Do you choose the people?

If I am still alive and taking part in the exhibition setup, yes. But the work was created to be independent. The institutions are advised to follow and handle the work by themselves. My body is not present.

As for the people, the process is very simple—anyone can participate; once they understand the work's structure of concepts and precepts, the work may begin. I never rehearse. There are no theatricalization methods, nor is there any training to fine-tune the work, like in dance. Control does not lie in this approach. Risk is always part of it. I must develop a relationship with those beings that are part of my work, but this process is not structured like a rehearsal, it is not that kind of molding I propose. In most of my works, each time they are re-created, there will always be other people.

IA—But the fictional dimension you create makes you differentiate your work from performance, from philosophy, from literature, because it is a bit of all of them. The impression those living images give me is that in them there is always a depletion of representations, they are never representational. It is not only your relationship with the living construction and the idea of humanity; there is also something about the present, about this media age, these struggles and resistances with other images that are not living but are there in the commerce of images. Your work is a work that circulates and also imposes itself like images do.

Analu Cunha—The work happens there, at that moment, not as image—the real image is the one that happens in the experience.

I would not recognize my work in photographic or video documentations in an art exhibition. From a poetic point of view, I needed to experience the soul given by the presence of living beings. The work is simply not its picture. Photographs or videos are mere documentations, either for publication or as part of a collection in the form of information, but they would not serve me, not even when I use my *modus operandi.* When I talk to the people=

flesh, I do not even use videos of my works to show how they should function; when I give instructions to the person=flesh, not even a picture. I just talk. I cannot adapt someone's image to another's. Two living masses are never alike.

AC—There is an image construction there that is an image of the experience, but it is a mental image, which stays.

I have the ideas and, at first, the rest seems to be the rest, the concept has already been given. But it is not really this way; in many works, I can rethink it, construct it a bit differently. Could I then say that I rehearse when I watch together with the public my own work? In this way, everything is always a rehearsal, in a transformation sense.

The first time I applied this rule of never rehearsing was with the work with a child that jumps rope in a basin of gelatin. The work began, the girl stepped into the jelly and started to jump, all were looking at the work, including myself. I was realizing the work for the first time. She started to jump. She was wearing a white nightie, and I thought it was going to get dirty, but what happened was that the girl became covered with that red goo, the gelatin; it was all over the place— there was jelly even on her teeth—and I remember going into a trance! I could not believe what I saw, I did not expect it to be so intense.

RD—Returning to the subject of *RhR*—this is a work that achieves a fictional weight, but it is ultra real.

You are talking about representation—
do you know where *RhR* comes from?
"Representative hyphen Representative," the abbreviation of the letters
became a growl, a guttural, visceral
word. The hyphen brings together two
ways of representing the world, whatever they may be, but in the case of *RhR*
it is the hyphen we are interested in.
In the middle, a hole, an abyss uniting
representativity.

The first time *RhR* appeared, its
first "Movement," was in 1999. I was
already having exhibitions. I was creating those poetic situations with living
beings and constructing the conceptual
system of the work, this internal
glossary. I believed it was aimed at an
art space, a gallery, museum, etc., or
some other obvious space. There was a
whole arsenal, there was a bubble
that ensured understanding, the certain knowledge that this was indeed
art. I had a philosophical universe that
remained there in my own practice—
this one thinks like that, the other one
doesn't—that whole struggle for power
and ideas typical of philosophy schools.
In this interview, in my work, in language, I talk all the time about this construction between poetry, reason,
meaning, madness, language, existence,
and power. I was thinking precisely
about this construction of meaning.
I had to ponder about what I had been
doing thus far, to restructure myself.
I prepared the first conversation with
people who invited other people, and
I founded *RhR*.

RD—While you were talking about all that, I was
remembering the power of *RhR*, its presence,
grasping the core, the feedback, the impetus that
your work presents time and time again. I think
that *RhR* makes this very clear because it seems that

you access a collective unconscious of images,
a status quo of images, for example the monk,
or the Muslim—or, in general, a sense of religiosity
or the power of a physical presence.

There was a kind of caution in *Uni-
forme-Desenho (Uniform-Drawing)*,
and when one got closer and people
asked, "What are you?," there was no
satisfactory answer, so people went on:
"How come there is no specific function or purpose?," "Why are you wearing that?" and so on. The participant
would eventually answer that it was a
"uniform-drawing," etc., etc. The noise
created by the meaninglessness of
the situation: in the case of *RhR,* this
was a hyphen. People are always looking for meaning in things.

The organism begins with geometric progression. I prepared a meeting
to present something I wanted to initiate, and I called a few people who
brought other people. This is already
fiction, I cannot recall any details, but
I told the ones who did not yet know
me that I was an artist and explained
the context of this whole story I am
telling you. I said I did those things, put
them in glass cases, always in artistic
environments, but that I needed something else to continue or to understand. I said I had to do that, to begin
something that was not an artwork,
but that, as an artist, I would donate
things from my faction, from the art
universe, from philosophy (a term for
the glossary) to this "Organism" (the
most amorphous word I could find). And
they asked, "But what uniform is this?"
and I said that we would bring that
uniform into daily life. I made *Uniform-
Drawing* as a donation as an artist.
I had already made some drawings like

that on white fabric and called them drawings, so there was a precedent there, of the plane, the cut. So much so that the *Costumes,* which I would make later, are all like that: no matter how much one sees the details, they are all surface; there was a whole conceptual construction to get to that point. And the *Uniform* is like a stain that is interspersed in the city, in life, in things.

IA—I do not understand—is it a plane?

Uniform-Drawing comes from the two-dimensional realm: the folded and cut-out fabric is glued on the edges and filled by a body; it is not a tailor's cut, which is more three-dimensional. The costumes also come from the plane—a roll of vinyl—and are folded countless times and cut out. This is how I got the idea of drawing in my works, drawings constructed with scissors, with the cut. We could say that the tailor's fabric is also a plane that does that, but it creates three-dimensionality. It creates something different that is a kind of verticality in this geometry. The "uniforms" reach actual space through the space of the body and social body.

Whatever *RhR* became, it started with vague questions, ideas about meaningless rituals, long conversations about the "organism." Those who came to *RhR*'s headquarters could find empty capsules (the "uniforms") and take them. The "uniform" gradually changed, the same way the insignia gradually modified the sense of time. The members multiplied. There were new members from other countries who had access to *RhR*. We are talking about a

time when there were no social networks or emails. We thought we were an initiatory society, but it was not at all like that—anyone who wanted to hold, not simply wear, the "uniform" became a member. "Intention" was another term I developed. *RhR* gradually emerged: it was a stain, the insignia was a stain, it had to spread out in an organic geometry, in a social architecture, and start to create noises that are the hyphens. The glossary gradually emerged from this contact with no precise answers.

IA—Did you always meet?

In many places in the city, in the world; we also went to art exhibitions. Sometimes people asked if that was an artwork and who made it, and we answered that it was not an artwork, it was a "uniform-drawing." As I said, there were people who thought I had an initiatory society, but the intention was just the opposite, to spread contamination! We frequently went to airports, because airports have zones with no legislation. We went there with no purpose. Sometimes it was to say goodbye to members from other countries who were going back home, in their transatlantic journey to wear the "uniform" in a geographic hyphen.

AC—The first time I saw your work, it was *O Puxador Paisagem (The Landscape Puller)* at Fundição Progresso (Rio de Janeiro, 1999). I felt a strong poetic impact with that work, and I thought about how nice it was that you had brought the landscape—a category from art history (that was my interpretation)—into real life. You are constantly talking about bringing such experiments into daily life, into real life, placing them in (the Rio neighborhood) Copacabana, moving them around. I want you to talk a bit more about that.

This is what *RhR* is, an experiment in a field that aims to be undefined and which is bound to disappear, because everything that exists does not need merely to endure or win. *O Puxador (The Puller)* had that indeed: I wanted to bring the landscape into an exhibition venue, like painters have done for so many centuries.

RD—All this has so much soul, so much power, that it escapes your emotional control.

I wanted it to escape. My management of *RhR* was not about control, but about a bureaucratic accumulation of information. Let us not forget about the touch of irony in it. In the case you were talking about, it had something in common with Flávio de Carvalho, with the social aspect. In *RhR,* I did not have that dimension in relation to Flávio, I did not know his work in depth, nor did I know what the "organism" I was founding would become. Philosophy and production of meaning was what I really wanted to experience with *RhR*. I remember that this appeared a lot in the *Costumes,* and it works in this way in relation to life, but already inside the field of art. *Loja de Costumes (Costume Shop),* is a shop because it is a recognizable place, it is where I place those garments one wears on the body as ornaments. And it has to go from the shop to life. I made two collections, the *Costumes,* first in blue vinyl in 2001, and then the second collection with transparent vinyl. The viewer gets to the place and recognizes a shop. Something should seem familiar. They recognize a set of behaviors there: mirror, hanging things, and an attendant who approaches them and asks if they need any help—she is trained to do that. The place is recognizable. It creates a situation of behavior, and when you get close, you realize what it is. There are ornamental possibilities, even if they are really unexpected, like ornamenting the knee, uniting neck and elbow with visual voluptuousness, folds and cutouts. The same thing is different in *RhR,* because it is directly related to ornamentation and decoration in art history. The title *Costumes* (in Portuguese, it means both "costumes" and "customs") implies clothing and the act of getting used to something, getting used to ornaments in one's life. The construction of the *Costumes* is another important fact: I fold, cut out, and create layers with the plane. It is not by chance. My consciousness is constructive, concrete. Excess and voluptuousness generate the ornaments. After one century of Conceptual Art, decorative ornaments sound like a sin, a crime, and nonsense.

SM—You are talking about the word "behavior." Previously we talked about the body. Is there anything bigger that pulls you toward this production, this meaning, this knowledge, with your interventions in life? The question of behavior, the relation between humanity and this behavior: Can you think of something that could be the main point of your research, or do you see it as something more diffuse, more undefined?

Behavior is the political inclusion of this body, where it belongs, the measure of its values and gestures. In *HcMc* it is a person, person=flesh. I recognize in the person their belonging to something or to themselves, their identity. I understand my process through locations and the power of the artist to determine. Those are all categories of behavior: repeating or creating in art is always a way of talking about its meaning. It is all about fittings, political and social fittings. The themes appearing in *RhR* are the contributions of belonging, of knowledge.

FS—It is interesting to observe in your speech that the record is not used as an archive, it always wants to be real. Even if it does not become real, it seems that at some point it might. Any of us could have a work that will never be executed, but in your case, I get the impression that it is an archive that is not formed by lines or words but by images, and this is also interesting.

For example, with *Faisões com Comida (Pheasants with Food),* I wanted to do something—I did not know exactly what. After the notes, it became a banquet served to living birds, a 2005 work with living pheasants. Looking at still life paintings, there was this element of beauty in the dead animals, hence the inversion, giving it a soul. The work really existed as a banquet eaten by the birds; it was an inversion that was somehow self-sufficient, and at the same time, it was a service elaborated by someone, a human being, society, the bourgeois, power, beauty, decoration, the chef de cuisine. Ornamentation, power, voluptuousness, gold, ecstasy, all became issues inherent in the ideas of "Ornamental Philosophy" found in many works, such as *Galinhas de Gala (Gala Chicken), Costumes, Ouro Flexível (Flexible Gold),* and others.

RD—You have a gigantic private glossary because you recreate the world, and you have a plurality inside your work, a freedom of possibilities. There is a book by Noam Chomsky about freedom of knowledge which talks about this same situation:

leaving a place thinking that you will find knowledge somewhere else, but he says that you knew everything before leaving the place where you were. This displacement is the feedback to know what one already knew. I always regard your work from this viewpoint.

I could talk about a work that has something to do with this universe you are discussing and which has some element of representation related to art history, *Nômades (Nomads).* Everyone can accumulate landscapes, even of the places one has not been to but only saw in books, places that perhaps do not even exist anymore. In *Nômades,* paintings made by a copyist are worn as masks, forming a strange ethnography. After the landscape is painted, I cut it out, fold it, and create ornaments with plants coming out of the painting, plants that the same copyist copies from botany books. The person looking at the work simultaneously sees the mask and the landscape. In the midst of daily life, people become storms, rough seas, dense forests, or inverted landscapes. This iconography of people as landscapes illustrates the idea that the landscape exists or is understood because we name it so—if we did not give it a name, it would be an endless horizon.

FS—But your latest works are also references to art history?

Yes, since back then, in *Homem=carne/ Mulher=carne – Pelos + Rede (Man= Flesh/Woman=Flesh – Hair + Hammock),* when one looks at the man's body hair with elongated eyebrows and the woman with elongated pubic hair—it has a *tableau vivant* atmosphere, and the references are automatically planted. I am not saying it is a reference to a specific painting, though. With the others, they are direct references, like the *Três Graças (The Three Graces),* for example. I looked into art history and observed paintings and sculptures that have to do with the three graces. I separated them and constructed all those movements with fabric, and the only task given to the participants is to stand, quietly and relaxed. The references to art history are a search for an etymology that becomes a cartography of domestication.

SM—Talk a little about your work *Baile (Ball).*

It appeared in 2003. Thinking about this issue of the dominance of painting, I was leafing through a book from the Louvre, and I saw this anonymous painting about a celebration: *Ball at the Court of Henri III,* 1581. The problem in understanding other civilizations is that one cannot recreate mimetically what one sees and cannot totally understand (even when mimesis is not the purpose). The anthropologist's problem is the same as the narrator's: the way he narrates something that he was not part of and may not even know, this is his drama. It is something we have to be careful with and recognize that we do not know, otherwise one is a tyrant or too careful. But the celebration, either in life or in death, exists, and the people in the painting from the Louvre book were celebrating. I decided, then, to take that image to a carnival group in Rio de Janeiro. They recreated it in their own interpretation, using the garments and other details from the painting. The work turned into a party.

This interview was originally published in a longer version in Portuguese in *Revista Arte & Ensaios – Journal of the Postgraduate Programme in Visual Arts – EBA/UFRJ,* no. 21/2010 (Rio de Janeiro, August 2010).

Appendix

181

Laura Lima

Born 1971 in Governador Valadares, Brazil
Lives and works in Rio de Janeiro

SOLO EXHIBITIONS (SELECTION SINCE 1998)

2014   Bonniers Konsthall, Stockholm
2013   *Bar Restaurant,* Migros Museum für Gegenwartskunst, Zurich
2012   *Cinema Shadow/Second,* Fundação Eva Klabin, Rio de Janeiro
2011   *Grande,* Casa França-Brasil, Rio de Janeiro
2010   La Centrale Galerie Powerhouse, Montreal
2009   Mercosul Biennial, Porto Alegre
       Galeria Luisa Strina, São Paulo
       Galeria Laura Alvim, Rio de Janeiro
2008   *Fuga,* A Gentil Carioca, Rio de Janeiro
2007   *Filosofia Ornamental,* Hardcore Art Contemporary
       Space, Miami
2005   *Paisagem,* Museu do Estado de Pernambuco, Recife
2004   *Instâncias,* Chapter Arts Centre, Cardiff
2003   *Costumes Loja,* Casa Triângulo, Sao Paulo
2002   Moderna Galerija Ljubljana
       HOMEM=CARNE/MULHER=CARNE e COSTUMES,
       Museu de Arte da Pampulha, Belo Horizonte
2000   *Laura Lima a Serviço do RhR, 24 dias em Madrid,*
       Espacio Uno, Museo Reina Sofia, Madrid
1999   *Puxador,* Fundição Progresso, Agora/Capacete, Rio de Janeiro
1998   *Projeto Digestão,* Centro Cultural São Paulo

GROUP EXHIBITIONS (SELECTION SINCE 2001)

2013   *Circuitos Cruzados – Centre Pompidou encontra MAM,*
       Museu de Arte de São Paulo
2012   Havana Biennial
       *From the Margin to the Edge – Brazilian Art and Design
       in the 21st Century,* Somerset House, London
       X-hibition, Marianne Friis Gallery, Copenhagen
       The Circus Crew, LARM Galleri, Copenhagen
       Aire de Lyon, Fundación PROA, Buenos Aires
2011   Lyon Biennial
       The Street, MuHKA, Antwerp
       The Spiral and the Square. Exercises on Translatability,

Bonniers Konsthall, Stockholm
11 Rooms, Manchester Art Gallery
Host City, Kunstverein Wolfsburg
2010   *Clube da Gravura,* Museu de Arte de São Paulo
2009   *Paisagem Ready Made,* Museu da República, Rio de Janeiro
Atenção: estratégias para perceber a arte, Museu de Arte
de São Paulo
Nus, Galeria Fortes Vilaça, São Paulo
2008   *Seja Marginal, Seja Herói,* Galerie Georges-Phillipe &
Nathalie Vallois, Paris
2007   *Panorama de Arte Brasileira,* Museu de Arte de São Paulo
Close to Me, Galleria Via Melzo, Milan
Universid'Arte – artista convidada, Universidade Estácio
de Sá, Rio de Janeiro
Portraits, Marc Selwyn Fine Art, Los Angeles
2006   São Paulo Biennial
Alegoria Barroca na Arte Contemporânea, Museo de Arte
Contemporáneo Santiago de Chile
Daniel Reich Gallery, New York
2005   *Limite como Potência,* Museu Nacional de Belas Artes,
Rio de Janeiro
Troca Brasil, Pacific Northwest College of Art, Portland
Educação Olha, A Gentil Carioca, Rio de Janeiro
Rencontres Paralleles, Centre d'art contemporain
de Basse-Normandie, Hérouville-Saint-Clair
2004   *Como en la tele,* Museo de Bellas Artes de Caracas
Acervo, A Gentil Carioca, Rio de Janeiro
2003   Mercosul Biennial
Spectacular, Kunstpalast, Dusseldorf
2002   *Photos,* Casa Triângulo, São Paulo
Panorama 2001, Museu de Arte de São Paulo / Museu
de Arte Moderna da Bahia / Museu de Arte Moderna do Rio
de Janeiro
2001   Tirana Biennial
Mercosul Biennial
H=c / M=c Machado / M=f / W=f Hatchet, Fundição
Progresso, Agora/Capacete, Rio de Janeiro
Mostra do Redescobrimento, Museu de Arte Moderno
de Buenos Aires
A Little Bit of History Repeated, KunstWerke, Berlin

Authors

SARA ARRHENIUS — Is a curator and writer based in Stockholm. She was the director of IASPIS (International Artists' Studio Program in Sweden) from 2001 to 2004. In 2005, she became the director of Bonniers Konsthall in Stockholm. Previously curated exhibitions include Tomas Saraceno, Monica Bonvicini, Rosa Barba, Ming Wong, Tarek Atoui or *A Trip to the Moon,* a group show around the status of film in contemporary culture, with Ryan Trecartin, Douglas Gordon, Lindsay Seers, and others. Currently she is preparing the extensive project *Art of Memory,* including solo presentations of, among others, Gerard Byrne, Raqs Media Collective, and Alina Szapocznikow. She is a frequent contributor to international and Swedish art magazines and has written and edited several books on contemporary art and culture. Among her most recent publications are *More Than Sound, A Smile for You, Tomas Saraceno: 14 Billions,* and *Translatability.*

HEIKE MUNDER — Studied cultural studies at the University of Lunenburg. She has been director of the Migros Museum für Gegenwartskunst Zürich since 2001. She co-founded the Halle für Kunst Lüneburg e.V., which she co-directed between 1995 and 2001. Previously curated exhibitions include *Geoffrey Farmer* (2013), *Ragnar Kjartansson* (2012), *The Garden of Forking Paths* (2011), *Tatiana Trouvé* (2009), *Tadeusz Kantor* (2008), *Rachel Harrison* (2007), *Marc Camille Chaimowicz* (2006), *Yoko Ono* (2005), and *Mark Leckey* (2003). She holds a number of regular teaching positions, including at the University of Lüneburg, Goldsmiths College (London), the University of Bern, the Zurich University of the Arts, and the Jan van Eyck Academy (Maastricht). Since 1995, she has written extensively for art magazines and catalogues. In 2012, she served on the jury for the Turner Prize.

VICTORIA NOORTHOORN — Is the director of the Museo de Arte Moderno de Buenos Aires (MAMBA). She holds an M.A. in art history from the University of Buenos Aires, and an M.A. in curatorial studies from Bard College, New York. She has served as projects coordinator for the International Program at MoMA, New York; assistant curator of contemporary exhibitions at The Drawing Center, New York; curator at Malba-Fundación Costantini, Buenos Aires; in addition to working as an independent curator from 2004 until being named to the MAMBA in 2013. She collaborated on the presentation of León Ferrari at the 52nd Venice Biennale (2007); and curated the

29th Pontevedra Art Biennial (2006); the 41st Salón Nacional de Artistas in Cali, Colombia (2008); the 7th Bienal do Mercosul, Porto Alegre, Brazil (2009); and the 11th Biennale de Lyon (2011), alongside numerous other exhibitions.

JOCHEN VOLZ — Jochen Volz is head of programmes at the Serpentine Gallery in London. He is also a curator at the Instituto Inhotim, Minas Gerais, Brazil, since 2004, where he has co-curated a series of large-scale site-specific projects on art and architecture with such artists as Adriana Varejão (2008), Dominique Gonzalez-Foerster (2010), Doug Aitken (2009), Lygia Pape (2012), Matthew Barney (2009), Rirkrit Tiravanija (2010), and Tunga (2012), as well as numerous exhibitions from the collection. He has contributed to many exhibitions, including *Planos de fuga,* Centro Cultural Banco do Brasil in São Paulo (2012); *Olafur Eliasson: Your Body of Work* as part of the 17th International Festival of Contemporary Art—SESC Videobrasil in São Paulo (2011); *The Spiral and the Square* at Bonniers Konsthall, Stockholm (2011); the Aichi Triennale in Nagoya (2010); and *Cinthia Marcelle* at the Biennale de Lyon (2007). In 2009, he organized *Fare Mondi / Making Worlds,* the international section of the 53rd International Venice Biennale together with Daniel Birnbaum. In 2006, for the 27th São Paulo Biennial, he guest-curated a special exhibition project in homage to Marcel Broodthaers with Juan Araujo, Mabe Bethônico, Marcel Broodthaers, Marilá Dardot, Tacita Dean, Meschac Gaba, Goshka Macuga, Rirkrit Tiravanija, and Haegue Yang. Between 2001 and 2004, he was curator of Portikus, Frankfurt am Main. As a critic, he writes for magazines and catalogues and is contributing editor to *Frieze.*

This book was published on the occasion of the exhibition
Laura Lima: Bar Restaurant, at the Migros Museum für
Gegenwartskunst, November 23, 2013–February 2, 2014 and
Bonniers Konsthall, September 2–November 23, 2014.

The exhibition at the Migros Museum für Gegenwartskunst
was curated by Heike Munder.

The exhibition at Bonniers Konsthall was curated
by Sara Arrhenius.

Migros Museum für Gegenwartskunst

Director / Curator of the
Exhibition
Heike Munder

Head of Administration
Catherine Reymond

Curator
Raphael Gygax

Collection Curator
Judith Welter

Head of Press and Public
Relations
René Müller

Registrar / Scientific
Researcher, Collection
Anna-Lena Gugger

Scientific Researcher,
Public Programs
Alena Nawrotzki

Administration Assistant
Katja Jaisli

Interns
Jasmin Eckhardt
Cornelia Huth
Yvonne Mattern

Head of Technical Services,
Exhibitions
Monika Schori

Technical Services,
Exhibitions & Events
Markus Bösch

Head of Technical Services,
Collection
Roland Bösiger

Technical Services, Collection
Muriel Gutherz

Technical Services, Exhibition
Cristina Golland
Steffen Kuhn
Monika Stalder
Basil Kobert
Emanuel Masera
Carmen D'Apollonio
Konstantinos Manolakis
Oliver Wahmann
Tanja Roscic
Athene Galiciadis

Coordinator Media Archive
Gabi Deutsch

Coordinator Visitor Services
Robin Bhattacharya

Visitor Services and
Public Programs
Kathrin Bentele
Robin Bhattacharya
Pascal Good

Visitor Services
Luisa Baselgia
Yuko Edelmann
Niria Frey
Max Heinrich
Christa Michel
Dominique Stalder
Eva-Maria Wilbs

Migros Museum für
Gegenwartskunst
Limmatstrasse 270
Postfach 1766
8031 Zurich
Switzerland
T +41 (0) 44 277 20 50
F +41 (0) 44 277 62 86
info@migrosmuseum.ch
migrosmuseum.ch

MIGROSMUSEUM
für Gegenwartskunst

An institution of the Migros
Culture Percentage.
migros-kulturprozent.ch

Director / Curator of the
Exhibition
  Sara Arrhenius

Project Manager
  Björn Norberg

Curator
  Camilla Larsson

Assistant Curator
  Caroline Elgh

Communications Manager
  Sofia Curman

Event & Sponsorship Manager
  Thérèse Dyhlén

Project Coordinator
  Li Erlandsson

Technician
  Niklas Johansson

Public Programmes
Coordinator
  Yuvinka Medina

Host Coordinator
  Katya Sandomirskaya

Communications and
Event Manager
  Weronika Witakowska

Bonniers Konsthall
Torsgatan 19
113 90 Stockholm
Sweden
T +46 8 736 42 48
info@bonnierskonsthall.se
bonnierskonsthall.se

◥Bonnierskonsthall

A site for contemporary art in
central Stockholm. Bonniers
Konsthall supports the newest
Swedish and international art
with an active program of exhibitions, artist conversations,
performances, seminars and
publications.

Publication

Published by: Migros Museum
für Gegenwartskunst,
Bonniers Konsthall, and
JRP | Ringier

Editors
    Heike Munder
    Sara Arrhenius

Managing Editor
    Raphael Gygax

Intern
    Jasmin Eckhardt

Translation from German
    Gerrit Jackson
    (Heike Munder)

Translation from Portuguese
    Renato Rezende (Interview)

Copyediting and Proofreading,
English
    Raphael Gygax
    Anne O'Connor

Visual Concept &
Graphic Design
    Studio Marie Lusa

Lithography & Production
    Odermatt AG, Dallenwil

The Migros Museum für
Gegenwartskunst and
Bonniers Konsthall would
like to thank:
    Laura Lima
    Marcio Botner
    Victoria Noorthoorn
    Jochen Volz
    Ulf Wuggenig

Laura Lima would like to thank:
    Lúcia Lima
    Sebastião Lima Filho
    Orfeu Lima
    Bernardo Ortiz
    Tete Paletta
    Ana Torres
    Cadu d'Oliveira
    Alexandre Lima
    Guilherme Lima
    Ernesto Neto
    Marcio Botner
    Luisa Strina
    Bojana Piskur
    Tonico
    Marssares
    William Vorhees
    Neida Lima
    Lene Werneck
    Luisa Adamis
    Marcio Ramalho
    Córa Soares
    Sebastiana Coelho
    Isabel Barcellos
    Heike Munder
    Sara Arrehnius
    Jochen Volz
    Victoria Noorthoorn
    Raphael Gygax
    Monika Schori

Printed in Switzerland

Distributed by

JRP|Ringier
Limmatstrasse 270
CH–8005 Zurich
T +41 (0) 43 311 27 50
F +41 (0) 43 311 27 51
E info@jrp-ringier.com

jrp-ringier.com

ISBN 978-3-03764-344-0